ore Praise for *My Black Country* and Alice Randall

ndall is the perfect trailblazer to shine this light. In her book *My ntry*, she hits all the notes of a great country song. She makes , makes you cry, makes you realize the difficulty and beauty of y human stories. The profound influence Black artists have had nre is so eloquently described, beautifully encapsulated in her blazing role as the first Black woman to cowrite a number-one nit. She's a treasure."

—Brad Paisley, Grammy award–winning country artist

Bottom Saints:

engaging, and often wise."

—*The New York Times Book Review*

rgeous swirl of fiction."

—NPR's *Fresh Air*

Bottom Saints is a tour-de-force."

—Tiya Miles, author of *All That She Carried* and *Wild Girls*, Professor of History, Harvard University

Wind Done Gone:

pirited reimagination . . . [Randall's] insights are frequent and sharp."

—*Publishers Weekly*

illiant."

—*Booklist*

ways fascinating."

—*Library Journal*

M

“Alice Ra
Black Cou
you smile
these ver
on the g
own trai
country

for Black

“Lively,

“[A] go

“Black

for The

“[A] s

“[B]r

“[A]

MY BLACK COUNTRY

A JOURNEY THROUGH COUNTRY MUSIC'S BLACK PAST, PRESENT, AND FUTURE

ALICE RANDALL

Alice Randall

BLACK PRIVILEGE PUBLISHING

ATRIA

New York · London · Toronto · Sydney · New Delhi

Vanderbilt

ATRIA
An Imprint of Simon & Schuster, Inc.
1230 Avenue of the Americas
New York, NY 10020

Some ideas, language, and events included in this book first appeared in the author's earlier publications.

"Linda Martell's 'Color Him Father'" appeared in the *Oxford American*, April 2010.

"Beyonce's 'Daddy Lessons' Is Classic Country" appeared in *American Songwriter*, October 2016.

"That's How I Got to Memphis" *Woman Walk the Line,* University of Texas Press, 2017.

"From Lil Hardin to Lil Nas X" *Rivers of Rhythm*. National Museum of African American Music, 2021.

"Music from the Magic Box" appeared in the *Oxford American*, Winter 2021.

"Mailbox Money" in *Whose Country Music?* published by Cambridge University Press in 2023.

First Black Privilege Publishing/Atria Books hardcover edition April 2024

BLACK PRIVILEGE PUBLISHING / ATRIA BOOKS and colophon are trademarks of Simon & Schuster, Inc.

For information about special discounts for bulk purchases, please contact Simon & Schuster Special Sales at 1-866-506-1949 or business@simonandschuster.com.

The Simon & Schuster Speakers Bureau can bring authors to your live event. For more information or to book an event, contact the Simon & Schuster Speakers Bureau at 1-866-248-3049 or visit our website at www.simonspeakers.com.

Interior design by Dana Sloan

Manufactured in the United States of America

1 3 5 7 9 10 8 6 4 2

Library of Congress Cataloging-in-Publication Data

Names: Randall, Alice, 1959- author.
Title: My black country : chasing the hidden roots and flowers of black country music genius / Alice Randall.
Description: First Black Privilege Publishing/Atria Books hardcover edition. | New York : Black Privilege Publishing/Atria, 2024. | Includes index.
Identifiers: LCCN 2023054033 | ISBN 9781668018408 (hardcover) | ISBN 9781668018415 (paperback) | ISBN 9781668018422 (ebook)
Subjects: LCSH: Country music—History and criticism. | African Americans—Music—History and criticism. | African American country musicians—United States. | Country musicians—United States.
Classification: LCC ML3524 .R34 2024 | DDC 781.642089/96073—dc23/eng/20231208
LC record available at https://lccn.loc.gov/2023054033

ISBN 978-1-6680-1840-8
ISBN 978-1-6680-1842-2 (ebook)

Dedicated to my daughter Caroline and the city where she was born—Nashville.

CONTENTS

PRELUDE

BACK TO THE STUDIO

I have eaten in studios, made love in studios, suckled my daughter in a studio, rocked somebody else's baby who grew up to win a Grammy on my hip in a studio, saw knives pulled and guns waved in studios, cussed folks out in the studio, *got* cussed out in the studio. Stopped by to gossip and visit with old friends and shoot the breeze, like all I had was time and no labor. Worked so late I slept on the floor of a studio mesmerized by the lights of the high-tech mix console that was never turned off, only to awaken to the sight of mice skittering across the floor reminding me that we in the South are never far from the wild. (Which made me laugh in a studio and not for the first or last time.) I've done a lot of things in studios.

Cry wasn't one of them. Until my fortieth year in Nashville, 2023.

The Bomb Shelter studio has a vibe that is part old-hippy group house or grow house, part warehouse industrial, part museum of analog recording gear. You enter through a much-used kitchen that announces the gut-bucket funk of the place.

The tight quarters are chock-full of old amps, vintage instruments, classic sound mixing boards placed for maximum performance not maximum pretty. On my first visit, tornadoes were twisting through the middle Tennessee skies. Some of the musicians had left to check on dogs, or homes, or to grab kids from school. Others were ordering or making lunch. Walking through the kitchen toward the control room, I heard voices in the live room—one singing, one encouraging.

Two folks were still working. I heard it before I saw this: Ebonie Smith, dressed in stylish sweats, her part-shaved head crowned with long faux locs, was fearlessly guiding a young Black mermaid with a voice like Dinah Washington and multiple shades of purple hair through the nuances of "Get the Hell Out of Dodge," a song I wrote shortly after my first divorce in 1991.

I had never seen or heard a Country singer who styled herself as a Black mermaid, until Ebonie invited Saaneah into the studio, after years of stalking Ebonie on Instagram, to work on what was being called the "Alice Randall Black Country Songbook" project.

I was instantly beguiled by Saaneah's siren song. Over the years, "Get the Hell Out of Dodge," which I co-wrote with Walter Hyatt, had been recorded at least five times. Walter recorded it himself in 1993. Honky-tonk legend Hank Thompson recorded it in 1997. Then two badass babes, Toni Price, in 2003, and Eden Brent, in 2014, took a crack at the song. Finally somebody was serving up this truth with salty sweetness: you have to leave with your mind, before you can leave with your body.

Thirty years after the first recording, here was Ebonie Smith guiding Saaneah into an interpretation of the song that was retro and Afro-futuristic. Instead of luring listeners to rocks, and death, the Ebonie/Saaneah collaboration lured listeners to an understanding that liberation is first an act of the mind, then an act of the body. The fragments of the siren's song I heard walking down the short hall were washing over me with proof of what I had long hoped: songs can be weapons. I was smiling big. Didn't even have to say hello. I walked into the live room, looked at the two brown women working at the mike, and happy hollered, "You got a mermaid singing my song!"

Ebonie was so much more than the producer on this session. She was the engineer, composer, and activist who was bringing the magic and the thunder, not just her Grammys, her Barnard degree, and her ridiculously impressive résumé. She had scrolled through her Instagram and found a Nashville-born, Country-song-loving, jazz-belting mermaid. And that wasn't even the big moment of the visit. They were just getting started. Just breaking through the top layers of what had been painted over during previous recordings, which had effectively erased me from my own co-write. They burned just enough incense to get all the femme and round and sweet they wanted in the room and all the edgy grunge out. Ebonie wanted to give Saaneah space and privacy to stretch into her interpretation. She invited Saaneah to take a break. She invited me into the control room. She wanted me to hear something nearer to finished.

Ebonie settled on a stool at the sound console. I settled into a couch. Ebonie pushed play. The guitar started, and then came a voice, a Black woman's voice. Adia Victoria was singing the first words of "Went for a Ride": "He was Black as the sky on a moonless night," singing my words, from the place I had written those words, a Black and feminine place, a Black and Western place, a Black and haunted place. I wept tears of joy. It was the end of imagining. Sometimes the end of imagining is a very good thing.

I no longer had to imagine one day somebody who looked like me would sing "Went for a Ride." It happened. I didn't have to imagine someone would sing the words "He was Black as the sky on a moonless night" and they would be Black, too. Didn't have to imagine an artist would sing those words and they wouldn't be *othering* the hero of the song, they wouldn't be talking about the Black cowboy as a novelty, as a curiosity. When the words "He rode with the best, hell he rode with me," were sung by white PBR world champion bull rider Justin McBride, it was understood that Justin McBride was the greatest cowboy in the world and this Black cowboy in my song was good enough to be recognized by Justin but was no Justin. When Adia Victoria sang those same words, "He rode with the best, hell he rode with me," it was one great Black cowboy acknowledging another great Black cowboy. That was the story

I intended to write, and that my co-writer only barely understood, the day we worked together as staff writers in a writing room in a Country publishing house in the nineties. In the twentieth century I had to slip my best ideas in sideways.

In the twenty-first century, Adia Victoria put all my ideas on front street. She swaggered through the song, found the secret door I hid in the lyrics, and walked through it into my American West—past and present—that she alters by her Black and Country presence. Adia obliterated some stubborn old myths. With every syllable and sound, she raised our new myth. When I thought I would never get to that, I got to that. When it had come, I couldn't bear to listen to most old recordings of my songs. I had been so whitewashed out of them, the racial identity of my living-in-song heroes and sheroes so often erased. Then, in rode Ebonie, and her posse of Black Country genius, galloping to the rescue. That's good funky eclipsing all the bad funk. That's my, Alice Randall's, Black Country.

WHAT IS BLACK COUNTRY?

Harlan Howard said that Country Music was three chords and the truth. I've said Country Music is three chords and four very particular truths: life is hard, God is real, whiskey and roads and family provide worthy compensations, and the past is better than the present.

That last truth is one of the places where Country experiences a racial split. In the world of white Country, the past that is better than the present exists in a longed for and lost mythical Dixie. In Black Country, the past that is better than the present exists in a longed for and lost Africa before colonization. In my life it was the Detroit past that was better than the Washington, D.C., present.

My ancestors come from Cameroon, Nigeria, and Mali and they come from Scotland, England, and Ireland. A common way to define Country Music is that it is American folk music that has Celtic, African, and Evangelical Christian influences.

Twenty-eight percent Scottish, twenty-one percent English, sixteen percent Cameroonian, and fifteen percent Nigerian is the rough estimate I've been given of the ethnic identities of my ancestors based on an analysis of my DNA. I am embodied Country Music.

The earliest Black Country song I know rose from the shores of the Chesapeake Bay and dates back to sometime before 1838.

We raise de wheat,
Dey gib us de corn;
We bake de bread,
Dey gib us de crust;
We sif de meal,
Dey gib us de huss;

We peel de meat,
Dey gib us de skin;
And dat's de way
Dey take us in;
We skim de pot,
Dey gib us the liquor,
And say dat's good enough for nigger . . .

We is the Black folk, Dey are the white folk. And the specific "we" is enslaved Africans and the specific "dey" are Scots. Frederick Douglass was owned by people, the Auld family, whose lineage traces back to Scotland. They were likely Ulster Scots who made up a lion's share of the migration to the eastern shore of Maryland starting in 1649.

The lyric to this early Country song was included in *My Bondage and My Freedom*, the second of Frederick Douglass's three autobiographies. Published in 1855, it details Frederick's escape to freedom in 1838. So, we know the song was being sung by enslaved Africans in these Americas sometime before that in the days between Christmas and New Year's, when it was heard and remembered by young Frederick.

The song caught by Douglass is seminal. It evolves over time. It transforms. It becomes hard to recognize. But I believe I hear an echo of it in the Bob Wills classic, "Take Me Back to Tulsa":

Little bee sucks the blossom, big bee gets the honey.
Darkie raise the cotton, white man gets the money.

Is that a sweetened-up twentieth-century riff on the nineteenth-century song? Another line in the iconic Country and Western dance hall tune:

Let me off at Archer and I'll walk down to Greenwood.

Archer and Greenwood are streets in the Black neighborhood of Tulsa. The neighborhood that was destroyed in the Tulsa Massacre. "Take Me Back to Tulsa" is not a blues song. It's a labor protest. It's African and Celtic and it tells a story. "We Raise the Wheat" is a Black Country song that gave rise to other Country songs. How many others are there?

It's hard to know. So much trauma disrupting so much memory. So much never documented. So much was never recorded. And so much yet to be recovered. Let me give you but one concrete example found on a federal website:

> *Despite the best efforts of the Library of Congress and other sound repositories around the world, innumerable items from the world's recorded sound history are believed to be lost. For example, it is estimated that only 2% of the 3000-plus cylinder recordings produced by the North American Phonograph Company (NAPCo) between 1889 and 1894 have been accounted for . . .*
>
> *There is always, however, the possibility that one or more of these may turn up in attics, basements or elsewhere. The Recorded Sound Section of the Library of Congress is currently searching for the following titles. Have you seen—or heard—any of these? (They may exist as test pressings or commercial releases, and on cylinder, disc, or other media.)*
>
> *If you have, please contact: codell@loc.gov.*

A difference between Black Country and blues? Black Country, because of its embrace of Evangelical Christianity, embraces hope. It makes a plan. Because it is Black, it deals with the real. Looking for lost treasure is real.

If you know of a boarded-up house in your community that you can safely and legally make arrangements to poke into, look in those attics and basements. You're looking for Edison Wax Cylinder boxes. They look something like a biscuit can. They may be about 4 1/2 inches tall and have about a 2 3/4 inch diameter. They will say Edison Records some kind of way on the outside of the can. They could be in a wood box that looks something like a big doctor's bag—that would be an Edison phonograph player. If you find one of those, you are more likely to find some cylinders.

On the list of artifacts the Smithsonian is hoping to find are twelve tunes recorded by the Bohees. One may have been recorded as early as 1890. Yep, three decades before the recordings of the Bristol sessions that have been called the big bang that created Country Music, the Black Bohees recorded "Banjo Duets."

In 1973, "Dueling Banjos" peaked at number five on the Billboard Hot Country Singles chart. The way I see it, that Country hit, and all recorded banjo wars, are descended from the Bohee Brothers.

Watching *Deliverance*—the film set in Appalachia that featured "Dueling Banjos" and starred only white people—I had never heard of the Bohee Brothers, let alone known they were early Black banjo recording artists. Didn't know James and George were born in Canada in 1844 and 1857, before the end of slavery in the United States. That they would move with their parents to New England before crossing the Atlantic to make a home and musical life in England, where they became banjo stars and banjo teachers to the aristocracy.

"Dueling Banjos" started off as "Feudin' Banjos" and was written in 1954. I first heard it in 1963 when it was performed on *The Andy Griffith Show.*

My father loved Andy Griffith. He appreciated the humiliation of Barney Fife and the weekly reveal of the incompetent, weak, puny soul hiding behind the powerful structure of white supremacy. Years later, at the millennial gathering of Southern writers in Nashville, which included precious few Black writers—Yusef Komunyakaa, Natasha Trethewey, and I may have been the only Black folk invited—Shelby Foote moderated a closing ceremony and somehow the discussion turned to the whiteness of *The Andy Griffith Show*, and I pointed out Blackness was hidden in plain sight in the banjo.

I didn't even begin to get to the point about jug band music. White Briscoe Darling courting Aunt Bee plays the jug originating as a Black tradition with strong roots to Louisville. Jimmie Rodgers recorded with the Louisville Jug Band.

When you are up in your attics or down in your basements looking for Bohee Brothers tunes, see if you don't find some early lost Black jug band recordings. I suspect Black jug band music didn't start with the amazing Louisville Jug Band. I suspect that's just where erasure begins to end.

So much erased it is hard to say when and where Black Country and Country began.

PORTRAIT OF A BLACK MAN PLAYING AN EARLY AMERICAN BANJO

I have imagined Black Country and Country to be born as an art form, as an aesthetic, in the year 1624 near Jamestown, Virginia. William Tucker, the first Black infant born in the British colonies that would become America, was born that year near that place. I have imagined his mother weaving English ballads she heard with African melodies she knew and singing to her son.

The inaugural catalog of the National Museum of African American Music was published in 2021. After failing to persuade museum leadership that they needed a gallery devoted to Black Country, I succeeded in convincing them to include a chapter in the catalog that reflected the phantom gallery that I wished existed. At the center of the imagined exhibit is a painting that hangs in fact, I believe, in a museum in Williamsburg. In lectures and in that catalog, this is how I have described the painting:

The Old Plantation is an eighteenth-century watercolor painting that chronicles a group of enslaved Africans in community dancing and singing as part of a religious experience or part of an entertainment—we do not know. What is clear is that they are engaged in an activity of their own creation under their own direction; some are in couples, some are solo, some are part of a larger group. Their purpose seems serious given their unsmiling faces, their reflective miens. In the center right of the work is a Black man wearing a dark hat with a white rim playing the banjo. His gaze is direct, confident. His feet are firmly planted. His fingers precisely placed. His beauty and power evident. He is the artist, leading with his instrument. Far in the background, small, less than the size of the head of the tallest man depicted, is a white house. Can this be the birth of Country Music?*

Here is loss. Here is home. Here is family. Here are the rural acres. Here is the love in a couple's gaze. Here is music. Here is all that is compensation for that loss. For me the blues is about a somehow sweet engagement with a bitter world. Country Music at its heart is elegiac and mournful, even when it dances; it is a sad engagement with a world promising sweet, a place where profound loss coexists with profound hope.

I won't call the founding of recorded Country Music something no one living has heard. So, it's not the Bohees. And I will acknowledge when we speak of Country Music and Black Country in the twenty-first century we are speaking of commercially available recorded music, so I cannot place the founding of the genre in seventeenth-century Virginia, though that is where I find the root and seeds of the aesthetic.

THE BIRTH OF BLACK COUNTRY

According to me, Black Country was born December 10, 1927, when DeFord Bailey played "Pan American Blues" on *Barn Dance*, a Nashville radio show blasted out on the WSM airwaves. Listeners couldn't see this, but DeFord was a short, handsome, dark-skinned man who wore a three-piece suit and brightly shined shoes to every recording session, performance, and when just sitting, waiting for death. In his last days his family would tease DeFord that they could just put him in his casket when he passed. He dressed that clean and sharp.

Bailey, who would become acknowledged as the first superstar of the Grand Ole Opry, entered the world in 1899. His daddy, John Henry Bailey, was a farmer. John Henry's father, Lewis Bailey, was a noted musician in Smith County, Tennessee, who performed what DeFord would later call "Black Hillbilly Music" in an all-Black family band.

That's been told by DeFord in his own words in an audio interview in the 1970s: "In the slaving time, my grandaddy and my great-grandad, they all were musicians back there. They say he was a good harp player. I would like to have heard him, see what he sound like."

That Black Hillbilly Music DeFord's granddaddy was playing in the nineteenth century in a family band didn't get recorded or acknowledged in the white or Black press, didn't make it into the historical record, doesn't leave a date that I can claim and document as the day Black Country was born. It just gets told in the whispers of the community and handed down as lore in the housing projects where DeFord spent his last years.

My daddy was the person who hipped me to the fact it was a Black woman, Lil Hardin, playing on that big, old Country record, and that there were probably a lot more Black folks *passing for white* on other Country records. He was the one who would look at some sheet music, or some hymn in a hymnal, then over at me and ask, "What you bet *Traditional* was a colored girl?" And he was the first to tell me the banjo was an African instrument, after all.

Other folks with other fathers tell a different story. It's often said that Country Music was born with a big bang. When the story is told this way, typically Jimmie Rodgers is the papa, Mother Maybelle Carter is the mother, and there is a magical and immaculate conception that culminates in Ralph Peer—a traveling representative of the Victor Talking Machine Company turned producer—playing the role of the stork that brings the baby, Country Music. And all this happens in 1927, in Bristol, a town that strides the Virginia and Tennessee border where commercially recorded Country Music sprang, not from a cabbage patch, but from the Taylor-Christian Hat and Glove Company. In the last days of a hot July and a hotter August, Peer produced a series of recording sessions, some starring Jimmie Rodgers, some starring the Carters. That's the way some folks tell it.

What if my daddy was right? What if that white stork, Ralph Peer, didn't bring the baby? What if a one-legged, eight-fingered Black man, Eslie Riddle, was the stork? What if DeFord Bailey is the papa, Lil Hardin Armstrong is the mama, Ray Charles is their genius child, Charley Pride is DeFord's side child, and Herb Jeffries is Lil's stepson? You get a whole new way of looking at Country.

Bristol, Tennessee, calls itself the place "Where Country Music Began." The city holds a variety of tourist attractions from the Birthplace of Country Music Museum to the Carter Family Fold run by descendants of the Carter Family that offer proof of the claim. Another tourist attraction, the Burger Bar, infamous as the place Hank Williams, Sr., was last seen alive, establishes Bristol's ongoing connection to the genre. The two-day Bristol Rhythm & Roots Reunion Festival, established in 2001, includes a nod to Black influences on Country—but something is missing in Bristol. Where is the huge statue of Eslie Riddle?

Some called him Wesley Riddle, some call him Leslie. There's evidence his name was Eslie Riddle and he is the Black man who may have been the true founder of the Bristol musical festival.

How's that? Eslie Riddle taught the Carter Family a whole lot of songs. That's an established and acknowledged-by-the-Carters fact. What isn't acknowledged or even alluded to? While still in his teens, before he met the Carters, Riddle blew off two of his own fingers in a shotgun accident that might have been a suicide attempt. Recuperating from both the shotgun incident and a prior accident at a cement factory that ended with a leg amputation, one-legged, eight-fingered Eslie Riddle began playing the guitar using only his pointer, his baby finger, and the thumb of his right hand.

When Riddle played songs for the Carters, he picked the guitar with three brown fingers. He had innovated an adaptation to his physical circumstances that resulted in a new and appealing sound created by his new technique.

Mother Maybelle Carter is famed for her guitar playing that is a foundation of the Carter Family sound. Her technique has been named the Carter Family Scratch. It sounds and works a whole lot like how Eslie Riddle played the guitar, relying on his thumb and pointer finger. Coincidence? Collaboration? Erasure?

I found Eslie Riddle in the 1910 census. It wasn't hard to do. He was three years old and in there with his brother, Grady, who was two. They were living in Burnsville with their grandparents, Sullen Griffith and Sindy Griffith, their mother, Hattie Griffith, and four uncles. Maybe the story of the Carter Family children naming him Eslie because they couldn't say Leslie is a lie. How many other maybe-lies are in the story?

Eslie and Grady and their mama were being raised in the shelter of grandparents who had been born enslaved in North Carolina—but Sindy could read and write, create and nurture life, and face death. At the age of fifty-two, she reported having birthed fourteen children and buried four.

Who would I like to ask about Eslie Riddle's involvement with the Carter Family, about Eslie Riddle's name? His brother, Grady Riddle.

Grady Riddle pastored AME Zion churches in western North Carolina for fifty-four years. He died March 8, 2003, in Burnsville at the age of ninety-five. If people had wanted to know more about Eslie Riddle, he was the person to ask. Scholars late into the twentieth century lamented not knowing more about Eslie. But no one interviewed Grady.

How different it would have been to know Eslie through the lens of the person who grew up hearing the same music and who rose to be a successful minister of God? A man with a seventh-grade education to Eslie's four. But nobody asked Grady.

They asked the Carters. They asked Eslie, when he depended on the Carters for work and depended on white gatekeepers who revered the Carters for bookings. Eslie Riddle died in 1980. When he was safe in the ground, no longer seeking jobs or needing to curry good favor, it would have been very interesting to ask Grady Riddle to characterize the collaboration. How does lack of access to markets impact willingness to collaborate? What is creative consent? And how does lack of access to markets affect our ability to give it? How often were Black artists faced with a choice (after working with a white collaborator) between no public credit for what they brought to the collaboration or credit for a fraction of what they brought?

If Eslie had said he was the originator of Carter Family Scratch in the thirties, would anyone have believed him? Did Eslie Riddle teach Mother Maybelle how to play what came to be called the Carter Family Scratch? We will never know.

So, let's get back to the big bang, the Bristol sessions, starring the Carter Family and Jimmie Rodgers. Even if you don't buy into the idea that Riddle played a seminal role in the development of the Carter Family Scratch, there's no denying Lil Hardin's impact on Jimmie Rodgers.

On July 16, 1930, in Los Angeles, Lil made Country Music history as the first Black woman to play on a hillbilly record that sold a million copies, "Blue Yodel #9," also known as "Standin' on the Corner." Three geniuses played on "Blue Yodel #9"—Louis Armstrong, Jimmie Rodgers, and Lil Hardin. Only Lil plays on every bar of the piece.

Lil's performance on the piano proves that Country is not as Bill C. Malone long posited: a genre with Black influence but without Black presence. "Blue Yodel #9" refutes that twentieth-century lie.

If "Blue Yodel #9" represents the birth of Country Music, as many have argued, including Johnny Cash, then I argue the woman driving that session with her innovative approach to the keyboard and her intimate knowledge of the lyrics is Country Music's midwife, and that's Lil Hardin. And if it's true, as I suspect, that she brought the song to the session, that she shaped the lyrics, then she's not just the midwife, she's the mama.

Black women have been present in Country since the earliest days of Country's existence as a recorded and commercially marketed music form.

So, this is another lie: isolated Black men had some presence and influence in Country at its very beginning—DeFord Bailey, Eslie Riddle, and Louis Armstrong—but Black women are a new addition to the Country scene in the twenty-first century. Lil's presence on "Blue Yodel #9" and the decades-long denial of that presence pose very interesting questions.

What if Country Music wasn't Mother Maybelle's white-as-the-Appalachian-snow child, wasn't Jimmie Rodgers's white-as-the-Appalachian-snow child, it was their Black as Nuttallburg coal grandchild? And that's Black.

In the 1930s in the infancy of Country Music, there were fifty-five thousand Black men working in coal mines and living with their families in coal camps. Some of the forgotten mine and town names: Nuttallburg, Hawk's Nest, and Stone Cliff. How do we forget this?

Don't forget what I've told you. Jimmie Rodgers and the Carters learned songs and chords from Black musicians. The Carters likely stole from Eslie Riddle. Lil Hardin plays on every bar of "Blue Yodel #9." Ain't nothing always snow-white in Appalachia, where even the snow can come dusted with coal. Get you some books by Afralachian poets and read them!

My father, George Stanley Randall, understood the whitewashing of Country Music to be a bomb obliterating significant traces of Black genius. And Black genius he understood to be a liberation tool. That's why I spend so much time with Country. It's a hidden trove of Black genius.

What makes a song Country? I've got checklists. This is a remix and expansion of one that first appeared in *American Songwriter* magazine. Evangelical Christianity and African musical influences mixed in with English, Irish, or Scottish ballad forms? Check. Calling that mix of Scottish, Irish, and English, Celtic? Check. Concerns with female legacy? Check? Love of whiskey and guns? Check. Offering advice? Check? Feeling sentimental about Bible-thumping and open roads? Check. Putting child-rearing and sibling relations over sexual adventures with lovers or bonds with friends? Check? Honoring the patriarch? Check? Concerns with good and evil and a determination to be good? Check. Shouting out to Texas? Check. Horse-opera riffs that remind us that cowboy movies helped make Country, Country? Check. Hiding some lost British or American metaphysical poetry in the form of a tortured extended metaphor like, "Drop-kick me, Jesus, through the goalposts of life" or "I'm just an old chunk of coal, but I'm gonna be a diamond someday"? Check. Doing right by Mama and listening to Daddy? Check. Check.

What makes a song Black Country? One way of looking at it, any Country song that ticks the very first box, which is most classic Country, is Black Country because of the African-musical influences. To drill down further there's a choice to be made. Do we focus on Black audience, Black artists, or Black artifacts?

If we focus on the Black audience, we can make the case that any song any part of a Black Country audience recognizes as Black Country is Black Country. When I see a little Black girl in a hot pink cowboy costume twirling an imaginary lasso above her head as she dances to "Old Town Road" even though she's dancing in a sea of white children to beats that were bought for thirty dollars from Europe, that tells me "Old Town Road" is a Black Country song.

If we focus on Black artists, maybe any song performed by an artist who *considers themselves to be Black and considers themselves to be creating within the Country genre* is a Black Country song. And maybe any Black artist, say Al Green on *The Belle Album*, who portrays themselves within their performance as a Black person involved in activities associated with Country virtues and leisure—going to church, working hard in school, cooking from the family garden, fishing, drying clothes on a clothesline, making love to someone you love—is creating Black Country. And it may be worth considering that any Black artist who portrays themselves within their performance of a song as a Black person involved in activities associated with explicitly Country vices, from shooting people who dishonor you and still seeming soft and sweet (Beyoncé's "Daddy Lessons") to drinking whiskey in champagne glasses and still seeming soft and sweet (Reyna Roberts's "Country Club"), is Black Country.

If we focus on Black artifacts (instruments and recorded songs) we will consider a song performed by a Black artist utilizing an instrument closely and specifically associated with the Country genre (banjo, fiddle, steel guitar, fife, yodeling voice) a Black Country song. Finally, we will also consider any song performed by a Black artist, *whether or not they consider themselves to be working in the Country genre*, a Black Country song if the song the Black artist is performing meets our definition of Country song. This lets me welcome Tina Turner's "Nutbush City Limits" into the Country canon without having to debate whether by releasing *Tina Turns the Country On!* she was declaring a Country artist identity, or whether "Proud Mary" is a rock and Country anthem or a Country-rock album.

Black Country is a big tent with many entry points. My checklist is not a litmus test. It's a likeliness test. It's a way to educate your ears and your eyes. Is there Blackness you have refused to see and hear? Are there Southern, Black, and Country aesthetics, instruments, and theologies that migrated north and persisted, ignored but embedded in flowers of sound? If you strain can you catch the trace of the Black folk whitewashed out of the rural South, the rural West, out of rural America on Country radio and records but somehow still present in Country songs?

Country is "Black as the sky on a moonless night." Knowing that has everything to do with when, where, and to whom I was born.

IN A MOTOWN CHERRY TREE: LEARNING TO WRITE HILLBILLY SONGS

I was born May 4, 1959, in Detroit, Michigan, to George Stanley Randall, Bettie Jean Randall, and a large, up-from-Selma, Alabama, re-rooted in Motown, Randall family.

My grandmother, my mother, and my favorite aunt shared a single love. It was not me. It was not my father. It was not Motown music, the Pistons, gardening, cooking, God, or money—the common passions in the Black Detroit of my childhood. It was Country Music.

Beyond the fact that they each loved Country—an affection they shared with far more African-Americans than is commonly recognized—points of similitude are scarce as hen's teeth. Untangling the way they loved Country, the why they loved Country, and the who Country they loved has become, over time, a way I came to understand each of these women and some important complexities about the American South and race in America.

Country entered each of these women's lives and moved through their lives in disparate ways. They loved different artists. They sang different songs. They each had a different preferred medium to receive the music.

My grandmother, Dear, first heard Country as a Black female living-in with her white Alabama family in the rural South. My mother, Bettie, first heard Country living with her Black foster parents, the Jacksons, in a rural Michigan town called Farmington, full of German immigrant Lutherans. She was a Black female with her Black family surrounded by whiteness in the rural North. My favorite aunt, Mary Frances, first heard Country in Selma, Alabama, while living in the bosom of her secure Black family in a brick house with a dining table and a piano.

Dear's favorite song was Mother Maybelle Carter's "Will the Circle Be Unbroken." Her preferred medium was the unrecorded human voice. She sang Country aloud to me and encouraged me to sing back to her. Born Georgia Minnie Litsey in 1898, Dear was a woman of exquisite gestures. She would make a flowery rope by tying the sashes from four or five of her dresses together end to end with bows. When it was time to go to sleep, I was invited to spend the night in her room with its twin beds across from each other on opposite walls with a cross high on the wall in between. After we said prayers, after she kissed my forehead, she would tuck one end of the flower rope into my hand as I snuggled into the guest twin. Then she would climb into her bed holding the other end of the flower rope. Her last words were not, "Go to sleep." They were not, "Sweet dreams." They were always, "Now we can hold hands all night long." She froze cherries and orange slices into her ice cubes. She ironed my sheets and towels. She cooked me dress boxes full of stewed apples that she dyed preposterous fairytale colors, blue and purple. She dug a goldfish pond in her backyard, stocked it with fish we would name, then banked that pond with rosebushes.

Dear sang to me. The sound traveled a short distance from her lips to my ear because I was usually on her broad, rose-fabric-covered lap when she sang. Her repertoire was starkly limited. She had a song of longing and optimism, "My Bonnie Lies Over the Ocean." She had a song of promise and enthusiasm, "She'll Be Coming Round the Mountain." And she had a song of loss and wonder, "Will the Circle Be Unbroken."

For Dear, singing was an intimate act; a ritual, made for two, one old

and one young, an art as ancient and immediate as a lullaby. She turned every song she ever sang to me into a cradle song. Her intention was never to hush. Her intention was to awaken her tiny audience to the mystery layered between the notes, in the sound, in the details of story, in the truth that song was a pleasure that triumphed over death. Her cradle songs were not invitations to mindless sleep, they were invitations to vivid dreaming, wild imaginings, and wise knowing.

"Will the Circle Be Unbroken" was the song she used to integrate death into the center of life as a cause of sadness—but not fear. And it was a place she taught me to change the words to suit my meaning. When she sang the song she learned from a Carter Family recording, she didn't sing the words Mother Maybelle sang, "And I saw the hearse come rolling for to carry my mother away." She sang, "And I saw the hearse come rolling for to carry my sweet son away." Dear sang, "Undertaker, undertaker, undertaker please go slow that young man you are hauling Lord I hate to see him go." Or she sang, "That chi—ild." She could turn *child* into a two syllable word, or *baby*, saddest of all, she sang, "That *baby* you are hauling Lord I hate to see him go." Over the years, between singing her verses of this song, she told me over and over versions of the same two funeral stories, the funeral of her eldest son and her youngest son.

When she sang "baby" she could have been talking about either one. Her eldest son, Bill, died in 1958, in his thirties, ravaged by a toxic combination of tax law, illiteracy, angry wife, and alcohol. Her youngest, Ernest, died at the age of four of asphyxiation in a house fire on Black Bottom's Chene Street, shortly after the family moved up from Alabama in the early forties. Both were her babies. One of them, his casket fell out the back of the hearse. I don't know which one that was. The way she told the story, it could have happened to either. This shock, this theft, fragmented her memory into connected bright shards of grief. The death of one son became the death of the other.

Breathing became twisting a kaleidoscope as the same old pieces fell into new geometries of evolving sorrow. Using the fragments, Dear didn't narrate the events just as she felt them. She told them as she felt they would be most useful to me. She didn't abuse her audience, or use her audience, she served her audience. What could only hurt, she held to herself.

She narrated to me what she had processed, not what she needed to process. I was not her therapist, not her journal, not her diary. I was her chosen audience of her spoken word Black Country song.

This is Black Country, this was Motown: she was in the first car of mourners, following the hearse that carried her son's casket, when the back door of the hearse slowly opened, and the hearse kept rolling. Slowly the casket slipped out of the hearse and fell down into the road. The bumper of the car she was riding in almost kissed her son's coffin. She was riding in a car that almost rolled over her son's body. A casket in the road with your dead son inside it. Suddenly that. Witness that. Suddenly know there is no bottom. She thought she was at bottom. Then the casket is in the road and her car is still rolling. There is no bad as it gets. Things can *always* get worse, and after that day she would believe they will often get worse. That is the blues.

Witness this . . . Breaking light in her mind: *I am not this thing swirling round me. I am not this thing happening to me.* Let the coffin splinter. Let the brains splatter. Let the flames lap the skin and the hair. Let all of that happen and it could not change this, Ernest and Bill were beloved, their bold beauty was seen. In the center of the shitstorm, in the heat of the flame, in the middle of the road can't change that. And she knew her baby, both her dead babies, Ernest and Bill, knew it, too, because they had sat on her lap and heard her sing just for them. Let the falling of the coffin out of the hearse be her son jumping out to sign love to her one last time. This is Black Country in all its surreal sweetness: audacious hope, wild imaginings, and necessary lies.

She sang me "Will the Circle Be Unbroken" and told me that story because she wanted me to know that I was not the things that would happen to me, or on me, or even in me. I was someone beloved, even in the center of this madness. In the middle of the swirl, she was kept busy raising children, beloved and loving, walking, talking, singing, love.

For Bettie Country was Hank Williams's "Hey, Good Lookin'" and radio, it was distracting and distracted sensual pleasure. My mother, who was born in Ironton, Ohio, in December of 1937, probably first heard Country Music in that place and time. The year she was born the big songs were Roy Acuff's "The Great Speckled Bird," the Bob Wills and his Texas Playboys version of "Right or Wrong" and Patsy Montana's "He's a Wild and Reckless Cowboy." But shortly after she was born, her parents left Ironton, a blue-collar forge town that was ravaged by a flood, and landed on Hastings Street in Detroit's Black Bottom, a place my mother was very unlikely to have heard much Country at all. Live music and jukeboxes were the thing in Black Bottom—blues, jazz, gospel, big band, ragtime. When my mother was five, her mother died, her father vanished, and Bettie was placed in foster care. She landed in an almost all-white rural farming village where she heard hymns in the German Lutheran church and Country everywhere else. Her foster parents (who immediately enrolled her in a private all-white-except-Bettie parochial school) were Black, prosperous, strict, yet loving.

Hank Williams played the Michigan State Fair in Detroit on September 2, 1949, and it's possible my mother heard that performance. She said she did. It was the hundredth year of the fair. She spoke of it, but it wasn't clear if she remembered the event or had heard stories from friends describing the event. His sound of sorrow and twang was a comfort and an excitement. As she approached graduation and her last years of high school, the state of Michigan snatched Bettie from the countryside, against the wishes of the couple who had cared for her for about a decade, and placed her in another foster home in Detroit.

Country became the only connection to a world she had lost. She heard Country on the Detroit radio as a variety of shows were constantly going on and off the air after Goodwill Frolic launched in 1944 and had a two-year run. *Hayloft Jamboree*, *Big Barn Frolic*, *Lazy Ranch Boys Barn Dance*, *Michigan Barn Dance*, and *Casey Clark Jamboree* were just some of the local Country shows filling thirty minutes or an hour of the airwaves of a Saturday night, and *Sage Brush Melodies* was a Monday through Friday afternoon show in the fifties. She for sure heard Tennessee Ernie Ford perform in 1958 at the Michigan State Fair. Once upon a time she had pictures of that.

In 1962, WEXL was pure Country twenty-four hours a day, seven days a week, along with the national shows, the *Grand Ole Opry*, and the *National Barn Dance*. Alone together in the car or in the basement laundry room where she kept a transistor on the windowsill, Country on the radio was the good secret we shared. It wasn't the only secret, but it was the good one.

Aunt Mary Frances was Ray Charles's "Born to Lose" and the stereo. I was about six months old in October of 1959 when *The Genius of Ray Charles* album was released. I bet Mary Frances bought it within a week. She was an up-to-date and snazzy chick with a large and eclectic collection of selected LPs, 78s, and 45s. Daddy said she wore that album out playing it for me, her new niece. Then she taught me to talk.

The first word I ever spoke was "Scoobiedoobiedobaby." My aunt Mary Frances cooed those syllables, "scoobiedoobiedobaby," over and over to me, punctuated by tickles until I cooed the word back to Mary Frances. I don't remember that, but I remember being told it by my father. In his telling, Sister cooed and tickled as Frank Sinatra crooned. And when I learned to talk good, Sister and I would play "What's this?"

"Just for a Thrill" was the single released in February of 1960, peaking at 16 on the R & B charts just in time for it to be a bona fide hit by my first birthday.

Toddler Alice would wave a black shellacked disc in front of Mary Frances's face and ask, "What's this?" And she would read the label back at me. "What's this? What's this?" We would make our way through a dozen discs before she tired of that game and started playing records, and then we played the game we were never too tired to play: cha-cha-round-the-living-room.

To quote one of my favorite Country writers of all time, Kris Kristofferson: "Loving her was easier than anything I'll ever do again." By the time I was three or four we'd stack those discs on a gadget that let you play multiple singles at a time on the stereo and cha-cha ourselves into a happy oblivion.

I don't remember Mary Frances ever turning on her giant television in the living room. My aunt's stereo and her large collection of vinyl records were the heart of her house—my first home. We gathered around the stereo, singing "Just for a Thrill," and eventually all the songs on Ray Charles's *Modern Sounds in Country and Western Music* and we would cha-cha. Mary Frances loved to cha-cha, at least she thought it was the perfect dance for a little girl and her aunt. We would whirl to "Bye Bye Love." I didn't know what that song meant to her. I didn't know then about that house fire on Chene Street, that took her baby daughter and nephew. How much sorrow she hid. She knew what it was to say bye, bye, love; bye, bye, happiness; bye, bye, most innocent of sweet caresses; bye, bye, Baby Marilyn, burned up in a fire. Mary Frances rose from grief to love me, rose from drowning in a bottle to love me. She loved me so passionately that I have at times wondered if I wasn't her daughter. My daddy loved his older sister so truly I have wondered if they had not been in love.

But I think it was this wholesome crazy thing: Daddy, recognizing my mother's brokenness, needed a mother for his child, and she needed a child to mother, and so Daddy gave me to Mary Frances, and Mary Frances moved my father and mother into an apartment in her beautiful house on Parkside—a house with a yard on all four sides—that I came home to after birth in Detroit's Women's Hospital.

Whatever she may have needed after the Chene Street fire and deaths, Ray Charles's *Modern Sounds in Country and Western Music* was the only therapy Mary Frances got. She sang along with Brother Ray when he crooned, "I love you so much it hurts me." Sometimes she was singing those words to her dead baby, Marilyn. Sometimes she was singing them to me. All the time claiming the pain of loving allowed her to keep loving Marilyn and start loving me. But it hurt.

Modern Sounds in Country and Western Music was released on April 1, 1962. I was almost three years old when it dropped. Mary Frances had coped for a year with me reaching ages her Marilyn didn't see without the help of Brother Ray. For years, she played those records for me over and over. That album she worshipped like a shiny black miracle became my foundation text. An entire alphabet, a vocabulary of love, careless love, dying love, promised love, leaving love, arriving love, perplexing love, torturing love, blind love, seeing love, liberating love, all kinds of love.

The therapy I remember getting in Detroit? Edgewater amusement park. Amusement parks feature large in my childhood as places where it was safe to be adventurous, safe to explore, safe to scream, comfortable to feel afraid and disoriented. I particularly remember loving an Edgewater Park ride called the Rotor. You entered a cylinder, leaned back against the wall, and the cylinder started going faster and faster around until you were pressed into the wall and then the floor fell out and you were stuck to the wall. It was some kind of therapy for me to have the floor fall out from under me and have me be alright, to live to scream in delight at the bottom falling out—because I constantly felt like the floor was about to fall out from under me and dreaded it. On the Rotor we embraced the fall. On the Rotor I had some kind of visceral knowledge that things I feared like being home alone with Mama, could be survived.

Bettie's Charley Pride single, "Just Between You and Me," Mary Frances's *Modern Sounds in Country and Western Music,* and Dear's three songs ("My Bonnie Lies Over the Ocean," the Celtic ballad that may date back to the days of Bonnie Prince Charles; "She'll Be Coming Round the Mountain," the African-American folksong that functioned as a rail on the Underground Railroad; and "Will the Circle Be Unbroken," the Country classic) were my first and forever Black Country canon. Dear appreciated a song that worked, just like she did, on multiple levels; songs with a simple surface that hid complex depth. And so do I. What Black women taught me to love, I taught myself to write.

I started songwriting sitting in a Motown cherry tree, about the age of five, in 1966. But first I was sitting outside a bar in 1962.

Dusk in Detroit. Daddy parked his car, pocketed the keys, and invited me to play with the steering wheel while he "ducked inside." Maybe I frowned. He said he wouldn't be gone long, then pointed to a place on the clock and said he would be back before the hand got to that place. And I knew he would. Daddy *always* came back *before* the clock hand got to the place he pointed. But that evening that wasn't enough. The car was warm and comfortable, but I didn't want to be alone. I looked out the window. I saw familiar bright letters hanging in the darkening sky. Words Daddy had spoken, "Speak up, gal, you're not down South," so many times before were floating toward me. I spoke. I said, "Daddy don't go in that B-A-R."

Daddy looked at me and declared, "I have left you too many times in front of too many bar signs if you spelling that word out. Never again."

We walked into the bar holding hands. Soon I was seated on a high stool sipping something garnished with a maraschino cherry. That's the day I learned the power of language. After that day, whenever Daddy stopped in a bar for a quick shot he took me with him, because I had used my words.

In the house on Parkside there was a side yard with five fruit trees. By the time I was five years old many the summer afternoon I would climb up into the limbs of that cherry tree with a small jar of maraschino cherries secured to my wrist with a handkerchief. When I made my way to a secure perch, I would eat candied cherries, watching a sea of cars flow by on the John C. Lodge Freeway, and let songs—from my grandmother's lips, from my mother's radio, from my aunt's stereo—roll 'round my head.

And sometimes instead of munching I would sing out loud. I started off singing other people's words to the birds, then one day I started singing, "Daddy don't go in that B-A-R, please don't leave me alone in the car, Daddy don't go in that B-A-R." Twenty-seven syllables. My first song.

Fast forward. 1983. I moved to Nashville, toting a folder full of Country song lyrics with me. I only remember two of the titles. One of them, "Reckless Night," would go on to be my first cut when the Forester Sisters recorded it. The other was an expanded version of my original "B-A-R."

The lyric folder traveled with me to all my early days meet-and-greets to find potential co-writers. When Archie Jordan (who has won fifteen

ASCAP awards and wrote the mega-hit Country classic "What a Difference You've Made in My Life") agreed to have breakfast with me at Pancake Pantry, I felt lucky. At the diner, as Archie silently looked through all the typed sheets lyrics twice or maybe three times, I felt nervous. Finally, he pulled out the sheet with the title "B-A-R."

"This one's the hit."

"That happened to me."

"I know."

That song never got recorded because I could not, would not, let go of the singsong little melody that I made up in a Motown cherry tree. And I didn't know how to share the story of my daddy leaving me outside of bars to duck inside for a drink without pathologizing my childhood, in particular, and pathologizing Black childhood in general.

I didn't need to worry about that. Much to my frustration, whenever I wrote a Country song that got recorded the audience assumed the characters in the song were white unless it was explicitly stated otherwise. Even that song that Adia sang that begins, "He was Black as the sky on a moonless night" when it was sung by Radney Foster, some fans (I know, because I've talked to them) failed to notice the song is about a Black cowboy. They thought "black" was referring to a mood not a man, or an outfit.

I could have written "B-A-R" and, even if it was sung by Charley Pride, few if any would be imagining a little colored girl speaking up, reading out the letters. And the song might have been a hit as Archie Jordan predicted. When the characters are white in Country songs some very questionable and some absolutely unacceptable parenting is lauded.

Guy Clark's "Desperados Waiting for a Train" features a grandfather figure who teaches his "grandson" to drive so the very young child can drive them both when the grandfather is too drunk to drive. In Bobby Gentry's "Fancy" a hard-pressed mother whores her daughter out with the words, "Just be nice to the gentlemen, Fancy, they'll be nice to you." Even more startling is Tanya Tucker's genius performance of "Blood Red and Goin' Down." A daddy leaves his ten-year-old outside a bar and goes in and shoots her mama and her lover. The girl sees their bodies "soaking up the sawdust on the floor." Tucker's performance convinces the audience there's something wild and wonderful and brave about having a passionate mother, a justice-seeking father, and being gritty enough to witness it.

A thing I love about Country? Country understands that people can be very imperfect and still be worthy of our empathy, our concern.

A thing I hate about Country? For the most part Black characters must be exemplars of striking virtue to be worthy of empathy. There are exceptions to be sure, but these Country classics reveal the unwritten rule: Reuben James, the hero of Kenny Rogers and the First Edition's "Reuben James," is heroically self-sacrificing and self-effacing as he cares for a white child; the old gray Black gentleman is magically wise in "Old Dogs, Children, and Watermelon Wine"; and Curtis Loew in "The Ballad of Curtis Loew" is not a talented musician, he is "the finest picker to ever play the blues."

If Tanya Tucker had sung B-A-R it could have been a great big hit.

THE SUPREMES SING COUNTRY AT THE COPACABANA

About the time I wrote my first Country song in a cherry tree, I heard my first Country song performed live on stage, "Queen of the House."

I was what my father proudly called "ringside," in a tiny shell-pink and shimmering silk-satin dress expertly tailored to frame my slight forty pounds when the Supremes played their very first run at New York's famed Copacabana in August of 1965. "Queen of the House" would appear on their album *Live at the Copa*, but it was the live performance that besotted me.

The Supremes were the first Motown act to play the Copa, the first of what would be considered R & B singers to play the Copa, and the first very young singers to headline the Copa. Their performance accelerated the change of Motown music from being the sound of Black Detroit to being the sound of young America in the mid-twentieth century and the sound of country club dances, old Black folk house parties, and so many weddings in the twenty-first century.

Impresario and record label chief Berry Gordy culled from the American songbook to create a set list featuring standards and show tunes intended to appeal to Copa's swanky New York audience. "Queen of the Hearts" was a departure from the central plan.

It was the Supremes working behind enemy lines as freedom fighters according to George Stanley Randall. And they sang a Country song looking straight at me because my dress "caught their eyes," Daddy said.

The dress, the most magnificent dress I had ever worn, or have ever worn, was a gift from and creation of Aunt Mary Frances, the woman who introduced me to the sounds of Ray Charles and to the words of Lil Hardin, to the fact that Lil Hardin was a couturier, and a costume designer, just like Mary Frances. Daddy knew Lil made important music. Aunt Mary Frances knew Lil made Louis Armstrong suits and dresses for socialites.

My dress was me reimagined as a young mermaid, shiny, powerful, and modern; me imagined to catch and delight the eyes of three extraordinary, very young women: Diana Ross, twenty-one, Florence Ballard, twenty-two, and Mary Wilson, twenty-one. The Supremes. When they saw me Mary Frances hoped they would see they had stepped into the future and were bringing brown gals with them.

That was the big point of my one-of-a-kind dress. There was another point. Mary Frances couldn't trust herself to go to New York with us. Ringside in a club, she couldn't help but drink too much and start talking to any brilliant woman on stage. She had had full-on arguments with Billie Holiday when she was on stage and Mary Frances was ringside, but she had found a way to applaud the Supremes with fabric.

And she was doing a little bit of what Lil did for Louis with the dress. And she told me. She was sewing me a costume that might entice somebody to take my picture and would look good in a picture. Mary Frances sewed for me just like how she had understood Lil to have sewn for Louis.

I still have the black-and-white glossy photograph of me at the Copa in the little shiny dress. I am sitting around a table with my mother, my father, and my babysitter Beverly Jasper, who would later become a judge. In the background of the picture is another child who had probably gone to the World's Fair. A white child, a boy. I wonder if he will be at the Beatles concert the next day. I will be at the Broadway musical *Golden Boy* watching Lola Falana dance with Sammy Davis, Jr.

It was a big music weekend even by New York standards. The Supremes were playing the Copa, Sammy Davis was headlining on Broadway, and the Beatles were playing Shea Stadium. That last was the big deal for most folks. For me the big deal was the Supremes. Even though I toted a Beatles lunch box to kindergarten at St. Phillip's Lutheran School (the first Aladdin lunch box that featured a Black person wouldn't go on sale till I was in the fourth or fifth grade), and I liked to sing one Beatles song, "I Want to Hold Your Hand," and I liked one Beatle, Ringo, the Beatle who would eventually give my beloved Lil a posthumous cut when he recorded a version of "Brown Gal" he called "Bad Boy" in 1978. But I *loved* all three of the original Supremes, and there were three Supremes songs I never got tired of: "Baby Love," "Come See About Me," and "Stop! In the Name of Love."

I could perform those songs complete with lyrics and original hand gestures. I didn't just love the Supremes, I adored them and not from a distance. The Supremes had shown up at my dancing school, performed at the school dancing recital where I, too, had performed, and they were just back from what the press (my family didn't read to me from books, they read to me from *Jet*, *Ebony*, the *Michigan Chronicle*, the *Detroit Free Press*, and the *Detroit News*) called "globe-trotting." They were the first young Black women I personally knew who crossed an ocean in a plane in what looked to me like a three-person friend group that wasn't so different from me, Anita, and Norice, the best friend group formed during my kindergarten days at the all-Black St. Phillips Lutheran School.

Part of the just-like-us thing—they were Country and city. The city part was all the sleek and modern shine and polish, like a hard Detroit car surface, the synchronized dancing that signed working an assembly line. The Country part was the soft Southern accents, the wide-eyed wonder, the sober joy.

With lyrics written by Mary Taylor, a tune by Roger Miller, and published by my future publishers, Tree, "Queen of the House" was a Country-as-calico Answer Song. "Queen of the House" was the answer to "King of the Road."

Many Answer Songs exist in a kind of contentious marriage with the songs they are coupled to. "The Wild Side of Life" and "It Wasn't God Who Made Honky Tonk Angels" are the iconic example of that subgenre.

"Queen of the House" and "King of the Road" share a coupling that is more like a twinship. The Supremes cover of "Queen of the House" is a complex call and response—and a profound answer to "King of the Road." They perform the divide between wives as people who "don't pay no union dues" yet work long hours, and husbands who do pay union dues and work long hours.

"Queen of the House" as initially performed by Jody (no relation to Roger) Miller parses a gendered-divide in a precariously middle-class space. This woman plays bridge while wishing she was married to a rich millionaire.

And as performed by the Supremes, "Queen of the House" parses a gendered-divide in racialized space. Their version slyly spotlights the divide between those who serve strangers as maids and nurses, and those who serve their own families as maids and nurses; as well as the divide between those who have sex with the king of the house inside of marriage and by choice; and those who have sex with the king of the house outside of marriage and without choice.

"Queen of the House" was a big song in 1965, burning up the pop and Country charts and earning Jody Miller a Grammy Award for Best Female Country and Western Vocal Performance in 1966. In 1965, before the Grammys, the Supremes found this song and made a few changes and let it float into my six-year-old ears. I clapped with my hands almost as loud as Mary Frances's dress. I felt Mary Frances's power and my own. I sparkled like a photon.

Mama didn't like that. And Mama didn't like the Supremes at the Copa. She liked them when she thought they were being groomed to look like her. She didn't like them as they started to go globe-trotting, leaving her behind. By the time we got to the World's Fair weekend she was done with the Supremes and wanted everyone else to be done with them, too. Mama had a way to one-up the Supremes, she started talking about Scott Joplin's mama. She was the person Mama wanted to add to the Supremes-sing-Country conversation.

FLORENCE JOPLIN, ERASED FOREMOTHER OF BLACK COUNTRY

There was another Florence, a better Florence, an earlier Florence, Scott Joplin's mama, Florence Joplin.

Bettie loved Scott Joplin music. His rhythms and melodies entertained and uplifted her with ease. When she played them on Mary Frances's stereo, his ragtime bounce was our singular, shared, wholesome delight.

What my mother knew about Scott Joplin's mother would have come from Black showbiz gossip that she heard in the Club DeLisa in Chicago, hanging around Ziggy's (more formally, the Ziggy Johnson School of the Theater, a dancing school attended by many Gordy children and supported by numerous Motown acts) or at Detroit's Gotham Hotel. The Gotham Hotel attracted so many old troupers who had collected so much gossip. What I know comes from chasing that gossip down and this is what I found.

Scott Joplin's mother, Florence, played the banjo and sang. His daddy played the fiddle. Florence was born in Kentucky in 1841 and born free. It should be more widely known that her free Black parents, Susan and Milton Givens, took her to Texas where they settled in a cotton farming community with other Black families, the Crows, the Shepherds, and the Smiths, in northeast Texas. In Texas, Florence met Giles, a slightly younger man who had been born into slavery in North Carolina and had arrived in Texas enslaved but managed to achieve his freedom before the war. Perhaps with the assistance of Florence's family. Giles and Florence managed to marry before the war. Their first child, Monroe Joplin, was born about the time of the battle Southerners called Manassas and Northerners called Bull Run. Scott wasn't born until 1868, three years after the war ended. Scott and his younger brothers, Robert and William, started off playing fiddle like their father. How I would have loved to hear the Joplin family band.

The disbanding was sudden. Giles ran off. Florence supported the family by doing domestic work with son Scott sometimes accompanying her.

When the Scott Joplin story is told it is often said that Scott taught himself to play piano in a home where his mother cleaned. The Black press told a different story. A paper called the *Freeman* covered the career of Scott's brother, Robert B. Joplin, noting that when he played the Lincoln Theater in Knoxville, Tennessee, in late 1907 or early 1908, he played to "packed" houses and offered up a number that was a rendition of "Montana-Anna" "assisted by the company in real cowboy costumes and brought down the house." Black Detroit remembered Will Joplin, reputed to be the best singer of the group; he died in Detroit in 1928.

Many scholars write of the formal lessons Joplin received from a Mr. Weiss and say *nothing* of what Florence Givens Joplin taught Scott and of what Giles Joplin taught their second son. Even without the father there was a banjo, two fiddles, and a piano in the second incarnation of the Joplin family band. I want to hear that.

My mother talked about the cradle songs Florence sang. The Black Country cradle songs that rose in the air of Texarkana, or wherever it was she thought his mama sang to him. My mother gave me that. She played me Scott's ragtime and made me curious about his mother. She walked the streets of New York looking so beautiful and talking about Florence Joplin.

The sound of Scott Joplin, the sight of Bettie gleaming ringside at the Copa, beauty. These were things about her I could love. A place she touched me that didn't hurt. A light she shined I wouldn't choose to unsee. For the beauty Bettie gave me I would not let her go.

For most families, the World's Fair, which we were also going to, was the big deal of a New York weekend in 1965. The only thing Daddy liked was the big globe that showed how big Africa was a lot better than a flat map did. For my family the World's Fair was secondary. Music, including Country Music, was the big deal.

I heard Diana Ross, Florence Ballard, and Mary Wilson sing on Friday night. And on Saturday, when I was supposed to be staying in a hotel room with my babysitter, I was on my daddy's lap, thanks to a scalped ticket bought at a high price, watching beautiful brown Lola Falana dance half-naked. And I began to imagine, Mama, Daddy, and me being happy forever after.

In years to come beautiful brown Lola Falana, following in Herb Jeffries's footsteps, would star in a Western, a horse opera, as Lola Colt, the horse riding, gunslinging, song singing, Black heroine in an Italian-imagined West, and I would see that film and remember her being a golden-colored girl in *Golden Boy*.

The weekend Daddy, Mama, and I spent with the Supremes, Florence Joplin, and Lola was the very best weekend I would ever spend with my parents. Music, dance, and imagining were the center of my World's Fair weekend. And Black Country was at the center of it.

If I wanted fair warning that my world was about to unravel, I should have paid a little closer attention to that ringside photograph. I might have seen that my father looked a little like the cat who swallowed the canary, that my mother looked strained. Or maybe children never notice things like that. If I paid close attention, I might have noticed my babysitter was disturbingly beautiful. A copy of the photograph blown up to poster size leans against a window in my office. When I look at it now, I wonder if my father was having an affair with my babysitter. And I worry for the giddy girl, me, oblivious to the drama at the table.

By the time the Country Music Hall of Fame (founded in 1961) opened its museum doors on Music Row in April of 1967, I, and probably a lot of other people with roots in Detroit's Black Bottom or connections to Motown, could have named two Black women who deserved to be hanging in any hall honoring Country, Lil Hardin and Florence Joplin, and at least three more who deserved to be contenders, Diana Ross, Mary Wilson, and Florence Ballard, the original Supremes.

To this day, there are no Black women in the Country Music Hall of Fame Rotunda and no Black women in the Nashville Songwriters Hall of Fame.

D.C. DAZE: SMALL TOWNS (ARE SMALLER FOR GIRLS)

I didn't know what an area code was.

I knew Sun's favorite number, 020, but I didn't know the area code for Detroit was 313. I knew my phone number. I was the star student of the third grade, but I couldn't phone home.

I have not forgotten the day Lena arrived at the door of my little all-Black Lutheran school, St. Peter's, asking to have a word with me. She was wearing a pantsuit with snowflakes appliquéd on the shoulder and four gold bangles. She was wearing pumps. I stepped out of the classroom into the quiet hall. The door clicked shut behind me. She said, "I'm leaving your father. You can stay here or you can go with me. If you stay here, he will take good care of you. If you stay here, you will never see me again."

Her detachment was contagious. That's how it looks to me now. What it felt like then was that the queen was quitting the castle and the princess felt compelled to run after her.

"Where are you going?" I asked.

"I'm not saying till we get on the plane. In case you change your mind."

The worst decision of my life was not hard to make.

I published that scene the first time years ago, in a novel, *Pushkin and the Queen of Spades.* But only three things in it are fictional: the mother's name; the mother's clothes (I remember a black mink coat but not what she wore beneath it); and the school's name (Greenfield Peace Lutheran School). What is absolutely true? The worst decision of *my* life, circa January 3, 1968, was not hard to make.

I believed I would never see my mother again. I believed she had nobody and my father had everyone. I believed she needed me.

And I thought she had changed. It had been a long time since she had hurt me. After the time in my last year of preschool when my father confronted her, with his mother's accusation, "your wife is hurting your daughter" and Daddy threatened to beat Mama if she was hurting me and I lied and said she wasn't hurting me, my mother stopped afflicting my body. She never hurt me again in Detroit. I wanted to know the new Mama better. I wasn't ready to lose the woman completely. And I believed what she said; my mother never lied. If I didn't go with her, I would never see her again.

And I knew Daddy would find me come hell or highwater. There was no risk of losing him. We had a "Ain't No Mountain High Enough" kind of love, a multigenerational commitment to resisting disruptions of Black familial bonds. No force in nature would keep him from getting to me—if I would just call out for help—and signal my location.

Unfortunately, for a hot moment the area code thing and fear that my mother might calmly and effectively strangle me with her bare hands kept me from making the call. I was lost in a completely foreign-to-me world.

We settled the very first night into Southwest Washington, D.C., a white-collar planned community on the Potomac River of contemporary high-rises and townhouses that functioned as an almost self-contained small town where I would live for the next three or four years. I could walk to church, to my public school, to a grocery store, to two different movie theaters, and, if not to a swimming hole, to three or four different swimming pools one could enter—if you had the right pass. And I, and my new fancy D.C. friends—most of whom attended private schools—had the right passes.

Detroit was, at the time of my birth, a big and majority white city; my Detroit was a majority Black metropolis. D.C., according to the census, was a majority Black metropolis; my D.C. was a majority white small Southern town.

Like most small Southern towns, there was an "across the tracks" area where the poor Black people were relegated to living. Southwest Washington was built in an era of "urban renewal" that included a lot of razing Black neighborhoods and "Negro removal" into housing projects the city neglected and underfunded.

The first joke/riddle I *heard* on a third-grade playground when I arrived in the late sixties? "Ain't Aunt Jemima on a pancake box?" A brown girl with soft-heavy-Southern drawl was posing the non sequitur. I answered, "Yes." Other girls with Southern accents jabbed their fingers toward me laughing and exclaiming, "Her mama on a pancake box!" and "She say, 'Ain't, ain't yo'mama on a pancake box?' and you say, 'yes.'" They expected this brown newcomer with two long braids and glasses to be torn down. The facts of life they knew? The White House itself was a white columned mansion where a whole lot of uniformed Black men, some of whom they even knew or were related to, attended to a white man, President Lyndon Johnson. They knew a whole lot of Black mothers and aunts who worked as domestics flipping pancakes in wealthy white households. "The Aunt Jemima" riddle was a potent taunt because it was rooted in the familiar, even to a child, rural Southern realities.

Coming from the northern urban realities of Detroit, the snap didn't slap. I didn't know one Black woman who worked as a domestic. I knew women who worked on tire factory assembly lines, women who worked as teachers, a whole lot of barmaids, women who worked at Motown and sang for Motown. I had seen a lot of "whores out on the stroll" even if I didn't know them. But I didn't know a single Black woman working in a white home, had never seen a Black woman in a uniform walking to a bus stop to ride across town to take care of someone else's house and children.

The defining taunt in my Detroit playground days? "They said the best was Sugar Ray, that's before they all saw Clay!" This meant: Time's up! You over! But it also meant, you may not be as pretty or powerful as Cassius Clay, but you are still somebody! Sugar Ray Robinson is sweet! That snap is rooted in Northern urban swagger and pride.

It was hard to be proud when you're a Black girl in the "overgrown Southern town" that was Washington, D.C., in 1968. Many Black people wouldn't go into Garfinkel's department store because they remembered not being able to try on clothes there, not being able to eat there. They felt shamed by the elegant edifice, and they shamed some of the Black folk who chose to enter the space.

In Detroit, dessert was homemade sweet potato pie that started as potatoes set to boil on the stove or apple crisp from the dessert section of the TV dinner tray. My first dessert in D.C. was chocolate mousse served chilled in a champagne flute. I knew how to make the recipe by the end of the week. We moved into the fancy high-rise building of Carrollsburg Square. Thurgood Marshall, his second wife, and two sons were our neighbors in the townhouses there. My Detroit clothes that came straight from the pages of *Children's Vogue*, included a little coat of gray rabbit fur that would have fit in with clothes from the court of Louis the XIV, looked completely out of place in ultra-contemporary southwest Washington, D.C., where the kids dressed like hippies, preps, or ragamuffins. The weather was a little warmer. The cars were different. Volvos. Volkswagens. Mercedes-Benzes, Jaguars, and some regular cars. We soon had a new Ford, a Duster, that was so unlike, so dowdy, compared to the Ford Mustang we had had back in Detroit.

Songs were my ongoing connection to Motown. Every time I heard Tammi Terrell and Marvin Gaye singing "Ain't No Mountain High Enough," the George-and-Alice theme song, I was reassured that Daddy was coming.

I had sung along with him so many times to that Tammi and Marvin duet, too many times for me not to believe he was coming. That melody was written, I believe I knew this back then, by a brilliant young Black woman, Valerie Simpson.

"She's sharp, Valerie Simpson's sharp, almost an Anna," Daddy said. Or, he could have told it to me later, when Simpson was having bigger successes and the memories were folding over on each other.

What I knew for sure? Daddy compared every brilliant and pretty brown woman in the music business to his adored Anna Gordy, who, he reminded me, founded Anna Records with her sister before Barry founded Motown. To say Valerie Simpson was almost an Anna was to say she was someone I needed to know, someone important because she created. And she didn't live in Detroit, she lived in New York where we had gone to see the Supremes. New York being were Valerie Simpson "stayed" made New York more interesting for this (and I suspect a few other) colored girls from Motown and other Midwest burgs.

In the early weeks of 1968, every time I heard "Come See About Me," a Supremes song that never meant anything at all to me before I was kidnapped, I knew Daddy heard it, too, not at the same time I was hearing it, but he heard it, too. And I just knew that song was doing for me what Daddy wanted me to do for the world, "Speak for those who cannot speak for themselves." That song was telling Daddy I was crying and lonely. That song was urging him to "hurry up" and "come . . . see about your baby." I trusted the song to speak for me when I couldn't speak for myself. I trusted the song to be me when I couldn't be me.

The song worked. It took a few months, but Daddy found me. He was a fine investigator. He hired lawyers to try to win me back. He lost. I no longer lived in Detroit. I was a visitor. But if Valerie Simpson could make visiting Detroit work, so could I. But not Mary Frances.

Mary Frances died within the year, drowned in drink. She didn't survive my mother stealing me away and sequestering me someplace no one in the family knew where, or even if I was alive. She tried to leave me her favorite diamond cocktail ring. My grandmother took it. She didn't want my mother to get it. When my daddy, who desperately wanted it for me, tried to take it from his mother's hand, Dear had seemed to throw it over the backyard fence and into the alley. All Mary Frances managed to leave me was Lil.

Time has proven I could do far more with Lil than with a diamond ring.

SAVED BY LIL HARDIN AND *THE JOHNNY CASH SHOW*

On April 4, 1968, Martin Luther King, Jr., was assassinated. I had lived through the righteous fires of the 1967 Detroit rebellion, and then I lived through fires protesting MLK's assassination. I was still shaking from all of that when Bettie announced I would be leaving my new school, Amidon, and had been admitted to Georgetown Day School.

A strange solace came in the form of a Country song when it was announced that "These Boots Were Made for Walking" would be performed by third-grade girls in the Amidon talent show to celebrate the end of the school year.

I had already danced to that song at Ziggy's. After Nancy Sinatra had performed her mega hit on the Ed Sullivan show, my mother had been one of the women encouraging Ziggy to include "that Country number" in the dancing school extravaganza he called the Youth Colossal. He took the advice and come Father's Day 1966, Black girls in Detroit were dancing on stage at the Latin Quarter to a Country song that would be recorded that year by Loretta Lynn, Kitty Wells, Hank Williams, Jr., and the Supremes.

As the young teacher running and choreographing the Amidon show taught us our much simpler moves, dancing the pony on diagonals across the stage, she started talking about Women's Lib. She said "Boots" was all about knowing we could walk away from anything that wasn't good for us. I ponied across the Amidon Elementary School stage wearing little white go-go boots with fierce focus. I wanted to pony on back to Detroit city.

With no oversight from the Randalls, Bettie became a carefully vicious mother. She didn't leave many marks, but she inflicted physical pain and intended to inflict mental anguish. She didn't get so very far with that. I, who had once dreamed Mary Frances was my real mother, began to dream Lil, whose words explained my mother's peculiar passions and proclivities, was my mother. When Mary Frances left me, Lil Hardin was enough—if I held on to every fragment. I held on tight to the sound of her words as sung by Ray Charles, to the sound of her words as sung by her, to her sounds alone in strutting through some melody as proof of Black girl genius and power. I held on tight to the few facts I knew about her, that she had gone to Fisk, that she had played on "Blue Yodel #9," that she sewed and designed clothes, like my aunt Mary Frances. That she knew hundreds and hundreds of songs from all the bands and clubs.

I became more and more like my good mama, Lil. I tried to learn to sew. I wrote songs. Soon "These Boots Are Made for Walking" was not the only Nancy Sinatra song that danced in my brain, I had "Sugartime." I had a child's understanding of the song. For me, it was not about escaping into sex or romance as it was likely written to be, it was escaping into the bubble Lil led me to, the one where I bounced without trouble or effort, lifted on the wings not of a snow-white dove, but on syllable, and sound, and rhythm, on song. Only now in Washington, D.C., the soundtrack of my girl world was more Dusty (Springfield), Janis (Joplin), and Nancy (Sinatra) not Diana, Mary, and Florence; and the classic artist was Bob Dylan not Ray Charles.

My mother loved her some Bob Dylan. One of her Detroit friends told me decades later that Mama left Daddy to see if she could hook up with Dylan. They had met backstage in Detroit when he was just starting out. I guess if you were Mama and you had turned Belafonte's head and made James Brown want to squeeze you and scream, you sure as shit thought you could capture that scrawny boy in jeans.

But shortly after arriving in D.C., Mama, a quick study, realized musicians were not the thing there. Politicians, professors, journalists, consultants—they were the thing. That's why she was willing to pay the money for private school.

After a spring semester at the public elementary school in Southwest and a summer that included a visit back to Detroit and migrating with a pack of neighborhood kids from morning swimming at one pool, to lunch at someone's house, and afternoon swimming at another pool, I started riding a kind-of-hippy-sort-of street Volkswagen bus service uptown to Georgetown Day School in the fall of 1968.

Fourth grade at Georgetown Day School brought a major influx of new hyper-local Country Music influences. A bluegrass band called the Country Gentleman was popular with both the parents and older siblings of my new friends. Their music was played and talked about, and they were significant local celebrities. Unlike the musicians I knew in Detroit who didn't have prestigious day jobs, I believe the original members of that band included a doctor and a scientist. One of the songs that crashed into my Washington ear waves was Glen Campbell's anti-war Country classic "Galveston," which includes the lines "I am so afraid of dying . . ." and "I clean my gun and dream of Galveston."

Teachers (and parents) were called by their first names and the big days of the school year calendar were Christmas, Seder, Country Market Day, and Chinese Kite Day. (If your kite wouldn't fly someone might attach a helium balloon to it.) At lunch we danced to Jimi Hendrix, Janis Joplin, and sang along loudly to Three Dog Night. "It's a one two three four . . . I don't give a damn, next stop is Viet Nam!" We wore shoes as seldom as possible and our hair as long and shaggy as could be. We wore overalls and jeans and painters' pants, but no one's daddy worked on an assembly line. Most were psychiatrists, psychologists, consultants, elected politicians, or lawyers. Some of those lawyers worked for unions. Few or none were union members.

People at my new school thought the Supremes and the Temptations were strange. They scoffed at their matching well-pressed costumes, well-coifed hair, and synchronized dancing. They hated their fancy citified ways. We were at a well-funded school in the center of the city doing our best to look like poor folks just up from the country and off the farm. No one noticed the irony.

I found a formal introduction to Black Country Music on TV. And I've written a little bit about it in the pages of the *Oxford American* in an article about me and Dear watching Lawrence Welk. Between June 7, 1969, and March 31, 1971, fifty-eight episodes of *The Johnny Cash Show* aired on Saturday nights. This coincided exactly with a period in early middle school that I spent many weekends in a strange little hamlet on the Chesapeake Bay called Fishing Creek, the guest of an eleven-year-old spitfire. My friend looked almost exactly like an eleven-year-old version of Liza Minnelli circa 1969 in *The Sterile Cuckoo*, which means she had pale skin and a spiky black Beatles haircut. Her bedroom in the Fishing Creek farmhouse was in an unfinished attic up rickety stairs. She had relations who lived next door full-time in what I remember as a modern and modest ranch house. One relative who lived full-time on the island was an oysterman we adored because he would loan two eleven-year-old girls a small boat that we could use to explore the bay and nearby sandbars and islands alone, and who was willing to zip us out to the barren islands and leave us for hours to play in the sand between the giant bleached-white driftwood sculptures and would reliably come to pick us back up. He adored Johnny Cash. The first Saturday night on Fishing Creek I got to watch *The Johnny Cash Show* changed so much for me. Some grown folks drank beer, we kids drank Coke, and Johnny and his guest sang, and I started singing along in my head.

Johnny had O. C. Smith, Charley Pride, Ray Charles, Louis Armstrong, Stevie Wonder, Mahalia Jackson, Edwin Hawkins, and the Staple Singers on the show. Watching them and hearing them was a little like a quick trip back to the Detroit before the kidnapping.

Much about the show was familiar, including the importance of gathering to watch it. My grandmother, Dear, had loved to watch *The Lawrence Welk Show* on Saturday nights, all the cool cats in Detroit watched *The Ed Sullivan Show* on Sunday nights and critiqued it all week long but especially at my dancing school all the Saturday after. It was familiar to me, this gathering with a sense of importance round a television to watch and hear music. This Country show was not just the Blackest thing on Fishing Creek, it was the Blackest art thing in my whole Washington world.

I knew O. C. Smith, Louis Armstrong, Stevie Wonder, Mahalia Jackson, Edwin Hawkins, and the Staple Singers from Motown. But Charley Pride was somewhat new to me. Charley was cooler than cool Country. He had that accent that was something like my mama's. And he had that jump-off-the-screen handsome that is a combination of genius, crazy, and athleticism. Charley Pride was intense. He was disciplined. He was pulling me to Nashville from the first time I laid eyes on him. He wasn't quite as wild and poetic as Cassius Clay, my first great and abiding public crush, but there was something about Charley that had me crushing on him hard.

And I was intrigued by the presence of women songwriters who were singing out in the public. In Detroit, there were women songwriters and there were women singers, but they didn't often come together. Lil was an exception. There was a divide on *The Johnny Cash Show*, too, but there was also Joni Mitchell. And there was Buffy Sainte-Marie, Jeannie C. Riley, and Lulu, who I adored from *To Sir with Love*, a film I had seen in Detroit before moving to Washington. And Cass Elliot, Dusty Springfield, Judy Collins, and there was stop my heart and make me blink Loretta Lynn. I got "Coal Miner's Daughter." I got that she had lost a world just like I had. Those were the singers I noticed and who made the strongest positive impression on me. Checking the guides I know the Carter Family, Linda Ronstadt, Brenda Lee, Patti Page, Lynn Anderson, and Tammy Wynette—who I would one day quote leaving my first husband—were all on the show, but they didn't make much of an impression on me then. I would find my way to Ronstadt and Wynette. The men who interested me most? Johnny Cash, Merle Haggard, and Kris Kristofferson. Kristofferson reminded me of the male teachers in my hippy school, Georgetown Day School. *The Johnny Cash Show* was my soul Country primer.

It was a next place I started hearing the Black in Country. "Son of a Preacher Man" was written for Aretha, whose father was a preacher. I could absolutely hear Aretha in that song and hear something Dusty brought to it that was worthy and original, something Country, something so blonde British girl visiting Memphis Country, something so much more interesting to me than Elvis. As a young person, I never liked Elvis, or the Beatles, or Mr. Rogers. I liked Jerry Lee Lewis, the Rolling Stones, and no children's television at all. I watched Julia Child and *The Galloping Gourmet* and *Dark Shadows*, and I loved *The Johnny Cash Show*.

Music mattered on *The Johnny Cash Show*. Music didn't seem to matter in D.C. the same way. In Motown and on *The Johnny Cash Show*, lyrics, the Bible, and sermons were the dominant literature. In D.C., novels, poems, legal briefs, foreign films, and old movies were the texts that got discussed. I started spending a lot of time in public libraries. When I got older, I got access to huge private libraries of paperbacks and hardbacks in the homes where I would babysit. Most of those houses didn't have a lot of records but they sure had a lot of books. More and more Country broke through on the radio. The Country songs I remember breaking through the loudest: "D-I-V-O-R-C-E," "Folsom Prison Blues," and "Skip a Rope," a Tree song that centers on the sidewalk wisdom of girls jumping rope. This song announces: the kids are not alright. They are waking up screaming in the middle of the night in a world where Mommy and Daddy hate each other, hate people with different color skin, cheat on their taxes, and have abandoned the golden rule. We turned that song up loud when it came on the radio. It fit our world and it said kids were important.

My family back in Detroit didn't fit into this new world.

When I heard my mother talk about the family and Detroit associates, she talked about escaping from a world of gangsters and hoodlums. That she had a former brother-in-law that was in the numbers racket, that a man who drove me to school had been a contract killer, that one of my father's best friends was the snow king of Detroit city, that my father owned a Laundromat and a dry cleaners and ran another one. She said laundries and dry cleaners sometimes cleaned more than clothes.

She didn't talk about all the great live music that we heard every week in somebody's house, or someone's bar, or dropping in at Motown Records, where I heard Gladys Knight sing in a practice room; didn't talk about the painter Jon Lockhard who would found African-American Studies at Michigan, creating my portrait in pastels and my cousin David's in oil; or the Black Lutheran school where Tiney Barnes from Alabama started teaching me some French and Latin in my very first classroom; and how her aunt Essie would feed us hot breakfasts every morning in a lovely breakfast room in a Black neighborhood where on summer afternoons we would collect Queen Anne's lace; or talk about my grandmother Dear sending me down the lawn to see the four-o'clock flowers open in the late afternoon and holding rosebud and blossom competitions with her neighbors—all Negro women up from Alabama living in homes they owned and growing roses for their pleasure and the pleasure of their families. All she said about those people was they couldn't read or write and they all carried firearms, even the women, who packed tiny guns in their purses.

CLOSE ENCOUNTERS WITH TRIPPY HIPPY COUNTRY

In 1969, the former Almond Joys released their first album, *The Allman Brothers Band*, announcing their new name, and it got played a lot at Georgetown Day School. In 1972, I fell in love with their most countrified song, "Blue Sky."

I didn't know if Gregg Allman played electric piano or B3 organ on that song, but I knew that the sound that boy-man played took me back home to Black Detroit. What I heard on "Blue Sky" was something that sounded like Black funeral parlor organ to me, the organ I'd heard at the House of Diggs Funeral Home. It sounded mournful, loving, and celebratory.

I can hear the ballpark influence in a lot of rock organ. That's what I hear in the Doors' "Light My Fire." I knew about ballpark organ because Daddy would take me all dressed up to see an afternoon game at Tiger

Stadium—once he even bought me a souvenir Willie Mays bat. And I knew about funeral organ because my grandmother would take me to funerals all dressed up because she didn't want me to be afraid of death or dead bodies. Both ways I came to love organs and organist. So "Blue Sky" was a bridge back to a world I had lost. It was a reminder that I didn't have any of what I once had plenty of, the jolt of joy I got off the blue sky of George Randall. Daddy's high-giving presence. I was still translating love songs into familial relationship songs.

In 1971, Charley Pride entered the pop charts (and blew to the top of the Country charts) with "Kiss an Angel Good Morning." Mama, driving morning carpool, stopped twisting the dial and sang along when that tune came on; sometimes we would sing out those lyrics when the song wasn't even on the radio. About this same time, the Seldom Seen, another bluegrass band, and Emmylou Harris started playing regularly at a place called the Red Fox Inn in Bethesda, Maryland.

And Little Feat released "Willin'." That song was so popular in the Georgetown Day School community some folks started calling me "Dallas Alice" and even on occasion, "Pretty Alice." I appreciated that. And I appreciated the fact the song paid respect to outlaws and the working class. I had not forgotten that most of my people back in Detroit were working class and some were outlaws. And had not failed to notice that my father, the hero in my life, was using "weed, whites, and wine" just like the hero in "Willin'." Only Daddy would have called his self-prescribed medications, "grass, pills, and hooch" and just like the hero of the song he would do all of that and keep working and keep loving and keep being willin' until one day he couldn't. But that day hadn't come yet.

"Willin'" came to me in 1971, appearing like a secret song for my daddy. And just about the time it might have disappeared, it reappeared when I heard the Guy Clark song "Let Him Roll." That got released in 1975, but I didn't notice that song till about 1987. It's a song about a man a whole lot like my daddy, too. It starts off "He's a wino, tried and true" and ends with true love and another Alice and Dallas rhyme. I think Guy was listening to Little Feat, too.

DOMESTIC POLITICS

There was more to Washington, D.C., than the small Southern town (the museums, the embassies, the spectacular diversity of architecture and languages, dazzled me), but the Southern small-town experience was an increasingly large part of my Washington life in expected and unexpected ways.

Women didn't get to be president, vice president, or on the Supreme Court. They usually didn't get to be senator or congresspeople. They got to be married to those people. Women didn't even get to work in the White House as domestic servants, or if they did, they got erased.

Sometimes the women erased themselves. I had a friend in school whose mother worked as a maid/janitor, we later learned, for a national security agency. My friend never knew where her mother worked. I didn't know either. We just knew she was child-proud, proud of her daughter and proud of me, her daughter's friend, because she said we were smart *and* fine Southern ladies. When I would spend the weekend with my friend, her mother would wait on us hand and foot, and when we didn't need anything, she tended her fastidiously clean house or verdant garden. The woman fried chicken, grew roses, kept all her furniture incased in plastic, and sewed clothes. My friend was never allowed to wear the same clothes to school twice. The mother was, by choice, her daughter's maid and cook. When I visited, she was, by choice, my maid and cook.

This was her invention: we were in the South and we were brown and we had a maid, a cook, a seamstress. It can be a powerful disruption of the received social order to inhabit expected categories in unexpected ways. She inhabited the category of maid in very unexpected ways.

She toiled at work and at home, day and night, weekday and weekend doing the invisible labor that allowed us to study, write, and imagine; allowed intelligence officers to collect, analyze strategize. She labored to make the world safer by doing her work so others could do theirs. She labored to make two Black girls' lives larger—by removing all chores. Our work was to think, to play, to imagine, to read. Only.

That mother gave her daughter the Southern childhood her relations had given some white child, while they left their own children home to do the household chores that stole their own childhoods.

SEEKING THE SAFETY OF FOREIGN SOIL IN A SMALL SOUTHERN TOWN CALLED D.C.

Before long, my mother was romancing a six-foot-something Black architect from Georgia who had appeared on *Ebony* magazine's most eligible bachelor list. With a degree from Howard and two graduate degrees from MIT, Jerome Lindsey, when I first met him, was teaching at Yale and Howard, and soon moved to teaching at Harvard and Howard. As the courtship advanced, Jerry moved Mama and me into a house he had purchased for our little family, the former ambassador's residence for the country of Czechoslovakia located at 501 Aspen Street N.W., near the D.C.–Maryland border.

When we moved in, Jerry was the associate dean of the Graduate School of Design at Harvard and commuting to Cambridge. He was a successful man by any public measure. As a child I noticed that the whole point of our house was that it felt literally foreign.

That house had a front hall with a staircase leading to the second-floor bedrooms, a third floor with servants' quarters, and back stairs that led to the kitchen from the upper floors. In addition to the living room, there was a dining room, an office, and a den. With dark wood and servants' quarters and a goldfish pond just big enough to float in, it felt like what it was—the residence of a minor diplomat from a minor country. He did everything to make our house feel like either being in an outpost of a struggling Eastern European country or a commune in Scandinavia. From the old European clocks on the mantel and the old oriental rugs on the floors to the hypermodern Bauhaus furniture and removing all the doors off the cabinets in the kitchen and filling the shelves with stark modern dishes, he worked to create a city home that was like nothing he had known growing up in any part of Dixie. Weekdays he wanted to feel far from the American South.

But he had grown up in Dixie hunting and shooting and eating from the land, sometimes squirrel or rabbit or deer, sometimes corn or tomatoes. He yearned to find a way to return to some part of that. We spent weekends scouring the countryside looking for Southern acres where Jerry believed a Black family could be safe and close to nature. Those acres needed to look somehow foreign, too.

This is what looked foreign to me. Tammy Wynette. The large television was in the den. It was there I saw a commercial or rerun of Tammy Wynette singing, "Stand By Your Man."

Wynette looked so foreign to me (nothing like the Ziggy dancing school mothers in Detroit or the Georgetown Day School mothers in Washington) yet sounded so significant I thought the lyric was, "Stand by Earthman." With her white shade of gold helmet hair, pale eyes hooded with blue eye shadow, she looked like a space alien to me. Remembering how exotic Tammy was, how foreign, it struck me strong, standing in front of the television, probably ironing clothes for Jerry, how very few white people I had met or even seen before I moved to D.C.

It was so rare that I remember my father once taking me downtown on a Sunday for an ice cream sundae at a place we called Sanders. He was wearing a silk suit and I was wearing a church dress. He carried me on his hip as we walked into the shoppe. I was so stunned by all the pale-skinned children that I reached out my small brown hand, pointed, and waved, "Look at all the little peckawoods, Daddy." Skip a Rope. I didn't know the word "peckawood" was a slur. I didn't know it was dangerous to call white people peckawood. I didn't know I was supposed to defer to white people. I didn't know there was a large number of white people in the world, because there was not a larger number of white people in my world.

I went horseback riding and I was the only Black kid riding out of that stable. In Detroit, I saw Black people riding at Belle Isle. Heard about Joe Louis's legendary horse riding stable and about the riding instructor at the Black lake resort, Idlewild. I wanted horseback riding to connect me back to Detroit, it didn't. Horseback riding in Vienna, Virginia, at a place idered new ones into the bits and pieces I recalled. untry songs I had inherited from my grandmother, other, including the works of Mama Lil; stimulated ntleman and Little Feat, then catalyzed by Prine, I ting Country songs in a small town in Virginia.

I would ever have recorded was born in that hot and gins, "It's a running out of luck town in old Virginia, s the new night air, in a churchyard stands a child com- seeking refuge from the shame she bears." I was follow- l's footsteps. She wrote her theme song, "Brown Gal," of Vim. I wrote mine, "Reckless Night," about cascades t, the song, the imagining, was the best way for me to

r I love Country. I know a whole lot about the past being e present.

CK AND AUDACIOUS BLACK COUNTRY LOVE

e enemy brought a library of music that included Country vnhouse in Southwest. Listening to Bonnie Raitt, I found Sip- e. Listening to Jimmy Buffett I heard the beach in Country d listening to more reggae. And always there was Little Feat at

"willin,'" I was livin', and one day I would be an angel who n from Montgomery and would be strutting with some fucking e.

il then I was growing asparagus. Waiting for my asparagus to pro- dible stalks I learned patience, to the tune of "Blue Yodel #9" the l played it. Tending two hundred strawberry plants, watching them ce plentiful fruit, watching that fruit ripen to almost perfection, ing to wait one more day for harvest, waking up that day to discover abbits had eaten all my berries but three, deciding to eat the remain- berries, washing them, biting them, savoring a flavor I had not tasted

called Potomac Equitation had everything to do with riding in England, with riding in the east, and only one thing to do with riding in the west and cowboys. Riding in the farm truck that picked us up from school and took us to the stable and later brought us back home, we sometimes picked up a Country station, and sometimes a Country song showed up on a pop station.

The very best thing about living with Jerry was that he convinced my mother to return to university to finish her undergraduate degree and pursue graduate work while continuing to work in various policy implementation roles. This kept her too busy to have much to do with me.

By spring of my freshman year of high school, Jerry had left Harvard to serve as the dean of the Howard University School of Architecture and Planning. When he was away on a multi-week business trip to Africa, Bettie met a man—a consultant who was instrumental in the invention of the zip code, or so he said. For the second time in my life, I woke up living in a strong Black man's house and went to sleep living under a white man's roof in Southwest Washington. Jerry returned and found us gone. Mother moved in with the new man. So, I was back in the small town of Southwest and spending time in an unincorporated Virginia town that was home to the depot where Stonewall Jackson's troops boarded the train for the Battle of Manassas and legendary nineteenth- and twentieth-century fox hunts.

DIXIE GOTHIC

A man raped me. In a modernist townhouse erected atop a razed Black neighborhood and in the Virginia countryside. In Southwest, I could escape on foot, run out the door and find shelter in another townhouse in the neighborhood. I could hike or take a bus to the shelter of the Smithsonian. And I did all those things. On fifty acres crossed by venomous copperheads and timber rattlesnakes, and trauma-triggering, blink-provoking other snakes, a ringneck with a lurid bright orange underbelly can look like a furious and slithering phallus when seen through dazed fifteen-year-old eyes. In those same eyes, a broken and benign shadow can often appear as the silhouette of a black bear or a bobcat. But not so very often, there is the flash of a sighting of what could be a bobcat, or there is bear scat. And always there are foxes. You tell yourself foxes don't bite and most of them don't have rabies. And most of the racoons you see don't have rabies. But you know of a kid down the dirt road in the house you are not allowed to visit that did get bit and had to have the shots. And you know about ankles that got broke trying to traverse the rough dirt to that shack, never to be properly mended. You've seen those limps in town, and the missing fingers from saws. So, sixty minutes by car back to D.C. when you don't have car keys, when the raggedy houses and the rich houses all have rifles and guns; and the strange girl new to the neighborhood is not accepted by the white or Black folk, is a distant too far to traverse. Nobody takes kindly to the crossing of their land without permission. There is no running away from this aesthetically pleasing A-frame cabin. There is no getting out of eye or earshot. There is way too much new and bad and it is not just the rape. It was when we ate in the local diner, every other word was "nigger" out loud and proud from other diners. It was growing strawberries and asparagus and sweeping floors. Another way that small towns are smaller for girls: girls get worked in the house and in the fields. My mother wasn't expected to work outside, The New Man wasn't expected to work inside. I was expected to labor alongside both of them, and before and after them. I was the labor and the entertainment. There was no television. No books. There was mainly labor, food, sex, and more labor.

I hated that farm. But it taught me some things. I learned more complete meanings of certain significant country words. Weeding strawberries I learned "back breaking" was a shooting pain, not a material split of bone. Getting raped to the sound of crickets, to the sound of rain, I learned that a plantation was not moonlights and magnolias, but crickets, rain, and blood.

But there w
A John Prine ta
Prine was sitting
He's wearing jeans
bales. Given the loo
player. Prine on that
pretty and I liked prett
like I read books from

I didn't like it. I didn
the motherfucker. This so
detail in the stories. Enou
around in it, pouring out
everything inside that song
stretch out like that, like I had
a Thrill"?

"Angel from Montgomery,"
burn up, abusive silences, destru
and the need to have one thing to

I lapsed into long silences. I spo
Hospital and scheduled for a spinal
eases. Then the tune came back to me
to me for me, "to believe in this livin' is
in my part of Detroit would have calle
that hard row. With "Angel from Montg
the hospital bed, walked to the nurses' stat
sentences, and was soon released with the s
study in Europe, far away from my torment

Prine's song had revived my ability to es
I would be an angel that flew from Virginia.
study in Europe. I gasped for dreaming like t
son gasps for air. Dreaming was my one thing
I rediscovered my unbreakable dream machine,
in my head. I couldn't remember lyrics of my favo

before and would not taste again. To the tune of "Struttin' with Some Barbecue," I did that.

I was a farmer for three years. Corn was our most reliable crop. If you pick it and cook it within twenty minutes of picking, it is so sweet. I was silent about the rape. I didn't tell anyone about Lil Hardin or John Prine. At the time I kept my best and worst things to myself.

We had moved from the Southwest townhouse to a house on the D.C.–Chevy Chase border by the time I returned from London to graduate from Georgetown Day School. That summer I found *The Joan Baez Ballad Book*. This double album set of Anglo, Irish, Scottish ballads included so many narratives of violated young women, of traumatized young women, of young despairing women, of young women who kill themselves and give direction for their own burial. These were narratives of hard and radical autonomy. If most of these young females ended up dead, I wasn't focused on that. I was focused on the fact their story got told and lived two hundred, three hundred years. That's what a song will do.

I lay sprawled on the floor of a den coloring in an Elizabeth the First coloring book and listening to *The Joan Baez Ballad Book*, half the equation for Country Music for hours, when I was shocked and awed by a return to joy. The colors on the page, the sounds in my ear, the nap of the carpet on my elbows, the scent of my own hair, the taste of nothing but my own saliva in my mouth, Black Vacation Bible School teachings rolling round my head, and an inkling that what I had suffered Elizabeth the First had suffered and traditional who wrote the ballads had suffered, swirled into a chaos of sound, color, history, and theology that brought a moment of piercing and particular pleasure. On waves of sound, color, and faith, I floated back to head-to-toe peace. I was loved. "Jesus Loves Me, This I Know" was the hymn sung most often in my Black Detroit days. I was no longer the devout Christian girl of my Michigan years. Inspired by Elizabeth the First, I took from the church what I needed from the church. For me that was love without end or beginning. Country

Music is Celtic ballads + African influences + Evangelical Christianity. All that was with me on the rug. But it wasn't on that stereo. It was in my head.

There was one good thing Bettie gave me in my D.C. days, and like her other best things, it was strangely Country. This good thing was Roberta Flack.

Mother loved to be out in the streets. She liked a bar. In Detroit, she liked the Black show bars. The Flame and the 20 Grand frequented by musicians, and gamblers. In Washington, she discovered political bars starting with Pitts Motor Hotel—chosen by Martin Luther King, Jr., as his base for the poor people march on Washington—and then Mr. Henry's, a political bar, a Capitol Hill bar, a proudly queer bar, where a North Carolina–born, Black schoolteacher played piano and sang.

"The First Time Ever I Saw Your Face" is a Country song that isn't recognized as a Country song. I recognized it. It is Celtic, written by an Irish songwriter, and it is Black. Flack carves layers of meaning into the lyrics with her interpretation. Ann Powers, one of the wisest music critics I know, wrote, for NPR:

> *One way Flack maintained this link was through gospel music—not the shouting Pentecostalism most rock and roll fans associated with that world, but the "long line hymnody" cultivated within Methodist congregations. Those indelible early hits, "The First Time Ever I Saw Your Face" and "Killing Me Softly," both invoke that style of sacred singing, one of the oldest forms of African-American sacred self-expression, in which leaders would spin out phrases like wool becoming thread, so that responders could absorb the words and find their own ways into the melodies.*

I felt an explosion of ineffable joy the first time I heard Flack sing the most elegant Country-pop song ever. Songs can be love bombs dropped in the heart. The listening explosion changed me. That song severed the strings that connected me to Lil's "Just for a Thrill." Listening to "The First Time Ever I Saw Your Face," memories of everything George told me about seeing me for the very first time, and falling in father-love with baby me came riding to my rescue.

The day I learned the meaning of the words *abortion* and *abortionist* was the day I asked my father about the first facts of my life. "When your mother told me she was going to have a baby, I told her I didn't want one. I told her she had to have an abortion. I took her to the abortionist." He described the scene in detail.

This is what I remember: the doctor took Bettie back to the room where he would perform the procedure. Daddy settled into a chair in an ugly waiting room. Bettie's pretty light-wool overcoat purchased from Saks by Bettie and paid for by Daddy was folded on the chair beside him. No one else was in the building. It was late, after closing time. He lit his first cigarette with a match and lit the second from the first. He had a fresh pack. Too soon the doctor came back out. Daddy thought Bettie was dead. The doctor shook his head. "She doesn't want an abortion," the doctor said. "I can't get her to relax," he continues. Daddy told the doctor to bring Bettie back out. Bettie walked out. Daddy put the coat on her. "We were having a baby." He wanted a boy. Someone he could name William and call Bill after his eldest brother and second daddy who had died around the time I was conceived. A baby girl was born.

Daddy was so disappointed I wasn't the second coming of Bill he didn't go to the hospital. One of his sisters found him on a stool at a favorite bar. She placed my picture on the bar top. The man next to Daddy hurled a racial slur and a charge of cuckoldry at Daddy and the photograph, "It looks like your woman laid with a Chink." This stirred the protective in my father. He made his way to my hospital bassinet. He let them put swaddled me in his arms. He was afraid to look down and see an ugly stranger, Mama's little baby, Daddy's little maybe. He pulled the blanket from my face and Daddy said, "I fell instantly and completely in love. Completely in love. Completely in love." He said it like a stutter. Later he explained, "You were mine, whether by birth or adoption." It was a decision he made *the first time he saw my face*. When I heard Flack's song, it was a reviving miracle.

So, that was another thing on the "Bettie wasn't only just an evil monster, even to me" scorecard. She didn't just give me Florence Joplin. She gave me Roberta Flack and Roberta gave me Daddy back. Just when I needed him most. Not Daddy's gun. Daddy's audacious love.

SWAMP DOGG, ESSENTIAL BLACK COUNTRY ECCENTRICITY

I found Swamp Dogg my own damn self. It was in a hippy boy's bedroom, an album library, on a shag carpet floor. Between an album cover with a giant peach, the Allmans, and an album cover with a giant tomato, Little Feat's, was a giant rat.

Swamp Dogg rides a white rat like a horse on the cover of an album. He's wearing a red striped shirt and a green jacket with cowboy western fringe and a porkpie hat. The effect is very red, white, and blue. He reimagined the American flag to sign not blue skies but economic oppression, and announced the patriot's duty to form and re-form the nation into someplace more worthy of Black cowboys.

Written in 1971, "God Bless America" is a peculiar patriotic song. It calls the Statue of Liberty a "joke." He spotlights "Indians own the reservation and Black folks still ain't free" as punch lines of Lady Liberty's sick joke.

He reframes the founders, the signers of the Declaration of Independence, as evil, claiming, "Hate, war and destruction is all *our* forefathers took time to sow." With that word *our* Swamp makes a sly but significant claim: white men fathered Black and white children. Swamp is Black and the founders are his forefathers. Dogg calls those daddies out. This is essential Black Country eccentricity.

Another eccentricity? This is one of the few songs in my Black Country songbook that emphasize a generation gap and generational conflict. What keeps it Country? The direct address to the Lord, the song is a prayer.

Over and over there is a direct address to God. This song can be appreciated in conversation with the old spiritual *welcome table*, where the singer promise-threatens when they get to heaven, "I'm gonna tell Jesus how you done me."

Swamp Dogg is not waiting for heaven, he is questioning the identity of the nation from his perch on Earth now, from the first syllables of the song. "Oh Lord, is this the land of the free?" And that might seem like a rhetorical "Oh Lord," or just a curse or a language tick, but it isn't.

I hear his close as a true prayer, a contemporary psalm. He calls the Lord's name five times, followed by a plea, "We need help!" Which he repeats. This is an urgent plea both for divine intervention and soul-searching. Over and over Swamp invites you not to sing along but to *think*.

The eccentrics of Black Country refuse to be seduced into a false sense of belonging achieved by adhering to established codes of aesthetics arising from either their home communities or the dominant culture. By flexing their connection to a globe not an acre, they flex their humanity, their universality, and their world making, then sign their own significance in the world they have made.

The eccentrics exploit the reality that Country is a hybrid form that draws from African, European, and Indigenous American influences. A global feast of myth, iconic stories, and elemental archetypes is offered up in their songs and life stories.

At Georgetown Day School, if you surveyed the student body, lawyer might have been the most frequent job of the fathers. If you took a survey of my friends, the most common occupations were psychiatrist and psychologists. We were surrounded by talk of analysis, group therapy, projection, and defenses. Swamp Dogg, Jimmy Cliff, Stoney Edwards, Herb Jeffries, and the other Black Country eccentrics made me proud to know Black folk were mining the collective unconscious then polishing the found jewels with defiant dandyish swagger. Even as a teen, I loved everything about that!

And I love this. The Black Country eccentrics are willing to make people uncomfortable. They are willing to demand that their listeners think hard and carefully. When you ride with the eccentrics you are going to do more than get entertained. It's the hard thinking that separates the Black Country eccentrics from the Black Country hippies. The eccentrics have a philosophy. The eccentrics embrace complexity and thorns. They are in conversation with Afro-futurism. They ain't trying to please everybody. You lucky if they trying to please one person beyond themselves.

Not trying to please folk has earned Swamp some pretty fantabulous international awareness. His most global Black Country song is "Synthetic World." It is explicitly political, explicitly philosophical, explicitly Country, and explicitly Country Afro-futuristic.

He wrote and recorded this song in 1970. He anticipates replicants, he contemplates room deodorizer as an instance of murder by capitalism, and he asserts with confidence his place of origin: "up from the Bayou where wildlife runs free" and his preferred identity, "Country." The whole song is pure, brilliant eccentric Country Swamp Dogg.

Swamp Dogg creates a rural Black center *for the world*. The whole world, all eight billion souls currently living on the planet. And thanks to Jimmy Cliff, that center is celebrated globally. In 1971 Jimmy Cliff recorded "Synthetic World."

In some other hippy boy's album collection in another room, perhaps in a stack of cubes reaching up to the air, I found Jimmy Cliff's *Goodbye Yesterday*. On it is Cliff's version of Swamp Dogg's "Synthetic World." I heard that song and maybe I knew one day I would be listening to it and trying to make a baby and a family. I was a girl who once on a backyard swing set looked up at the stars and thought the person I will love most in the world is looking up at the same stars. Swaying to Cliff's beat and Dogg's words, I knew one day I will be in love, and I will be political, and angry, and sweet, like Jimmy Cliff singing Swamp Dogg.

I want to steal the album from the boy and play it loud around my house as a coded denunciation of my mother and The New Man. But I don't do that. I, too, am tired of being patient. But I am also afraid The New Man might hear it as an invitation. And I don't do the boy in the room. I kiss his face. The turntable is spinning in a room with a waterbed as Jimmy Cliff swing-sings a calm denunciation of a "synthetic world" which I hear as "sin-pathetic world."

That was the world I was living in and a Country song denouncing that world while claiming Country identity, "you can say that I am

Country . . ." and frustration, "my patience is growin' thin" did me a powerful good. Swamp Dogg and Jimmy Cliff called out the D.C. of my hardest D.C. daze *evil and puny* while performing their own Black Country beauty. No wonder I made a magnificent baby, daughter Caroline, after listening to that track.

I identified with all of that. The more I heard in this Black Country gem a braiding of sound that encourages us to make love, to dance, and to chastise. The song breathes: political improvement is urgent and necessary and so is the dancing and the lovemaking. It breathes when you step out of your overalls. Understand you are wild, free, and wholly human because you are a preaching and political person. I looked into some sweet boy's eyes, and I didn't have to ask the question out loud, "How do we make the world less synthetic?" We both know.

In 1971 Swamp Dogg won a BMI Award for song of the year. He claims to this day he didn't get invited to the dinner. They sent him his award for "Don't Take Her (She's All I Got)" in the mail with a letter saying they were sorry he couldn't come.

Swamp co-wrote that huge hit for Johnny Paycheck. It's a great song. The male version of "Jolene." But it was recorded by an artist I cannot abide: Johnny Paycheck.

Paycheck served time for shooting a man in the head. And he faced charges of raping a fan's very young daughter the night he met her. And after that he was invited to join the Opry. How does he get forgiven for all of that? Even if you don't believe the rape, what about shooting someone in the head? Paycheck died broke at the age of sixty-four. On his 2020 album, *Sorry You Couldn't Make It*, Swamp released his new version of his old song. I'm glad there's a version of it I want to listen to again. To quote that other Swamp Dogg, "Your world is plastic, cities made of wood."

1976 BICENTENNIAL YEAR BLACK COUNTRY

The Black Country that was making its way into my Washington life was the Black Country strange enough to be noticed by and purchased by the left-wing hippy intellectuals I was hanging with at Georgetown Day School or what I heard driving out to spend a weekend at Deep Creek Lake, or to Annapolis to sail, or to that hard farm in Virginia.

It was in a car going someplace like that when I first heard Stoney Edwards sing "Blackbird." Released in 1976, the bicentennial year, "Blackbird" *is* a Country parental-advice-song like no other. It works like a dangerous live vaccine in a soundscape that understands racism as a deadly disease. In it a loving father inoculates his beloved son against racism with the N-word.

Stoney uses "Blackbird" to convey this message: *Y'all tried to destroy me with words but my father sheltered me with better words.* The child being dismissed as a "country nigger" is invited by the parent to imagine themselves as a proud and soaring "Blackbird" who in its flight is an indictment of the American Eagle being celebrated in the bicentennial moment. The song centers a Black child receiving tender and pragmatic care from a loving Black man.

Stoney's most famous song, "Hank and Lefty Raised My Country Soul," is often described as sounding hard-core *traditional* Country. What some folks seem to mean by that is Stoney sounds white. But Stoney sounds like Stoney: openly Black, loudly Black, tasty Louisiana Hot Sauce Black.

Two very different tall tales have risen and made the Music Row rounds about Lefty Frizzell's response to Stoney's performance and song.

One is that Stoney met Lefty and Lefty dismissed him as a "nigger." The other is Stoney met Lefty and Lefty was touched by the fact that he was being remembered, out loud on the radio, when he thought the music world had passed him by *and* appreciated the fact it was a Black person who was doing the remembering.

In the biography of Lefty's life, written by his brother, the story is told of Lefty learning chords from a "Black man" who lived down the street from their uncle Lawrence. Lefty's first guitar was bought off that man. Lefty's folks paid two dollars and fifty cents for it. We don't know what they paid for the lessons, but Lefty's brother states the unnamed "Black man" coached Lefty on playing and singing. When artists talk about the way Lefty influenced them, they need to know Lefty was taught by a Black man. I want to know that man's name.

A lot of crazy stories swirl around Stoney Edwards's life. He claimed he was originally named Frenchy for the bootlegger who stopped by his house the day he was born, December 24, 1929, to deliver moonshine for the family Christmas festivities. He claimed never to have gone a day to school. He claimed his mother was an Indian and his daddy was a mulatto. He claimed he was chased out of Oklahoma by revenue men who wanted to shut down his moonshine business. He claimed he shot himself in the leg during a quick-draw contest and had to have his leg amputated. This reminds me of Eslie Riddle. He claimed that was the second weird accident of his life. The first was when he fell into a locked container on a job site and got so poisoned on carbon dioxide that he had to spend two years in a hospital. The only thing ordinary in his childhood? He grew up Black and listening to the Opry on the radio and wanted to hear his voice on it, which means Stoney grew up listening to DeFord Bailey.

Stoney's son, Ken Edwards, is working to get his father's story told, which includes releasing six albums on major Country labels and landing a top twenty Country hit, "She's My Rock." On my favorite of his albums, the one named for that cut, Stoney wears black textured pants with a black-on-black stripe, red and black cowboy boots that feature a diamond pattern, a black leather vest, a tomato-red collared shirt, and a low black cowboy hat. He's sitting on a fallen tree. A field, farmhouse, and hills of green are visible in the background. In the foreground, diamonds sparkle on two of the fingers of his left hand. *That blackbird flew high!*

Me, Swamp, and Stoney know worlds and worlds about hard-won happy in the green countryside.

ENCOUNTERING: THE FIRST FAMILY OF BLACK COUNTRY AND OTHER ALLIES

I rode the rabbit theft of strawberries into college. I wrote my college admissions essay about strawberry farming. I wrote about saving myself some of the trouble of weeding by covering my strawberry patch in black plastic, and pulling the plants through and the weeds didn't grow because they didn't get light. I posted my applications from London, where I was spending spring semester of my high school senior year.

I wasn't on any established program. I was on a tiny budget, living in a shared room so small that the two single beds in it almost touched. I had taken myself to the British embassy library and started looking randomly through the shelves for somewhere I could go to study far away from harm. I found a little pamphlet for the University of London's Institute of Archaeology. I sent them a telegram asking if I could audit a class or two. Someone pleasant wrote back that there wasn't an established procedure for admitting, or refusing, someone with my qualifications. I wouldn't be officially enrolled, but I could attend. And they gave me the start date and a list of classes. I chose a seminar on Hadrian's wall and Roman Britain. I appealed to the head of my school, Gladys Stern, and she approved giving me the money my family had already paid that covered the second half of the year of my tuition. She asked me one question, "Do you need to go?" I said, "Yes." And that wise woman said, "If you need to go, I need to help you." I enlisted a friend to join on the adventure. I returned to D.C. in time to read William Blake's "The Tyger," the poem that asks, *Did the same God that created good, create evil?* at my graduation ceremony.

The fall of 1977 this blackbird flew to Harvard.

Five improbable things happened during my time in Cambridge that worked in concert to catapult me toward Nashville. 1) I met Gloria Messinger, the single most well-connected, well-educated, and business-brilliant woman in the world of Country Music. 2) I met Edith Gelfand, who had a taste for high-risk, high-return investments. And who had become interested in Country Music on ski trips to Colorado. 3) I discovered a little examined relationship between Country Music and British and American metaphysical poetry which boomeranged me back to reexamining my father's statements that "Black folk invented Country Music" and "Traditional is a Black woman!" 4) Boston got a Country radio station and I spent a lot of time typing English papers listening to it on the radio. 5) The federal government released a ten-album treasure chest—*The Smithsonian Collection of Classic Country Music*, omitting almost all Black Country.

If any one of these things had not happened, I likely would never have moved to Nashville.

I met Gloria Messinger early days on the Harvard campus. The Harvard housing gods assigned her daughter, Emily Mandelstam, and me to the same freshman suite. It took another few years to meet Edith. Her much younger cousin was in the class behind me and eventually my college boyfriend's roommate. When the boyfriend ran for Massachusetts state representative (while still an undergraduate), I held a fundraiser for him in D.C. that Edith attended.

Both of these well-educated lawyer women remind me something of Lil.

The Gloria-Lil connection was public. Lil and Gloria both had this "I am powerful, beautiful, and all about the music business, get with me, or get out of my way" glamour. Gloria looked, to me, like Katharine Hepburn in *Philadelphia Story*. She carried herself like a brain and a dame.

The Edith-Lil connection was more intimate. Lil wasn't my mother, but I wanted her to be. Edith wasn't my mother, but I wanted her to be. Edith, like Lil, didn't have children. Edith, like Lil, nurtured in music business space. Some of the ways Lil nurtured Louis resembled some of the ways Edith nurtured me. No small part of it was an ability to be ambitious for someone who was not sufficiently ambitious for themselves.

Messinger found her daughter's Black roommate's love of Country Music intriguing. I found her lived experience of being one of the first women to graduate from Yale Law School, and the first to graduate from Yale and enter the entertainment industry, intriguing. When we chatted, with wind blowing hot soup into my face at the Harvard-Yale game tailgate she hosted, Messinger was curious about what my appreciation of Country songs and Country radio might indicate about the rate of expansion of the genre's audience. In later conversations, she flattered me by stating I might be a major new songwriting talent. As I approached college graduation, she offered pragmatic assistance. She offered to introduce me to major writers who could help evaluate my potential and she offered to set up meetings with music publishers. She was impressed that I knew what a music publishing company was, that I knew Anna Gordy had owned a publishing company before Barry Gordy. I was impressed to learn ASCAP published Lil. We both agreed if I were to get signed as a staff writer for a Country publishing company, it would be a significant change to the business landscape of music.

So, I had the promise of connections and seeds of money almost from the get-go. All that remained to spark the crazy-for-Country fire? Failure to get a job was one part of it. I interviewed at *Essence*. I interviewed at *SAVVY*. I interviewed a few other places and all I landed was a very high-paying nanny gig. The family advertised in the *Harvard Crimson*.

The other part of it was I received a copy of *The Smithsonian Collection of Classic Country Music* for a graduation gift. Bill C. Malone, who wrote the liner notes and compiled the collection, believed there was Black influence but not presence in Country Music. There was so much beauty and strength in the collection and so much vicious erasure, starting with zero mention of Lil. No mention of the singing Black cinema cowboy, Herb Jeffries, whose portrait in full Western stage costume had hung in the Gotham Hotel. And the South and the West portrayed in the songs chosen for the album whitewashed Black people out of spaces where they had lived and loved and worked to the tunes of fiddle and banjo.

I would strike back. I would spotlight unheralded Black Country artists. I would publish excluded voices; and I would write songs about the Black South and West that were not getting written, songs about Black cowboys and Black frontier women, songs about brides and lynchings, songs about brown girls in small towns. I would found Midsummer Music and I had a very good idea who my chief investor would be. I accepted the nanny job as a base of operation.

In the summer of 1981, I moved back to the Southern countryside. I was living in a contemporary guesthouse on a contemporary estate listening to *The Smithsonian Collection of Classic Country Music* over and over, baby-tending, and plotting. I was ready to seed change in Southern space. I called Country songwriting "preaching to the unconverted." Most liberals I knew wanted to preach to converts. I was going to find a way to put some progressive ideas into the heads of people who didn't typically listen to them.

The nanny job didn't last long. I interned for a literary agent and eventually landed a job at the Wolf Trap Foundation for the Performing Arts. To commute to work I purchased an eight-hundred-dollar car. I was already sharing an eight-hundred-dollar-a-month house with three young men: an aspiring architect from New Haven who had just graduated from Dartmouth; an aspiring management consultant from the Upper East Side on his way to Harvard Business School via a dress shop; and an aspiring editor working at the *Washington Post*'s *Book World* who had grown up on ranches in Washington State.

This last roommate, found via an advertisement in the newspaper, bought me my first pair of spurs, gave me my first plug of chewing tobacco, and introduced me to the joys of Hank Williams, Sr. It wasn't quite kissing a cowboy, and it certainly wasn't my first rodeo, but my first taste of the wide Western sky once jumped out of a second-floor bedroom to save my honor—and he was plenty pretty.

I took him to the Virginia countryside. We picnicked in the graveyard. My cowboy and me didn't make love in the graveyard, though we may have gone there to do that; we made rhymes.

And I made up my mind to move to Nashville.

My first foray to Music City was a scouting trip. During awards season, I checked into a small-town, tall hotel, maybe eight stories high, with a guitar-shaped swimming pool.

The Spence Manor is a flat box situated in a very modest neighborhood of small houses distinguished by the people who slept there. Elvis. Me. Everybody in between. Willie Nelson and Robert Redford worked on the soundtrack to *Electric Horseman* in the presidential suite there. Sissy Spacek stayed at the Spence for the Nashville debut of *Coal Miner's Daughter.*

At the front desk I asked how far it was to Music Row, only to be told I was on it. Music Row is a neighborhood centered around two one-way streets: 16th Avenue that runs north and 17th Avenue that runs south. Back then both avenues were flanked by modest one- and two-story houses that had been repurposed to house recording studios, publishing companies, management companies, hairstylists catering to the music industry, and the occasional grander, bigger house or purpose-built office building, like Buddy Killen's Mexican hacienda-styled, three-story Tree Publishing.

Awards season in Music City was a seven-day extravaganza of breakfast parties, luncheons, cocktail parties, dinners, after-hours bashes, annual meetings, celebrity baseball games and bowling tourneys, and all manner of late-night debauchery scheduled to avoid four major black-tie Country Music award galas—the ASCAP dinner, the BMI dinner, the CMA (Country Music Association) Awards Show, and the SESAC dinner. A cross-section of everyone involved or wanting to be involved with Country Music attends some part of these festivities. Awards season usually falls in October.

It's not just the big stars that converge on Nashville in October, though the big stars come. Whether they're up for awards, or tapped to hand out awards, most come. And they don't come alone. They bring with them various, sometimes combustible, combinations of wives, girlfriends, husbands, boyfriends, parents, cousins, children, stepchildren, and old friends. And all the people aspiring to write, publish, manage, kiss, marry, or dress those big stars come; and everyone hoping to sell a car, a horse, a bull, a bank loan, or a house to a big star comes. Yep, one October someone tried to sell me a share in a bull and knowing so many of the current great bull riders are brown and Black Brazilians, I was tempted. Then I started worrying about the bulls. And the rising stars come, and the falling stars come. Whether or not you have tickets or are on the guest lists for the established events, the bars will be open. And during awards season, somebody is always picking up the tab for everybody in the bar with a half-familiar smile or name.

At twenty-three years old it didn't take me thirty-six hours in the city to discover all that chaos creates opportunity and dread. October in Nashville is the time of year people at the top fear some new arrival is going to topple them from their throne. Once that was me.

Gloria Messinger set up meetings for me with the most-prominent ASCAP members in Nashville. Every meeting Gloria set was with a white man, specifically Buddy Killen, Ralph Murphy, Archie Jordan, Wayland Holyfield, Bob Morrison, and Ronnie Gant—the men who would play a significant role in Gloria being able to announce a year later, during awards season, that ASCAP had collected two hundred million dollars.

I showed up to the Acuff-Rose office—the building where Hank Williams, Sr., had picked up his publishing checks—wearing a light gray skirt suit. Ronnie Gant, who ran Acuff-Rose Publications, was wearing jeans and a button-down shirt. He had his feet up on the desk and started peppering me with questions the moment I settled into the chair opposite him, ending with "Where *are* you from?" When I answered, he shook his head like it hurt. He had arrived at a conclusion: "I don't see it. I just don't see it. You need to go back to wherever it is you came from." Then, perhaps remembering who had gotten me into the room, he walked back the complete dismissal. He said he would show my lyrics to two of his younger writers who were more familiar with "raw" material.

A few weeks after I returned home to Washington, D.C., I got a letter from Ronnie Gant saying he had shared my lyrics with Mark D. Sanders and another young writer. All three men had come to the same conclusion. "You have no talent whatsoever." That was the day I decided to move to Nashville.

I was moving my Black and female body from Washington, D.C., to Music City, and I was going to find a way to make this truth known: Black women helped birth Country.

If Ronnie knew where I came from, he would have been afraid to tell me to go back there.

When my head was hung down low, Daddy would singsong-say, "What's wrong, little girl? Forty dollars nailed to the dope house door will get anybody killed. It may take a hundred dollars in the morning, but by late afternoon there's always a junkie who do anything for a forty-dollar fix. I got forty dollars. What's wrong, little girl?" I come from an unrecorded Black Country song, "What's Wrong Little Girl?" That's the tune that set me in motion to move to Nashville after Ronnie Gant tried to *bogart* all the new *Urban Cowboy* cash flowing into Nashville for the white folk.

No wonder Beyoncé's "Daddy Lessons" is a favorite Country song of mine. My daddy taught me some hellacious "Daddy Lessons."

I had been tottering on a brink about the move until I got the "No Talent Whatsoever" letter from Ronnie Gant. I was having a big time in D.C. "Tainted Love" by Soft Cell was the song in the clubs where we danced late into the night, and there was a place we loved that played "8th Wonder" by the Sugarhill Gang, produced by Sylvia Robinson, who had founded Sugar Hill Records. And I had discovered Rank and File. Heard them live, I think, at the 9:30 Club. I spent a lot of time there, heard that first album, *Sundown*, there. They were mixing punk and Country and I thought I could mix rap and Country. I tried to talk to Hal David about rap and he didn't even seem to know what it was. Buddy Killen liked that idea, but nobody knew what to do with that idea unless I wanted to perform—and I didn't want to perform, I wanted to write—Black cowpunk. And I wanted to publish Black cowpunk, too.

I wanted to start a Country Music publishing company. I wanted to spotlight Black artists. I wanted to write a novel. Maybe I was starting to think about producing a Country punk band inspired by Sylvia Robinson producing. Her rise sparked new ambitions. And I wanted this other win. I wanted to face and confront the only thing I had ever known my father to be afraid of, the thing forty dollars couldn't fix: the South.

To enter the world of Country would be to invade its citadel. To have a success in Country would be a way of exploding myths of Black inferiority and absence in the place where the myth was having an ongoing killing effect on Black people who had not been afforded the same privileges and advantages I had received.

The artist I was imagining singing the songs I wanted to write hadn't been born yet; and when she is born, she will be a writer, too. She will look and sound like Sunny War, an artist who enters the world in 1991. Maybe she will do a thing I wanted to do fuse punk and Country and create heart explosions. Maybe she will shock and awe with her voice that exquisitely excavates the lower registers of sound to bring us to the higher registers of insight. Maybe she will sing like a granddaughter of Nina Simone. If I had a crystal ball maybe I would see a single coming in 2023, "New Day." And hear Sunny confiding that she is love's junkie, love's addict. Then provide receipts, "stole . . . light . . . from my eyes, jarred it up like fireflies." Could an image be more punk and Country or piercing? Her guitar playing will be called "startling," idiosyncratic," and "unique." She will claim Chet Atkins as a guitarist who inspires her. Her lyrics are wildly original and vicious. Sunny War can be unabashedly nasty. Her first punk band will be called Anus Kings, but on *Anarchist Gospel*, the album that brings "New Day," she is bravely loving, spiritual, and raw. Named at birth Sydney Lyndella Ward, Sunny War will be the embodiment, voice, lyric, and guitar of the Saturday night/Sunday morning paradox: good and evil persist in coexisting.

I don't know that, couldn't know that, didn't have a crystal ball, but wanting to do something so exactly like that is what was pulling me toward Nashville. I didn't know what I wanted to do would be so hard to do that it wouldn't be done till 2023. I knew this.

Privileges and advantage came with some preferences and vanities that tethered me to D.C. I wanted to see my friends on the daily; I wanted brilliant *and* exceptionally well-educated lovers. I had discovered myself to be a person who fell in love with the habits of the mind then the pretty, pretty. I had discovered I liked a man with a lot of girl in his boy, who was still very much a man. I wanted to go to parties where food was served in courses before we dashed to dance in a hot, loud room to sometimes disco, electronic, R & B, and Country. I wanted to eat excellent and affordable Vietnamese, Ethiopian, and Afghan food; grab hot churros with coffee Sunday mornings and eat in world-class French and Chinese restaurants at least once a month. All of this and pop into museums every week, sometimes every other day, in D.C. and see a wide range of Black people talking a wide range of languages doing everything from being doctors, lawyers, and congresspeople to bus drivers and streetwalkers. I wanted to keep doing a whole lot of what I had been doing. And much of this would be impossible in Nashville.

Then push came to shove. Ronnie Gant had told me to go back to where I came from, that was the push. Daddy told me I was living the life of a very pretty, very intelligent, very *frivolous* person. That was the shove. I don't believe I had ever heard my father use that word "frivolous" before he used it against me. And then he had another surprise. He was talking about a song I didn't think he knew. He was saying he liked me better when I was hardworking, spotted, and nerdy, wearing overalls and painters' pants.

He told me he listened to Janis Ian's "At Seventeen" over and over again and prayed the only prayer he has ever prayed. He went into a kind of falsetto when he recounted this, "Please God, make her at least half–Bettie beautiful and half–Mary Frances good, I'm not asking for Bettie beautiful and Mary Frances good. Nobody gets all that and Randall smart, but, Lord, don't let her be unfortunate like the girl in 'At Seventeen.'" According to Daddy I got pretty and smart, but God fixed him and made me frivolous. And forty dollars wouldn't fix it.

Daddy's indictment made me belly laugh. That belly laugh shook me back to first ambitions. I didn't tell Daddy I was living so fast and crazy, making audacious choices, loving so hard and wild, to dilute what had been forced on me.

I just told him I was moving to Nashville to be the next Anna Gordy, to prove him right about Black people inventing Country Music, and to fund the writing of novels. I was going South and going deep.

It was a quick life-changing pivot. I wouldn't be frivolous. I wasn't letting somebody else's worst days define my best days. I was returning to my Black Bottom roots. I didn't say I would find me a prince of the Black South to marry, pretty as Daddy, pretty as Marvin Gaye, but that was a part of the plan, too.

I had the big, pull-the-trigger meeting with Edith. I came away with one hundred thousand dollars, three years to get a cut, leadership of the company, and majority ownership of Midsummer Music.

Almost the last thing I did before leaving Washington, D.C., for Nashville was attend a concert at DAR Constitution Hall with my first almost cowboy. On March 16, 1983, the Country Music Association celebrated its twenty-fifth anniversary in epic style.

On the bill: Willie Nelson, Barbara Mandrell, Merle Haggard, the Oak Ridge Boys, Alabama, Bill Monroe, Loretta Lynn, Charley Pride, Roy Acuff, Eddy Arnold, Anne Murray, Gene Autry, Glen Campbell, Ray Charles, Charlie Daniels, Jimmy Dean, Tennessee Ernie Ford, Larry Gatlin, Ronnie Milsap, Minnie Pearl, Merle Travis, Kitty Wells, June Carter Cash and Johnny Cash, Ricky Skaggs, Grandpa Jones, Pee Wee King, and John Ritter. Politicians in attendance: Jimmie Davis, who penned and performed "You Are My Sunshine" long before he was governor of the great state of Louisiana; Vice President George Bush and President Ronald Reagan. I was seated right across from President Reagan. When you go as the guest of Buddy Killen, the president of Tree International, arguably the greatest Country publisher, the publisher of "Heartbreak Hotel," you go first class.

It was a complicated night. The venue had something to do with it. DAR Constitution Hall was built by the Daughters of the American Revolution and was an infamous venue, one that had refused to allow a Black opera star, Marian Anderson, to perform in it. I took pleasure in seeing Charley Pride stride onto that particular stage in front of that audience.

The almost cowboy teased that President Reagan was staring at my breasts. That dress was a black silk Vicky Tiel warning shot that no one paid attention to. If Lil had been in the audience she would have noticed. She understood the importance of stage clothes. She knew how to read the rags and how to make an audience read the rags. She would have seen that barroom-gal bubble dress as an announcement that I was coming for a reckoning. I was coming to get some of my own back, I was coming armed with Detroit audacity and Cambridge shine to make Music Row acknowledge all the Black, all the African—from the banjo to Lil Hardin—that made the night possible and wasn't recognized. Not just Charley Pride. Not just Ray Charles, who would close the show singing "America."

It was not simple or easy for me to sit in the DAR Constitution Hall and listen to Country. It was flabbergasting. It was gobsmacking.

Roy Acuff announced that "nobody in Country Music is there alone . . . Country Music is a family" and everybody in Country Music can look back to someone who influenced them. Then he proclaimed Jimmie Rodgers "the father" of Country.

My First Family of Black Country was conceived in that moment. It was nurtured in the silence of missing names. Acuff found the space to mention Will Rogers, the comedian, but no space to mention Lil Hardin Armstrong and shamelessly no space to mention DeFord Bailey, founder of the Opry feast. The kicker was the closer. Ray Charles singing "America." Listening to and looking at that performance in DAR Hall caused me to understand that there was a First Family of Black Country. That he, Ray Charles, was Lil Hardin's and DeFord's genius child; that Charley Pride, on the stage as Ray Charles played and sang that patriotic anthem, was DeFord's side child; and Herb Jeffries, the great Black singing cowboy of film, who wasn't present in the audience of the auditorium but should have been, was Lil's stepchild. Always a stepchild not invited somewhere they had every right to be. In Country that's too often Herb Jeffries. In Country that's too often the whole Black audience.

I had been having second thoughts about actually heading to Nashville. Kurtis Blow was playing at the 9:30 Club and that wasn't going to happen in Nashville. But the absence of Herb Jeffries propelled me. Sitting in that vast auditorium with a sea of white people including the president of the United States, the vice president of the United States, Senator Teddy Kennedy, and the presidents of every major Country Music record label and performance rights organization, I had an inkling I was the only person in that room worried about Herb Jeffries, and wondering why, though *he was alive*, he wasn't in the room. It was time to change the room.

Soon, on February 18, 1983, I hit the road with three friends—one woman and two men—in a rented brand-new highway-ready car pointed South. I left the eight-hundred-dollar Opal rusting in the backyard. On the twelve-hour drive, we sang along loud to the radio. The song that had me mesmerized? "Faking Love." "Only temporary lovers as we lie here to each other . . . faking love." Buddy Killen had produced "Faking Love" and told me all about its co-writers, the legendary Bobby Braddock who wrote "D-I-V-O-R-C-E" and my favorite all-time Country song, "He Stopped Loving Her Today," and the eighteen-year-old songwriter phenom, Matraca Berg. I listened. Buddy was the one person in Nashville who believed it was so important for me to be at that concert, he spent hundreds of dollars on two tickets and a lot of goodwill to snatch two prime seats up for me when hit writers and publishers were crying without invites. Matraca and Bobby would prove to be bigger gifts than the tickets.

SCALING MUSIC ROW CITADEL: SCREAMING LIKE A BANSHEE IN BELLE MEADE

My first night in Nashville I slept in a seven-story brick building in a neighborhood, Belle Meade, that should be associated with DeFord Bailey but most often isn't. The Wellington Arms, built in 1939, is located at 4225 Harding Pike, walking distance (except no one walks in Nashville) to 540 Belle Meade Boulevard, a house DeFord Bailey's harmonica virtuosity—blasted across the country via the WSM airways on the Grand Ole Opry radio show—helped purchase.

When I arrived in town, 540 Belle Meade Boulevard was inhabited by a very fine lady, Margaret Ann Robinson. Her father founded WSM Radio; her husband was the CEO of National Life and Casualty who helmed the building of the Opry House, Opryland USA theme park, and the Opryland Hotel.

I would spend a lot of time in my early Nashville days in those three "Opry" venues that were inextricably yet often invisibly tied to DeFord's art and audience.

The invisibility was not benign happenstance. For more than half a century Roy Acuff was a highly visible presence in the Opry universe and on the Opry campuses. He obscured more often than he revealed how much DeFord contributed to his early success as an individual artist and to the early success of the Grand Ole Opry as a platform.

In the 1930s when DeFord Bailey's audience was much larger than Roy Acuff's, DeFord helped launch Acuff's career by appearing on the same bill and sharing the stage. When they were both starting out, DeFord was the draw that got the larger number of tickets sold at live shows. He was the draw that got a lot of folks tuning in to the Opry.

My apartment was also walking distance to 530 Belle Meade Boulevard, another home with a DeFord Bailey connection. 530 Belle Meade Boulevard was long inhabited by J. C. Bradford, Sr., the first Nashvillian to buy a seat on the New York Stock Exchange. When Bailey first arrived in Nashville, he toiled (in a smaller house) for J. C. as both a "houseboy" and as musician employed to entertain the Bradfords' guests. Reminiscences of hearing DeFord blow his harp moved with the Bradfords to "the Boulevard."

To give you a taste of what DeFord may have experienced in his first weeks in Nashville back in the first quarter of the twentieth century, let me tell you what I experienced in the last quarter. I walked into the Wellington Arms laundry room wearing the crimson Calvin Klein sweats I had purchased to lounge in Oak Bluffs, Martha's Vineyard. A middle-aged white woman wearing khaki pants and a crisp white shirt walked in with a basket of laundry, smiled, and asked me, "Who's are you?" When I didn't answer the woman repeated her question adding, "Do you belong to Mrs. ____ in apartment ____ or Mrs. ____ in apartment ____?" The way the woman snarled "belong to" made her subtext question clear, "Who's property are you?"

I didn't mind being mistaken for a maid; I have a whole lot of respect for maids. What incensed? This witch thought working for someone meant, more or less, they owned you.

That was my welcome to DeFord's world and the world DeFord,

unacknowledged and underpaid, helped build. I wasn't recognized as a neighbor; I was recognized as servant. This required a response.

My favorite phrase in Lil Hardin's "Brown Gal" is "breaking all conventions." My favorite word in the song is *vim*. I was in the land of Country Music and Country values authenticity. I knew what vim would have me do. I looked right in that woman's face and screamed at the top of my lungs with a wide-open mouth. And I didn't move an inch. I held my ground and screamed like a banshee.

Some of that screaming was for me, some of it was for DeFord; I had been hearing and thinking a lot about DeFord. Those first weeks in Nashville it seemed every time I walked into a building some older writer or producer would narrate DeFord's death to me as a cautionary tale.

The nature and wording of the warning varied. I remember clearly the two most common variants. Those who wanted to encourage me to work hard described DeFord's demise something like this, "And he died in poverty because he was too lazy to write new songs." Those were the folk who *wanted* to encourage me.

Those who took one look at my twenty-three-year-old Black body and agreed that I needed "to go back to wherever it is you came from" told me the story of DeFord's end, "And he died in poverty, living in a housing project, shining shoes, because he was too lazy to write new songs."

In those days in Nashville, on Music Row, "housing project" and "shining shoes" were code for Black. Poor white people, in the mythos of that time and place, lived in trailers, preferably a double-wide, or on the family's defunct and imperiled farm. They, white folks, didn't live in housing projects. They, white folks, were independent. They, white folks, didn't depend on government aid. They, white folks, persisted. The implication was Black people, exemplified by DeFord, didn't persist. In all versions of DeFord's story I heard on the Row, DeFord's death was a tragedy of DeFord's making.

When prodded to stop talking about his death and tell me something about his life, the folks I was meeting on Music Row at the very beginning described him as a feeble man, addled by polio and misshapen, who didn't exist in music before he played on *Barn Dance* in 1925 or after he left the Opry in 1941.

Except to die. They always got back to the death. I stopped asking white men to talk to me about DeFord.

Fortunately, white men were not the only folk on the Row. It was Shirley Washington who helped me day-to-day navigate the sharks on the Row in the early days of getting Midsummer Music the publishing house established and getting myself established as a Country songwriter.

I first met Washington, one of the Black women who helped birth Country Music, on the scouting trip to Nashville I took in the fall of '82 before I made a permanent move in the winter of '83. She worked at ASCAP "taking care of the building" and "welcoming visitors," some said. Others said she was "the maid." I think of Shirley Washington as the Nashville office of ASCAP's secret weapon.

She didn't know a lot about DeFord Bailey, but she knew he was a "Big" with a capital B. She knew he was respected in the neighborhood. And she knew Music Row overlapped a Black neighborhood. Shirley was the first, but not the last, to tell me that.

People didn't talk about this much, but Music Row was built on the edge of (and sometimes right on top of) an old Black neighborhood. In 1954, the white Bradley brothers, Harold and Owen, opened the Quonset Hut, a recording studio on the western border of the Black neighborhood called Edgehill.

Black churches, two Black-owned pharmacies (one, Clemons Drug, boasting a soda fountain), funeral homes, shoeshine shops, and Black families all thrived in Edgehill. With the churches came music. Long before the Quonset Hut was opened by the Bradley brothers in 1954, Greater Bethel AME was founded in 1866; Kayne Avenue Missionary Baptist in 1882; Bass Street Baptist in 1887; and Lea Avenue Christian opened its doors in 1903. All these institutions took an active part in seeding music into the neighborhood that would become Music Row through their choirs and the wide range of secular music enjoyed in their homes.

By the time I arrived, one of the most prominent Black families to live in what was considered the heart of the Row neighborhood was the Forrester family. Fourteen Music Circle South was and is their address, but hundreds of Black families lived walking distance to my new work home and thousands had been displaced in the forties during Negro removal movements.

Shirley knew all of this. She knew Connie Bradley, her big with a capital B Boss, was Owen Bradley's daughter-in-law, wife of his son, Jerry. She knew Music Row was a small town within a city where who you knew mattered as much as what you knew.

Who Shirley knew was Della Riley. And she raised Della up before me as a progenitor. She made me know I was in Della's debt. I hope telling this is a beginning of repayment.

Shirley came to work in an ambiguous uniform that she herself devised and got the office to accept. She wore a brightly colored Hawaiian men's shirt and nurses' slacks. Della worked at ASCAP in a literal maid's uniform.

Della worked six days most weeks, seven days some others. When Ed Shea, the former Nashville Chamber of Commerce executive, was tapped to head up the Nashville office of ASCAP in a move to connect the music industry to mainstream Nashville business, he took Della with him. When ASCAP moved into its first big and fancy office building on Music Row, Ed and Ms. Riley moved, too, except he was called Mr. Shea and she was called Della. In very different ways they both fueled ASCAP's aggressive press into Country. Della worked cleaning up the ASCAP building—including cleaning the glass walls of the stunning lobby and those walls were tall and wide. Thinking of Della cleaning all that glass, I came to hate those walls.

To understand how much work Della did, one must know that the Sheas had seven children, six girls and a boy. A person who helped open the original ASCAP office on the Row and who was often referred to as the "mayor of Music Row" reported to me stopping by in the evening to pick up Ed Shea to go to a showcase. Mrs. Shea was cooking in the kitchen. Della was cleaning the house. And this was at nighttime. To understand Della's seven-day workweek, one has to know that ASCAP threw big, late parties using the round reception desk in the middle of the all-glass lobby as a bar. After the parties, after everyone but Della left, she would clean. Clean the floors, the glass walls, the reception desk bar, the refrigerator, and the bathrooms. She would clean it all.

To truly understand that Music Row was located at its founding in a Black neighborhood, ponder this: Della's church was close enough to the ASCAP building that she could walk to it and bring back a steaming plate of chitlings for lunch—and on more than one occasion she did just that.

Setting Della ahead of me was a good thing Shirley did for me. It wasn't the only thing.

She always found a room for me to write in whether or not I had reserved a room. Sometimes Shirley elevated me to the boardroom whether or not I had an appointment with one of the "official" writers' representatives. Shirley was my most able writer's rep. She always had a seat and a cold Coca-Cola for me. And she always served the soda with a chaser of insight into which writers I should avoid and whom I should pursue. She knew who was too racist or too sexist to write hits with me. She knew better than anyone else in that building. She knew which people would make an appointment to write and not bring their best lines. She knew their best hooks, their best melodies. She knew which of my outfits worked and which didn't work. And she wasn't afraid to tell me. She had waited a long time to serve someone who looked like her. She hard-wanted a big hit for me.

A thing, not the only thing, Connie Bradley, Della Riley, and Shirley Washington had in common was being assaulted by misogynistic language on the Row. Della and Connie were taunted with words. Executives crowed to Della about the attractions of Della's booty and of Della's boss. She heard these words a thousand times. I've spoken directly to the man who recalled saying this to Della: "Connie Bradley had a body Ajax couldn't keep clean . . ." Language was vicious back then on the Row if you were a woman. I heard it all.

Della and Shirley survived all that, and Shirley helped me survive it. Their fingerprints are on everything ASCAP accomplished in Nashville. That's the other thing Shirley, Della, and Connie have in common. But everybody talks about what Connie contributed and hardly anybody talks about the myriad small and large ways Della and Shirley contributed to ASCAP's success on the Row by supporting publishers and writers in their quest for success.

Shirley side-eyed me into knowing I arrived dressed all wrong. My style was part too punk grunge, part too preppie Harvard. My hair was the wrong kind of wild for "the Row." Fortunately, my very first weekend in Nashville, exploring the riverfront way downtown (an area at the time of pawnshops, a seed store, places to sell blood plasma for cash, and a few very cool shops) I discovered Goodies and its proprietor, Barbara Kurland.

DRESSING FOR SUCCESS AT THE UNIQUELY QUIET BLUEBIRD CAFÉ

Looking through the Goodies racks was like moving through an art gallery. The pieces had attitude, intelligence, they were highly original, and out of sync with commercial style you might see in magazines. At her shop, Barbara curated an inventory that helped to define a new, distinctly recognizable Music Row insider uniform. I can still remember some of those one-of-a-kind, artsy, and affordable pieces.

I purchased most of the clothes I worked the Row in from Barbara Kurland—the first woman to mount a real campaign to be mayor of Nashville and a go-to source for insider information about songwriters and recording sessions. I chose dresses from her collection that slyly referenced dresses Black banjo playing women, Black fiddling woman, Black blues shouting women, and Black gospel singing women might wear; dresses my grandmother wore. Most people may not get that, but most got this: the dresses came from Goodies, the only place selling anything like them in Nashville at the time. Those dresses allowed me to walk in and announce, without a word, that I was connected.

Barbara's husband, Shelly Kurland, was one of the most in-demand session players and string arrangers in the city. Barbara's daughter, Amy Kurland, had just opened the Bluebird Café, which was fast becoming the gathering spot for working songwriters.

After spending my second night in Nashville at the Bluebird, I spent a lot of nights there. Located in an upscale strip mall where you could buy hand-smocked children's clothes and expensive copies of antiques, the Bluebird looked from the outside more like a suburban-ladies-who-lunch-between-school-drop-off-and-pickup café than a honky-tonk. Inside it was a new kind of show bar.

Growing up in Motown—where the bars typically served up some form of live music with the booze—and with a father who dashed into some watering hole every two or three hours for a drink, I was well familiar with every commonly known form of show bar. From holes in the wall with only a single piano to multilevel silk-lined interiors containing stages large enough for an orchestra, I was familiar. Within minutes of entering the Bluebird I knew this place was something fundamentally different.

It *looked* like some bars I had known. There was a single largish room filled with small tables around which were crowded ladder-back chairs providing seats for about seventy-five people. Dark and stylish teal-blue walls were hung with framed and autographed publicity stills of the artists who had performed on the barely elevated stage, more of just a riser big enough to hold four musicians and their amps. Across from the stage was an imposing dark wood bar just wide enough to fit six or eight barstools. To the left of the bar were a few rows of church pews.

But it didn't *sound* like a regular bar. It sounded hushed. At the Bluebird during a performance the audience did not talk. Ever. You could make a sound, you could clap. That was it. If you talked, first you got shooshed. To be shooshed by Amy Kurland was a stinging public shaming. Few made a sound after their shooshing. If you persisted? You always got shooshed again; sometimes you got removed.

The Bluebird did not play, it was about serious business. It might have looked like a pretty tearoom with those patterned curtains at the window, but as I learned to say as a girl at Ziggy's, "Pretty kitty got claws."

And secrets. On the other side of the wall across from the plate glass windows, essential conveniences shared a single, crowded short corridor: the Bluebird's refrigerator, a men's toilet, a women's toilet, and a pay phone.

The women's toilet had one commode. This meant there was always a line. And there was often a line for the phone. The toilets were not even primarily used for a quick pee, there was a lot of career-making or breaking, primping, strategizing, and sex going on in the toilet, as well as some plain romantic sex, and some got-drunk-sick. The line for the women's toilet was so long on many a night that I and other females needing a commode for a quick pee used the men's. Even more nights I "held it."

The Bluebird was a place young people came to practice their art, further their craft, compete, dream, and scheme in the company of others some who had just succeeded, some who had achieved superstar status, and some who were falling stars looking for their next cut or their next lover. In the quiet dark of the Bluebird every good song-thing seemed possible. If you could get drunk, stoned, and tripping people to quietly listen, what couldn't you do?

During my Bluebird nights, most of the audience was made up of songwriters and the people directly involved with servicing songwriters: publishers, managers, record label folk, performing rights licensing people. Only a small percentage of the audience was made up of what we respectfully called "civilians." The world called them fans. We were fighting an art war to provide the civilians with the soundtrack to sustain their lives and fund ours.

There were exceptions to this, of course. Fan Fair week, DJ week, the charity fundraising nights. But on a regular night in the eighties and early nineties, that's how it was. My first weeks at the Bluebird, I usually knew no one but the bartender and the person on the door. After I had been in Nashville a year, I knew almost everybody in the room.

Usually, the shows started at 9:00 or 9:30 p.m. Typically there would be three sets. My routine was to drink coffee and take notes. I didn't drink out in the world in my first years in Nashville. I was there to learn. I didn't steal lines from others, didn't use them in my songs, but I scribbled down other folks' lines so I could study them. Graph the stresses and unstresses, the patterns of the rhyme, analyze the uses of alliteration and metaphor with the care I once applied to Shakespeare and with so much more excitement.

When you hear a song on the radio, it is already probably a year or two old already. At the Bluebird, I heard songs so new their authors had barely memorized them. I heard where the music was going, not where it had been. I heard where the music would never go but should. I heard truths so hard they couldn't be told on the radio or on a record. And that was just from the stage.

In the chairs, waiting in the bathroom line, from the very first night, I heard every kind of *Baby, please don't go* at the Bluebird. There were common variations. *Baby, don't leave me. Baby, don't jaunt down to your dealer. Baby, don't clock-in on that job that's killing your art. Baby, don't leave Nashville.* And every so often the saddest tenderest *Baby, don't go* of all. *Baby, please don't die.* Sometimes it's silent. Once I sat in the pews between Townes Van Zandt and Guy Clark squeezed in so tight their jeans-clad legs touched my naked knees and Guy stared *Baby, please don't go* into his best friend's eyes.

In April of 1983, the Twenty-Fifth Anniversary of the Country Music Association concert aired on CBS. I didn't watch. I was probably at the Bluebird. About a month later, *Motown 25: Yesterday, Today, Forever* aired on NBC. I watched with intense focus. The label and I were born the same year. These Black people had to change music, change dance, change politics, change economics, and *succeeded*. Michael Jackson succeeded in changing dance during the show. There's an emotional armor called Detroit chin-up swagger. The special reminded me to wear mine, in Nashville, like a light garment.

Dressed for a new brand of success, and with head full of the hottest songs and the weirdest Country songs ever, from attending all those writers' nights and hanging out in tape copy rooms, and memorizing the lyrics I was writing, I checked in with Bob Doyle, then the youngest and brightest writers' rep at ASCAP, the person who picked me up at the airport when I came for that first scouting trip. He had someone he wanted me to meet, Diana Reid Haig.

Diana was working at House of David as a studio manager and occasionally as recording engineer. The Sarah Lawrence graduate arrived in Nashville in 1981 and has been called the first female sound recording engineer on the Row. She took a job at Quadrafonic Studio thinking she was going to work for Elvis's keyboard player, David Briggs—but David had already left to open his own studio which would become closely associated with two of the greatest writers of the period: Will Jennings and Max D. Barnes. Max of "If You're Gonna Do Me Wrong (Do It Right)" and "Red Neckin' Love Makin' Night" fame would be the only man to ever attempt to woo me with chewing tobacco and the last songwriter to chase me around my apartment. After trying to co-write with Max D., I never let another male writer into my apartment.

Everything about Diana, including the sexual harassment we endured, was fifties vintage. She drove a two-tone 1956 four-door Chevy Bel Air that was the dark gray and cream. She was producing an edgy remix of a fifties-era variety television show, *Belle Meade Beach*. She gave me a cooking spot. On one episode I flamed plum pudding made with plum baby food—a very fifties recipe. Her front room boasted an extraordinary collection of fifties-era television sets that a mutual friend, debutante turned singer-songwriter Marshall Chapman, claimed were never turned on.

Diana and I created our own code of conduct. We worked. We didn't drink liquor. We didn't do drugs. We swilled coffee. Our mantra was: work works. Even though we knew it didn't always.

Our first song, "Dangerous Curves," a cow-punk version of a fifties doo-wop, was completed to our satisfaction. Armed with the knowledge, probably from Barbara, that Steve Earle (an up-and-coming rockabilly singer-songwriter from Texas) was cutting soon, it made sense to us for me to call Bob Doyle, talk him out of Steve Earle's phone number, then cold call Steve at his home to pitch "Dangerous Curves."

It did not make sense to Steve. He started cussing. He called me everything but child of God. He started whining about the trials of his day, which included having a broke car. Soon I was picking him up at a house on Belmont Boulevard and driving him to the nearby LSI Studios. When he was out of the car he leaned through the open window to shake my hand and thank me. I pressed a cassette marked "Dangerous Curves" in his hands. Whatever kind of "crazy bitch" he hadn't called me over the phone, he called me then. I mashed down the car door lock, then rapidly cranked the car window up. A week later he rang me on my rotary home phone, "You're going to be a hit songwriter one day and I'm going to help you."

Steve and I set up standing writing appointments. The finished songs, "You Tear Me Up," "Halfway Home," "You Can't Break My Heart," were my co-writing 101 class.

Diana Haig and Steve Earle were among my best wild allies when I hit the Row. I needed them. The big deal muckety-mucks who were running the town wanted to preserve standard operating procedures.

Buddy Killen would only do so much for me when he realized I was starting my own publishing company and at that time had no interest in signing with Tree as a staff writer.

Don Henry, the songwriter working in the tape copy room, didn't care. He liked the same thing about my lyrics that Hal David, the president of ASCAP and a songwriting icon, had liked—my crazy ideas. And I liked Don Henry's. We hatched multiple plans to get those ideas on the airways—one involved studying the wildest and weirdest songs, cut or uncut, in the Tree catalog—and figuring out why they worked or didn't. We were going to get rooted in something other than the radio: the interior of our own heads. Don made cassette copies for the pluggers to pitch. Don worked in a windowless room lined floor to ceiling with reel-to-reel tapes in cardboard boxes. We listened to whole lot of them. We spent hours, what felt like whole days, listening to demo-reels. This was my songwriting graduate intensive.

CHARLEY PRIDE AT A BLACK-TIE BANQUET IN A NASHVILLE BALLROOM

My very first ASCAP dinner, it would have been 1983 or 1984, I saw Charley Pride seated with his wife, Rozene. Making my way to his table (that may have been the year the carpet in the Opryland ballroom was strewn with silk autumn leaves), I was intercepted by Jimmie Davis, or someone who looked like him and didn't correct me when I said, "Governor Davis?" He stuck out his hand and I believe he said, "If you're in this room I need to know you." I already knew who he was, the man who wrote "You Are My Sunshine," the former governor of Louisiana. Because I was from Washington, D.C., people pointed out Jimmie Davis to me, assuming I would be interested. Looking back, I wonder if he thought I had to be a Charley Pride relation. I didn't stay long enough to figure any of that out. I just told him I was a songwriter, a song publisher, and was on my way to introducing myself to a great song singer, Charley Pride. Davis got out of my way.

This is who I was moving toward: as long as I had been consciously listening to radio, I had been hearing Charley Pride's voice on it. Charley Pride's first single was "The Snakes Crawl at Night," released in 1966. About that time he briefly became the talk of my world, Black Detroit, and the talk of the big three assembly lines, when he wowed more than ten thousand white fans—who were not expecting a Black singer—with his performance at his first stadium show.

A year later he would become the first Black artist to appear on the Grand Ole Opry since DeFord Bailey. His first number one was, "All I Have to Offer You (Is Me)," released in 1969. In 1971, about the time I was peeking him on *The Johnny Cash Show* and crushing, he was voted CMA Entertainer of the Year. He was voted CMA Male Vocalist of the Year in 1971 and 1972. As I slowly made my way toward him across the ballroom his single "Night Games" was blazing up the charts. It would be his last song to land in the number one spot. I was meeting Pride, the artist who so directly followed in DeFord's footsteps, at a pinnacle.

Pride stood up when I reached the table. He may just have had somewhere to go, or he may have had what some of us call excellent home training, or it may have been his way of showing respect for a Black woman. As far as I noticed, Rozene Pride and I were the only two Black women in the room dressed to be guests at the banquet. I started gushing words of respect for him—my appreciation of his performance at the twenty-fifth anniversary of the CMA Awards in Washington at the DAR Constitution Hall. And gushing about my plans in Nashville, I wanted him to know he helped put me in the room.

Pride was taller and even more dazzlingly handsome in person than he was on television. He didn't say much to me. I talked so fast, and the room was so loud, he probably barely heard my name and wouldn't remember it if he had. But he hadn't forgotten how hard it was to get into spaces like this. He shook my hand and let everyone see he was welcoming me. Then he sat down, and I was dismissed.

MAKING A POWER MOVE AT THE WEENIE ROAST

Which was a good thing. I needed to get up early the next morning. It was write at 10:00 a.m. and write at 2:00 p.m., even during awards season. And it was attend all the events where there would be a lot of writers and artists that week and all other weeks. There was no better venue for that than the Weenie Roast.

The Weenie Roast was an annual Music Row good weather ritual. Everyone was invited, anyone could just show up, and most folks doing any kind of work on Music Row came. It was hosted by a bank that liked being known as the "musician's friend." I attended my first Weenie Roast wearing one of my Barbara Kurland purchases. A tall man with dark eyes struck up a conversation. He was an extremely well-read surfer from California and seemingly high as a kite on insight and ambition to be a hit songwriter. When he told me he wrote for Acuff-Rose, I asked him what his last name was. He said, "Sanders." When he discovered I was a songwriter, he invited me to write. I told him he didn't want to write with me because I had "no talent whatsoever." When he realized I was quoting his own words back to him, half-embarrassed, half-amused, he repeated the invitation to co-write. This time I accepted, eager to prove Mark and his boss wrong.

Our first co-write was the cringe-able and never recorded, "I Don't Want to Be Your No. 1 (I Want to Be Your One and Only One)." Mark had seen and rejected my best ideas. His publisher wanted love songs. I had veered from my established strategy not to write romantic love songs. The next time we sat down to write, I worked my original plan. I suggested we write a song about religious hypocrisy and unwed mothers. He liked the idea. I pitched a title, "Reckless Night," and lines from a rough draft he had previously seen and dismissed. This time he was intrigued.

By the time we completed "Reckless Night," a song that would get recorded, the song that began in that churchyard in Virginia, I knew I had found a radically underutilized and radically underfunded asset.

Mark was the perfect first Midsummer songwriter hire. We each had an unusual vocabulary of themes, imagery, and words for a Country songwriter. We both leaned into the King James Bible language and metaphor, not the theology. We had a lot of overlap. That was the start of it.

It wasn't the end. We were both writing from the perspective of creating a conversation in song with other American literatures, with fiction and poetry, more than writing in the context of the Country song tradition. I brought Emily Dickinson in the room, He brought Steinbeck. We both knew Faulkner and Zelda Sayre. We did meta-things—pointing our listeners to those authors, writing what we thought those authors left out. And we wrote to an audience the authors we loved often ignored: people who wouldn't or couldn't read difficult fiction or difficult poetry. Sometimes those folk could tolerate a difficult song. The music, the beat, can help some strong medicine go down.

We were also technically complementary. I could talk about a lyric in an abstract form as a series of stresses and unstresses, and he would understand what I meant when I talked about iambic pentameter. He could take a melody and then scan out the entire structure of the verse, chorus, and bridge in stresses and unstresses so I could write to the scan that fit the music. That saved a lot of time. In theme and technique, we suited one another.

And my emotional intelligence told me that Mark didn't love working with standard Music Row alpha males just because they held power positions. He liked writing with his friends. He liked writing with new voices. He would write his biggest song with someone I introduced him to who had been my daughter's Saturday night babysitter, and she had had precious few cuts at the time. Mark did great with a very smart, new to the game, writer and I was both new to the game and wanting to put new writers in the game.

To get his bills paid, Mark was working in a high school five days a week, then showing up at a publishing house writing room to write songs. I suspected Midsummer could lure him away from Acuff-Rose if Midsummer offered a big enough draw. And I believed if we encouraged him to start writing something other than the love songs Ronnie was hankering for, he might be the gold mine.

Mark wasn't ready to sign with Midsummer yet. We didn't have a plugger other than me. He believed I could write. He wasn't sure I could plug. He was only too aware three years earlier I didn't even know the word "plug" meant pitch songs to artists and record labels and persuade them to actually "cut," meaning record, them.

I found my song plugger, Karen Conrad, at a songwriter's night at one of the bars on 8th Avenue, either Douglas Corner Café or the Sutler Saloon. I was looking for a writer who would let me pitch. Karen approached me between sets. She came straight to the point, "I see you all the time. We should know each other. Come see me." Then she gave me her card. The way she went back to working the room, I knew I would take her up on the invitation.

One conversation convinced both of us that our interests were aligned. My business partner, Edith, and I contracted with Karen to pitch the Midsummer catalog. The woman who had pitched Jimmy Buffett and Jim Croce and had stepped out to form her own publishing company was now pitching me. Karen was thrilled to be, as she described it, "No longer hanging on by my fake fingernails," and to be able to use some of the money we were paying her to pitch to fund signing her own writers. At that time no bank in Nashville would loan a female independent publisher money for the purpose of running her business. It was a big win-win.

It was time to have another conversation with Mark Sanders. He had moved from Acuff-Rose to Maypop, a publisher owned by the band Alabama. We offered a big draw, I think I remember it was $37,500, with the stipulation he couldn't keep working in schools—he had to write full time. And we strongly encouraged him to write songs about something other than love.

Soon enough Mark was writing for Midsummer Music, Karen was pitching our songs, and we had an office in the cool Audio Media Building on 19th Avenue South.

IN THE RYMAN WITH ROY ORBISON AND A CHICKEN DRESSED UP LIKE JOHNNY CASH

I settled into my regular Monday through Friday rounds: write at ten and/or write at two; hit one, two, or three writers' nights each night to find new collaborators and get intel on the competition, other writers, and publishers; wine and dine managers and artists at breakfast, lunch, drinks, and dinner. On Saturday hit a bigger show. On Sunday study the previous week's Billboard Chart, making sure to listen to any new song that entered the chart, and study the listing of shows for the week in the Sunday newspaper, choosing which ones I would attend and strategize new ways to meet artists I could pitch.

One idea I came up with: park myself, uninvited, in the office of the Tennessee Film Commission. After the film commissioner had seen me sitting in her outer office for more than four hours, quietly reading, she invited me in. Soon I was working as a chicken wrangler on a Johnny Cash video in the then boarded up, but ever iconic, Ryman Auditorium.

My first task was driving to the airport in my little tan Ford Escort to pick up the "trained" chicken who would be starring with Johnny.

The critter was in a wire cage with a handle. You would think a trained chicken would be quiet. This one made odd little noises as I navigated the long way back to the Ryman that didn't involve the highway.

My second task was settling the chicken into the dressing room he was to share with Roy Orbison. I wasn't sure the great Roy Orbison would want to share space with a chicken or me. But I was excited to meet the man who wrote "Blue Bayou." Orbison was all in black and accompanied by his wife, Barbara, an ex-model, who was all in black, too. I think I had on a white peasant dress. I know I gushed on about "Blue Bayou." Orbison invited me to share some of my lyrics with them. Eventually someone from wardrobe showed up with the chicken outfit. It was a little tiny, shiny Nudie-style Western show suit. I started pulling the stunt chicken into the suit; it pecked me. I yelped.

The sound provoked one of the strangest non-tragic fifteen minutes of my life. Roy Orbison, Barbara Orbison, and I bent over that chicken and successfully pulled it into that show suit. It took six hands, but we got the job done—and the chicken looked pretty remarkable in the costume.

But all three of us in that room suspected "The Chicken in Black" video was a mistake. For more than an hour we waited to be called to the set and talked. After an hour of waiting and talking, this was coming clearer and clearer to me. I needed to be writing, needed to be finding the collaborators who would be as loyal to me as Orbison was being to Cash, as Cash had been to Orbison. Folks who would be there for the lows, and helping you get to the highs, for the first time or again. I checked on the chicken and it pecked me again. I abandoned it. I fled out of the Ryman. I ended up sitting on the sidewalk in downtown Nashville, literally butt on the sidewalk, feet in the street. There were production trailers and production lights and people who looked like they were filming something all milling about. Someone walked up to me and said, "You must be Johnny Rodriguez's daughter!" Someone else asked, "Are you Johnny Rodriguez's daughter?" When I said no, they didn't believe me.

When I said I was "a regular American Black person" they didn't believe that, either, but walked away probably believing I was crazy. I was still sitting on the sidewalk trying to make sense of this swirl of Orbison, chicken, and Rodriguez when an attractive Black woman who looked to be in her fifties, outfitted in a crisp dress with a matching suit jacket, walked up to me, hand extended, and asked, "And who might you be?"

I told her my name. She asked me more questions. She said I had to meet her godson. She said he had just told her there were no interesting women in Nashville. She said any Black woman sitting in the middle of the sidewalk in the middle of the day and working on a Johnny Cash video was an interesting person. She arranged to have us both invited to the same Fourth of July party.

But I wasn't headed to a party on the Fourth of July. I was working that day, which meant heading to an opportunity to hang with a new artist and some rising producers. I wanted to go to the party being hosted by Joan Elliott, a professor of German languages at Tennessee State University whose twin sister was a doctor in D.C.—she and her sister had been the first Black twins to ever attend Wellesley—but I regretted. Even the holidays are workdays when you're working for yourself, and the clock is ticking down on three years and the balance is ticking down on what began as a whole lot of money in the bank. Every day I had less money and less time. So on the Fourth of July, 1984, I hopped in a car with my friend, Ray Kennedy, RCA recording artist, engineer, producer, sometimes known as "guitar man," who owned two of the studios I did a lot of wild things in, including rocking the infant Hillary Scott, the future Lady Antebellum, then Lady A, on my hip while her mother, Linda Davis, sang a demo. Ray and I headed to a gathering at the home of an aspiring recording artist I will call Oogly Ugly.

We got there and it was a fairly interesting hang until I started noticing all the racist home décor. The scariest was a back scratcher that looked like an elongated, terrified Black person. I would get a new and cheaper apartment. I would sell housewares at the local department store. Money and time were ticking down, but we had to leave. I grabbed Ray's hand and we were out the door. Oogly Ugly was probably too drunk to care. He was, in my highly subjective opinion after I saw those "Black people objects," always drunk on hate and always ugly, oogly ugly, ugly as homemade sin in face, body, and voice. We left. And the motherfucker did me a favor. I met my daughter's daddy at that party—a brilliant, clogs on his feet, one earing in his ear, Black Zen Buddhist graduate of Williams College, and the University of Texas Law School. Avon Nyanza Williams, III, was talking about leaving the law and opening up a seafood restaurant on the coast in Mexico. Fleeing the chicken I dressed up in a Nudie suit and a racist backscratcher, I ran into my future.

THE FAIRFIELD FOUR, BLACK GOSPEL AT THE RYMAN, AND HALLELUJAH, MY FIRST CUT!

But next I had a close encounter with the Fairfield Four that changed the way I looked at the Ryman. Before I was born, the Fairfield Four played all-night gospel shows at the Ryman.

The first place I ever saw and heard the Fairfield Four live was a hotel ballroom in downtown Nashville about the time I was meeting Avon and getting married. Reverend McCrary was still alive. I believe the lineup Pam Tillis and I saw was Willie "Preacher" Richardson, Reverend McCrary, Wilson Lit Waters, Isaac Freeman, and Robert Hamlett.

I know it was a five-person configuration and that surprised me because I thought the four in Fairfield Four referred to the number of people in the group, not the number of parts in the harmony. Their sound was the backbone of Country. The song of theirs I remember most clearly has become a theme song for the My Black Country project, "Ain't Gonna Let Nobody Turn Me 'Round."

I listen to an eighties recording of that song and hear so many different things. I hear the blueprint for my writing. Multiple voices and rhythms. I hear the slide up and down of notes that sound like a siren, like a warning bell, sounds like an ambulance, like a human being shouting an alarm, shouting the power of gossip and conversation, wailing the death of the mother. And I hear theft.

That song sounds so much like "Elvira" and "Bobbie Sue," mega-hits for the Oak Ridge Boys in the early eighties. That song sounds too much like them and it comes long before them. The Fairfield Four were founded in Nashville in 1921. Rufus Carrethers, Harold Carrethers, and John Battle were the original three members. I can prove that. In 1937, the Reverend McCrary joined the group. Twenty years after their first performance, the husband of one of the founding members of my Links chapter, John W. Work, III, recorded the Fairfield Four into the Library of Congress during Sunday service of the Fairfield Missionary Baptist Church.

They got an even larger audience in 1942. A regular early morning fifteen-minute set sponsored by the Colonial Coffee Company that aired nationally via WLAC, a 50,000-watt station. Behind that exposure they toured rural areas and came home to sing in the Ryman Auditorium. When you think about Black influence on Country, the Fairfield Four blasting homegrown Nashville Black gospel across the country should be the first name to cross your mind. If you were getting up to go out to work in the fields in the forties, you likely started your day with their sounds. They were on from 6:45 a.m. to 7:00 a.m.

In addition to the all-night gospel shows at the Ryman, they played the churches. They played the small towns of the Jim Crow South until all that got too hard to do. Sleeping in cars because they couldn't sleep in hotels. Not being able to fill up their gas tank. Then suddenly in the 1980s, they reemerged playing around Nashville. The place where they started. The place they influenced more than was initially acknowledged. They were in the ballrooms. They were in the churches. And their sound was on the radio.

The Fairfield Four are present in the sound of the Oak Ridge Boys. I can't prove that. Who's to say that hearing "Elvira" and "Bobbie Sue" on the radio didn't propel them to come out of retirement to claim and reclaim their authorship of this Nashville sound?

The first time I saw them, they wore overalls and suit jackets. And that's what I call complex Black Country couture. They were signifying ownership. Signifying dignity. Signify rural identity—refusing to be redlined out of *Hee Haw*. Hearing them sing, "Ain't Gonna Let Nobody Turn Me 'Round" inspired me to keep on keeping on, even when I hadn't gotten that first cut yet. Then I got it.

Just shy of a year after we met on Independence Day, Avon proposed to me in a revolving restaurant atop the Hyatt in downtown Nashville to stop me from fussing at him. I said, "Yes." The same day he proposed, in a studio not so very far from the Hyatt, "Reckless Night" was recorded by the Forester Sisters and released by Warner Bros. Records. I got my first cut. A co-write with Mark.

Steve Earle helped get that done. One afternoon, he invited me and a visiting out-of-town friend of mine to hang out with him at the publishing company where he was writing at the time, Silverline-Goldline. His publisher, Pat Halper, joined the conversation. Before I knew it, my out-of-town friend was mansplaining to Pat Halper, one of the first women to be hired to pitch by a major publisher, why she needed to listen to "Reckless Night" and get it recorded.

Ever gracious and often amused, Pat listened to the cassette demo of the song. Then she opined that the song could be perfect for the Forester Sisters—and she was pitching at Warner Bros. for the Forester Sisters the very next week. Though she had nothing to gain financially, Pat pitched the song to her friend Paige Levy, the A&R (Artist and Repertory) executive at Warner Bros. who was working with the Foresters. I was on my way to having a song on their most successful album and the B-side of a No. 1 single. The album *The Forester Sisters* reached No. 4 on Billboard's Country Album chart. And in time they would prove to be one of the most successful all-female Country groups with fourteen top ten singles.

I gave myself three years from incorporation of Midsummer Music to first cut or I was pulling the plug and going to graduate school. Now, I was staying. I would run the publishing company and Avon would practice civil rights law with his father. Everything was better than according to plan—for a hot minute.

KOSSI GARDNER, UNHERALDED BLACK COUNTRY GENIUS WITH FUNERAL-ORGAN ROOTS

Because his father was suffering with ALS, Avon the third didn't go out much when he wasn't working in the law office. Much of Black Nashville gravitated to "the senator's house" to show their respect and to enjoy his free and excellent liquor. Avon the third wanted to be present both to translate his father's increasingly slurred, garbled, and energy-sapping speech and to anticipate his father's needs and thoughts so he wouldn't have to exhaust himself struggling to speak. I admired that. We did most of our courting in his parents' kitchen and I did some of my best early learning about Black Country in that same kitchen.

I knew my heart was steady in its waltz toward Avon when I met Kossi Gardner, who looked like a cross between Billy Dee Williams and Jimi Hendrix, and my heart didn't skip a beat. It was a late Saturday afternoon and the house was lightly crowded with guests.

Kossi was standing at the long high-top bar in the kitchen. I took a seat beside him and asked him if it was true that he played on Country records. He said it was and that the first song he ever released was "She'll Be Coming Round the Mountain."

One of Dear's songs. Kossi recorded one of the songs Dear sang to me. It was like a voice from the grave. He had gone to Fisk just like Lil. And he talked with a barbershop-talk rhetoric style, where the journey is as important as the destination. It was a "when the student is ready, the teacher comes" thing. We jumped right in. Was "She'll Be Coming Round the Mountain" a song about a female God? About Mother Jones the labor leader? About the Second Coming?

Eventually Kossi suggested it could be something more than all of that. What? An aural antidote to Jim Crow Alabama hidden in a nursery song. Was the song a wish and a premonition that one day soon, the nation would rein in white wickedness? Not whiteness but white wickedness? Kossi had a byzantine brain.

I have heard the Muddy Waters version of this song, and it is stone

Black Country, rural, celebratory, defiant, confidently Christian in its certainty that bad will be vanquished and goodness restored, if not on earth in song heaven, "We gonna kill an old red rooster, eat like we usta . . ."

Then he was off on a next tangent. According to the gospel of Kossi and me this was a difference between blues and Country. The blues exists in a world where Satan is real and God is dead, or in a world where there was never a God, or in a world that is hell on earth now. It exists in a world where often the best you can do is fly above the world and up to cloud nine with whatever gets you high.

Black Country exists in a world where God is love, and what violates love violates God, and God is violated daily. This is a place where reckoning, reconciliation, and righteous anger slow dance with love and beauty, creating the possibility that some sweet tomorrow, on earth, will be better than today. In Kossi's Black Country, imagination, invention, and bending the note a new way was heaven on earth now.

Heaven and hell and music were all tied up together for Kossi, maybe because he learned to play organ in his father's funeral parlor. It was caring for the dead. Playing organ at funerals had given Kossi a window into a wide world of Black lives split open by grief that sprouted joy. He had played songs for weeping mamas able to hold smiles in their eyes because they knew heaven was real. He had played marches for women who held their head high walking behind the coffin that carried their mother, carried their tiny baby, carried their lover, because they knew heaven was real.

Kossi had played for the living and the dead. Reminded me of Dear saying the coffin falling out of the hearse was her baby shouting love. Kossi had played for a lot of dead bodies. And he had played organ in the church, played the hymns that were meant to lead the congregation away from hell. All that got him thinking about things a little different.

My favorite Kossi Gardner album, *Kossi Gardner Plays Charley Pride*, has been dismissed as "altogether strange."

A 1978 article in the *Tennessean* by Walter Carter reads: "Gardner's attempts in Nashville as a solo artist have been unsuccessful, if not altogether strange. His two albums for RCA, *Organ Nashville Style* and *Kossi*

Gardner Plays Charley Pride, were practically collectors' items the day they were released."

I am one of the people that collected that album that features Kossi dressed and coiffed, resembling Jimi Hendrix sitting in what appears to be the middle of the woods. The cover, shot at Hills of Calvary, the cemetery his family owned, depicts a creek in woods that are a part of a graveyard. His then wife, the Texan Fiskite who gave him two daughters, did his hair by rolling it in large pink curlers, then brushing it out.

The cover is radically rural. Nature, trees, dried grass, rocks, and sky dominate the visual background. The title *Kossi Gardner Plays Charley Pride* appears in bright butterweed yellow in all capitals. The name Charley Pride, three syllables, twelve letters, is synonymous with African-American Country star. A falling-down, distressed, two-rail, unpainted wood fence is evidence of the hand of man, the generations before. Nature and name work together on this cover to say that this is a Country album. Then the image gets complicated. Sprawled across the center of the cover, staking out the majority of the vertical and horizontal space, is Kossi Gardner looking nothing like male Country is supposed to look.

He's not in cowboy clothes or blue-collar work clothes; not in rhinestones or flannel or all black. There are no boots on his feet, no cowboy hat or baseball cap on his head. He's in a pumpkin-orange, double-breasted, neo-Edwardian jacket, purple trousers, fine black dress socks, shiny black dress shoes, and is sitting on a tree stump.

And it's not just his clothes that are psychedelic bohemian, it's his parted-on-the-side sweep of thick and wavy African hair that falls long to his shoulders, crowning his head. It's the way his fingers are curved and outstretched as if he is playing an invisible instrument or catching an invisible ball or caressing an invisible body or talking with his hands or sculpting the air. His knees are splayed. He's confidently taking up a lot of space and smiling. He's looking anywhere but directly into the camera. What is he looking at? We don't know. We know this: he is acknowledging the woods as our place, and he has placed Charley Pride in context and conversation with two Black men, one visible and one invisible. By shooting his album cover at the cemetery his father, Gardner, Sr., built and owned at the time, on land that would be familiar to many Black Nashvillians, Gardner, Jr., entwines the Pride legacy with the Gardner legacy. By playing the Pride songs, Gardner, Jr., entwines Pride's art with Gardener's art—to an ambitious purpose foreshadowed by the ultracontemporary palette and clothing—he's taking the woods, his father, and Pride into the future.

The album sounds like almost nothing I have ever heard. The melodies are familiar, but the sounds are not. The mechanism for evoking emotion is unfamiliar and yet it is conveyed. Kossi called the sound "spacey."

Afro-futuristic.

He was creating *space music*. Country space music. By translating Pride's lyrics into pure organ sound, translating the tones of Pride's voice into pure organ sound, Kossi was sending Charley Pride songs, stripped of words, into the universe. Why? He was creating songs that might emotionally move intelligent life on other planets.

Kossi Gardner played to create heaven on earth now, honor Charley Pride, and communicate with space aliens. To use a Kossi phrase, "That's some wild shit." And he wasn't the only one doing Black Country wildness. He hipped me to John Betsch. One of those visits in the Williams family kitchen, he shared percussionist John Betsch with me and so I knew "Earth Blossom," that lost Nashville Black hippy Country classic. More wild shit.

And while he was doing the wild shit, he provoked some powerful Music Row insiders to hear and acknowledge that he was doing something significant and Country. John D. Loudermilk, inducted into the Nashville Songwriters Hall of Fame in 1976, started working as a producer with Kossi a decade earlier in 1966, the same year Loudermilk started working with Gregg Allman as a producer. Kossi played with the greatest Country guitarist of all time, Chet Atkins. Kossi played on Atkins's sides; Atkins played on Kossi's side. When Chet Atkins was living, he said he wanted Kossi to play at his funeral.

The Country songs he recorded included Loudermilk's "Big Daddy,"

"Take These Chains from My Heart," and "Oh, Lonesome Me," originally recorded by Hank Williams with his Drifting Cowboys; and the Ferlin Husky hit and Opry staple "Wings of a Dove." He also recorded "Fancy" and talked to me about Bobby Gentry. For Kossi, Loudermilk and Gentry were the great Country songwriters. He had two and one was a woman. That emboldened me. My favorite Kossi enigma? How much influence did he have on Gregg Allman?

Kossi Gardner and Gregg Allman were both organists. Kossi was born in Nashville in 1941. Duane was born in Nashville in 1946. Gregg was born in Nashville in 1947. Loudermilk was working with Kossi and the Allmans in 1966. When Gregg was starting out, gigging around Nashville, Kossi, six years older, had graduated from Fisk and was playing in all corners of the town. He played in studios on Music Row, on Jefferson Street, he played in Printers Alley, he played in emerging rock spots. Did young Gregg Allman hear Kossi's Black funeral parlor–inflected organ, and did it influence him? I asked but Kossi didn't tell. He just gave me a beatific and enigmatic wide smile. He wasn't claiming the Allman Brothers. He was a prince of Black Nashville; he was claiming a young Black organ player named Shannon Sanders and he was sure she was going to do something. He was claiming a white boy who played with him on Printers Alley, I think that turned out to be my friend legendary Country guitarist Biff Watson; but best he said, "I'm claiming you, baby."

For a hot second. Then he vanished. His family said he was always running from the cemetery, running from death, running from funeral parlor organ. One of Kossi's first singles was his cover of Loudermilk's "Big Daddy." It could have been Kossi's theme song. "Who's on the loose but cannot be found . . . Somebody ran off with the mayor's wife . . . Somebody tried to take the police chief's life . . . Somebody stole the judge's ragged old gown . . . police are searching but . . . he can't be found . . ." Even when Chet Atkins did die, and someone from Chet's family called wanting Kossi to play, his daughter, Keisha Gardner, couldn't find Kossi.

The one man who would have known that Chet Atkins played with the Carter Family, that Eslie Riddle taught the Carter Family, that though the Carter Family recorded a fine "Wabash Cannonball" in 1929, and Roy Acuff's version sold more than ten million copies, it was lost. Kossi himself recorded a most excellent version on his 1970 album, *Organ Nashville Style*, after he found the very best "Wabash Cannonball" of all: the stone Country "Wabash Cannonball" performed by Black and blind Willie McTell in 1956 that was released in 1960.

Without Kossi getting me to Willie McTell, I would most vividly remember the "Wabash Cannon Ball" not as a song, but as a roller coaster in Opryland.

UNPACKING OPRYLAND (THEME PARK, HOTEL, STAGE) CULTURAL WAR ZONE

The Wabash Cannonball, a double upside-down roller coaster at Opryland, and the Grizzly River Rampage, a water ride, provoked the kind of catharsis I had discovered on the Rotor. I became addicted to the thrill and rode those rides often. Roy Acuff, who had a house in the theme park, would sometimes sit outside the Grizzly River Rampage and wave. I saw him there doing that.

Just like it was promised in one of the Opryland brochures as I moved through the Opryland campus I saw, "real people, real animals, real things." Including Acuff, but also Charley Pride, also Ray Charles. I saw them both in the flesh on the Opryland campus. The train that looked like it was fueled by coal was, in fact, fueled by coal. I thought about John Henry riding that train. I thought about a lot of smokestack lighting on that train. They say that there were live buffalo, elk, deer, cougars, bears, and timber wolves in their natural habitats. I don't remember any of that. I remember live music publishers, music promoters, DJs, artists, fans, songwriters. And I remember a whole lot of Black people who were not stars.

Opryland USA, the amusement park, opened in 1972. It sprawled over 120 music-filled acres. The Opry House opened in 1974 and became the forever home of the Grand Ole Opry. The Opryland Hotel opened in 1977. The *General Jackson* Showboat launched with an Opryland pier in 1985. The hotel wasn't always as big as it is now. With ten thousand tropical plants in the conservatory, and a fake indoor river in the Delta Atrium that's so long you can take a twelve-minute inside-the-hotel-lobby boat ride, now it is huge. In 1984, the hotel was just under a thousand rooms, and the big attraction was the Magnolia Lobby that looked like the pages of *Southern Living* come to life. Through the years, it has always been something big and grand on the banks of the Cumberland River. Great as the hotel is, I loved the theme park.

You didn't spend a whole wild and wet day in the park without seeing Black folk. Black kids had jobs at Opryland. Black people rode the rides at Opryland. Black musicians got gigs at Opryland. Black stars played at the Opry House.

The rapid expansion of radio formats targeting a Black audience and playing Black music 24-7, and the advent of Black-owned stations ushering in a golden era of Black radio. African-Americans in the sixties had choices about what to listen to on Saturday nights and most didn't listen to the Opry even if their parents and grandparents had tuned in to WSM every Saturday. Opryland employed hundreds of seasonal workers, many if not most of whom attended local high schools. Some of these people were Black. Thousands of visitors came to the park. A significant portion of these were locals with highly discounted season passes, some of these were Black. This led to the emergence in Nashville of a small but significant population of Black people who knew a whole lot of Country songs and had heard a whole lot of Country stars. These were folks who were able to make their own connections between Country and R & B, Country and hip-hop, Country and gospel.

And some of these people had intimate legacy experience with Lil Hardin's history, had grandparents or great-grandparents who had gone to Fisk with Lil or attended performances by Lil, or owned records by Lil. Some had *lived* experience with DeFord Bailey. Some had lived experience with Charley Pride on the Opryland campus, which he frequented as a member of the Opry. Some had lived experience with Ray Charles, who performed in the theme park in 1976 as part of the *Music Hall America* show that was filmed, televised, and syndicated. Many had legacy experience with Herb Jeffries.

The small cadre of African-Americans living in Nashville and working at Opryland theme park, including DeFord Bailey, Jr., and the larger group living in Nashville and visiting the theme park, including me, were uniquely positioned to hear and see common and uncommon African-American influence and presence in Country Music, and to be aware of intentional erasure.

The move from the Ryman was announced on October 18, 1968, in the immediate aftermath of Martin Luther King, Jr.'s death. The Opry was moving out of downtown, away from Fisk and the Black neighborhoods of Edgehill, North Nashville, and out south. Away from Music Row.

Some say Opryland was conceived and then developed as an evolving effort to sanitize Country and remove markers of its African origins. Sever connections to the African-American experience.

Leading the charge were Roy Acuff and Porter Wagoner, but what they got was something different—they got a place where Maya Angelou encouraged a young, Black female Country songwriter to persist in the audacious ambition to enter Country space and honor Black folk who had entered it before her. They got a place where Ray Charles sat down to a piano in a crowded room one DJ week and sang "Seven Spanish Angels" so powerfully that those DJs went out and pushed the recorded duet version of the record to the top of the Billboard Country Charts.

And the Opryland campus itself became a haven of sorts for Black people visiting in the South. This is not an intended consequence. It is an unintended but felicitous consequence. When it opened in the early seventies (as a hotel and an entertainment venue that included rides, shops, and restaurants) it was the exceptional grand Southern hotel and high-end Southern entertainment venue *that had never been segregated.*

This gave the Opryland Hotel a unique appeal to local Black folk and

Black folks living across the region in Atlanta and Louisville and New Orleans.

With multiple HBCUs in Nashville (Fisk, Meharry Medical College, Tennessee State University, and American Baptist College) and so much recording, Black folk (particularly doctors, lawyers, professors, parents of students, preachers, and musicians) were used to coming to Nashville. They were not used to coming to Nashville and having someplace glamorous to stay, someplace upscale to eat—*unless* they were staying in a private Black home, perhaps one designed by Black architect DeBerry McKissack, or eating in a private Black home, say Mrs. Arna Bontemps's home.

Until the opening of the Opryland Hotel, if you were Black and coming to Nashville you wanted to stay with friends and dine with friends. If you were lucky enough to stay with, for example, the McKissacks and dine, for example, at Mrs. Bontemps's you could expect to enjoy some of the finest dining the city had to offer, sleep in one of the most original and efficiently designed contemporary rooms the city boasted, and you could hope to spy between room and board an Aaron Douglas painting, a William Edmondson sculpture, or perhaps an Elizabeth Catlett. Black Nashville was proud of the epicurean delights and graceful accommodation it was able to extend to visitors.

But Black people in Nashville, at the time Opryland opened, still stung from being refused accommodation at the grand Hermitage Hotel and the seedy but wild Loveless Motel. They stung from being refused admission to the Parthenon that was supposed to be the symbol of the city. Grandma Bontemps told me of inviting a group of prominent Black women from across the South to Nashville to view the Parthenon on the day a week that was set aside for "colored visitors." The day came. The local hostesses and their guests arrived only to be told that the day allocated for "colored visitors" had been changed. They were not allowed entry. Across the city, other stories were told of other attractions, restaurants, museums, motels, hotels barring Black visitors, or being openly unwelcoming of Black visitors, in some cases long after the laws on the books had changed.

MIDSUMMER'S FIRST HIT, THE LAST DAYS OF DEFORD BAILEY, AND OTHER VICTORIES

Mark sang "Reckless Night" at my wedding reception in Washington, D.C. Shortly after the wedding, my new husband joined the State Department at a swearing-in service in mid-October of 1985.

This was unexpected. Short months before the wedding Avon made an abrupt pivot. He went to the movies instead of the second day of the Tennessee Bar Exam. He couldn't practice law in Nashville at his father's law firm. We wouldn't be moving to the house next door to his parents, and I wouldn't be commuting ten minutes to my office on Music Row. He "had to" accept the position that he had been offered in the State Department.

In the blink of a young girl's eye, we were shipping out to the Philippines, where the Country standard, "Baby I Lied," performed by my friend Deborah Allen and written by Deborah and her then husband, Rafe Van Hoy, would become the theme song for the People Power Revolution. I was based in Manila but commuting to Nashville.

My first long summer writing trip I got invited to attend was Farm Aid, which in 1986 was still being held on Willie Nelson's ranch outside of Austin, Texas. Bonnie Raitt's mesmerizing performance of "Angel from Montgomery," that song that had helped me survive, would have been the highlight of that trip, but that got eclipsed. An acquaintance tried to pressure me into joining in the illicit druggy fun. I declined but ended up coaxing them into trying a jolt of sobriety. In the Austin airport, flying back to Nashville, the lines to "Girls Ride Horses, Too" began to take shape. It was a story song about a drug-running man who tries to intimidate a girl and ends up getting robbed and educated by the girl. Beneath those events it's the story of a girl who takes back her power—erotic, economic, and physical—from a man who attempts to seize and claim it. I knew a little something about all of that. And in Austin I chose to tell it.

As I remember it, Mark Sanders and I took about three days to get that song written right. Then Karen got it cut almost as quick. Her old friend Tommy West was producing an album for Judy Rodman, newly signed to MTM Records, a Country label founded by television star Mary Tyler Moore. Soon enough Mark and I had our first top ten hit—and the mailbox money was rolling in.

Good as that was, it wasn't the best thing about that summer.

In 1986, three years into my life as a Country songwriter and song publisher, I heard a very different end to DeFord's story. This time DeFord's end was victorious.

As told to me in the kitchen of 1818 Morena Street by then Tennessee State Senator Avon N. Williams, my first father-in-law, the man I called Big Avon, the last chapters of DeFord Bailey's life were spent with both Bailey's music and Bailey's experience in the music industry becoming secret weapons in the fight for Black political power in Tennessee.

How's that? In 1968, against all odds, Big Avon became the first Black state senator elected in Tennessee since Reconstruction. Six feet tall, keen featured, quick-witted, with an explosive temper, piercing eyes, light brown skin, close-cropped hair, and a smile with a slight gap, Avon Williams carefully cultivated an intimidating presence. He transformed good looks, legal acumen, righteous anger, political connections, blood ties, and marriage bonds into a dazzling aura that inspired adoration, fear, and hate.

In the summer of 1986, he was in a fight to retain the seat he had held for seventeen years.

Big Avon was afflicted with a rare disease he fought to the death, ALS, Lou Gehrig's disease, and it was rapidly advancing. Yet with his brain unimpaired, he functioned effectively, continuing to play a leadership role in the state Senate, communicating by typing.

A young Black lawyer, Richard Jackson, rejected the local wisdom in the Black political world, which declared that despite the challenges of ALS, Williams—with seniority on significant committees, unrivaled brain power, proven political acumen, and forged-in-fire political relationships—was the best advocate for the people in the 19th District. Jackson argued that the community would be better served by someone who wasn't, he didn't say the word, but he got across the meaning, crippled.

There were some who wanted to focus on these facts; each transfer out of or into his wheelchair was a major challenge for Senator Williams. He could not stand even for a second without support. Only a speech-therapist/translator and a very few close family members could decipher his increasingly labored and increasingly garbled utterances.

The younger man waged a vigorous and effective campaign. He outspent Williams three to one. He played every ableist card in the deck. Back then we didn't call it that. We called it the he-was-a-great-man-till-ALS-got-him card.

With the margin for winning the election tight and campaign money short, somewhere between jaunting off with Steve Earle to Farm Aid and writing what would become my first top ten Country single, "Girls Ride Horses, Too," which would one day be covered by the brilliant Sista-Strings, I wrote, produced, and recorded a campaign jingle for Big Avon.

The writing happened at Big Avon's house. The recording was done at Room and Board where Ray and I had co-written "The Family Hour," a song about a stepfather who attempts to rape his stepdaughter on a hunting trip and gets shot. The Room and Board Studio was so close to the old Sunnyside Plantation that we would sometimes walk the studio dog, Lefty (named for Lefty Frizzell and Lefty in "Pancho and Lefty"), on its grounds during recording breaks. My friend Ray Kennedy, who later produced Steve Earle and Lucinda Williams's albums, donated the studio space and the engineering time. The singer Scat Springs donated the vocals. Big Avon approved the text, "Don't send a boy to do a man's job."

Pleased as punch, I played the finished jingle for Big Avon and asked him how it felt to have his first political jingle on the air. The man looked at me (not for the first time) like I was ignorant, crazy, or both.

Then he schooled me. Slowly and laboriously, he pronounced, "DeFord Bailey wrote my first jingle, and played on it, too!" In the summer of 1986, every word was torture for Big Avon to produce. But he found the breath and the will to make that statement loud and proud. I was startled into recalibrating the significance of DeFord Bailey by Senator Avon N. Williams, Jr.

Election Day 1986, Williams won by 453 votes. That night he thanked "My loyal and beautiful supporters, my devoted family, and all the people of the 19th District for your love and inspiring work." High in Williams's pantheon of loyal and beautiful supporters was deceased DeFord Bailey.

And it wasn't just that DeFord played an unheralded role in his first election by writing that first jingle. Or that, after the Klan had burned a cross on Senator Avon N. Williams's lawn in 1972, DeFord Bailey stood by Big Avon as he had stood with him before. And it wasn't only that, Big Avon was *inspired* by the way DeFord performed in adverse circumstances on the stage of the Opry as he had performed in adverse circumstances in the Chamber of the Tennessee Senate. But none of that was DeFord's biggest impact in the summer of 1986.

Big Avon was being dismissed as "crippled" behind his back as DeFord had been dismissed as "crippled" right to his face aloud and in print. There was an excessive and inappropriate focus on the changes early polio had made on DeFord's body as there was an excessive and inappropriate focus on the changes late ALS was making on Williams's body. Knowing DeFord to be expert, excellent, and atypically but well-abled was some large part of Big Avon knowing he could be the same. Seeing DeFord as a power, as potent, exactly as he was, prepared Big Avon as he was flying through the hall connecting his Senate office to the Senate chamber in his electric wheelchair.

DeFord was evidence Williams wasn't a lesser power—he was a new power.

When I first started rattling on to and at Williams, before he was my father-in-law and after he was my father-in-law, about the possibility that the genius of DeFord Bailey was his engagement with *mimesis*, with his ability to translate the train, not imitate the train; that he gave folk an aural train out of town, Williams encouraged me with his corny humor to "chase that train of thought." I listened.

The first Black state senator in Tennessee had put himself through college playing a silver horn. He knew something about music. But it was more than that. His humor was often simple. His insight never was.

Big Avon knew a whole lot of Black folk lived within earshot of trains that they lacked the money to ride or the gumption to hop. Those people didn't need an *imitation* train sound, *they needed a sound that functioned as a train*. That's just one of the things I learned in the kitchen at 1818 Morena Street.

Black folk needed a sound that was an escape, a sound that was a positive possibility, a sound that took them away from where they were to some place better. We needed what "Pan American Blues" provided and DeFord Bailey delivered: reliable escape most Saturday nights for a good long while.

By 1932, WSM was broadcasting with 50,000 watts of power, which meant every Black person in America and some in Canada had a good chance of hopping a train out of town by listening to DeFord. And millions of white folk had listened to him, too.

DeFord isn't just the father of Black Country, DeFord is the father of Country, and was Country's first superstar. Period exclamation mark. How in the fuck does that get forgotten?

DeFord's obituary published July 3, 1982, the day after he took his last breath, stated: "In 1928, the first full year of the Grand Ole Opry, Mr. Bailey played on 49 of the 52 shows—20 more appearances than the next most-frequent artist." When he was on the Opry, DeFord had Black and white fans. Then he was fired off Country's most iconic radio show.

DeFord Bailey didn't vanish when he left the Opry. Even though that is implied in the materials the Country Music Hall of Fame have up about him at the time of this writing and on the version of his Wikipedia page up when I write this. In the wide Black world and in Black Nashville he continued to be part of the arts conversation. And he continued to be part of the political and legal conversation.

It was just his mainstream commercial Country career that was destroyed, his *white* Country career when he left the Opry. His life in Black Country that began when his mother and father handed him a harmonica not a rattle, his life as a *fourth-generation* Black hillbilly artist, as a citizen and a creative in Black Country, did not stop till death took him and he was laid in a grave in Nashville's Greenwood Cemetery.

There is an aural monument I want for DeFord: a performance of his "Evening Prayer Blues" by SistaStrings.

I am grateful to the thirty-year-old sisters from Milwaukee, Wisconsin, who go by the name of SistaStrings. Their performance of "Girls Ride Horses, Too" as a duet with the sisters trading verses has roots and wings. The roots are the sister harmonies most evident on the chorus; the wings are the verses with each sister giving the narrative a distinctly different interpretation and spin.

Monique and Chauntee Ross were born roughly around the time "Girls Ride Horses, Too" was written and recorded. The song is just a little older than they are. Their Milwaukee was very different than my Detroit. They were raised in a family of five children (they are the two youngest) who were homeschooled by their parents, who were both ministers. They were given instruments as young children and told the instruments would be their path to college. That prediction proved true. Chauntee graduated from the University of Michigan, Monique from the University of Wisconsin. No one predicted they would become, with their violin and their cello, essential members of a Nashville-based, urgent reimagining of Country into a more collaborative, less hierarchical, and more inclusive art.

Shared space, shared stage, coexisting in harmony and in counterpoint, is first nature to them. As members of the Rainbow Coalition of the Loving, Allison Russell's band, they take the stage and beam they are the lived reality of that ambitious name. Performing my first top ten, they find—with voice, with violin, with cello—the subtext: "Girls Ride Horses, Too" is about reclaiming what has been stolen. Every bar they play, these sisters reclaim present and historical excellence, and innocence, that wasn't recognized. Innocence can be pragmatic and vengeful. Another Black Country walking contradiction, like being raised Black in America to play classical instruments and finding your way into Country and Country adjacent.

My career in mainstream commercial Country publishing and writing took a radical zig then a zag about the time I got married. Midsummer was not making the big bucks yet. We were still ticking out of time and money. I had a plan to solve the problem. Bob Doyle was leaving ASCAP to start his own management and publishing company based on a new writer-performer he had discovered, Garth Brooks. I suggested we join forces in publishing. We did. It was a most excellent business decision.

BIG DREAMS: BIG HITS, BIG MISTAKES

But the balance of love and money was off, not way off, but off.

With me, Edith, and Karen helming Midsummer, we were chasing female artists, and working with a woman-owned record label, MTM (Mary Tyler Moore), as a frequent partner. Our tiny office was an oasis of female empowerment on the Row, and a bastion, we hoped, of nurture-centered capitalism. We wanted happy, healthy writers producing powerful songs that earned so we could employ more of them. Midsummer was a publishing company that centered a feminine perspective and was anchored by a Black perspective. That's what I built with those women and Mark Sanders.

We didn't push to make the most money possible, we pushed to get as much political poetry on the radio as possible. My Alice, not Midsummer, agenda was even more specific, to get people a little more worried about the world they were living in.

As the clock ticked closer to three years in, and the bank accounts ticked down closer to zero, the decision to share space and certain resources but not merge with Major Bob, Bob Doyle's new publishing company, put us closer to black ink—and into a new building—but Midsummer was no longer a women-centered or Black-centered Country Music publishing company. We were on the periphery of the Garth ride.

There was a big and immediate human and economic triumph. Mark co-wrote "Victim of the Game" with Garth, who put that song on his album *No Fences*. After that Mark didn't have money worries. He didn't have who to collaborate with worries. Everybody wanted to write with him. He was elevated into a whole new echelon of Nashville writers. His immediate family was launched into a whole new level of economic security. Those are things I wanted for my writers.

That doesn't happen unless we moved out of the contemporary Audio Media Recorders Building on 19th where Karen Conrad had the office adjacent to our windowless Midsummer writing room, and out of the arrangement for Karen to plug our songs. We moved into a gorgeous old brick house on Music Row with Bob Doyle and his crew, and into an arrangement for Bob and his team to plug Midsummer songs. Midsummer and Major Bob writers all end up hanging out together in the Major Bob downstairs sofas and in the Major Bob kitchen and Garth and Mark start swapping ideas.

This doesn't happen without that either: One day Garth went out to sing a demo and he came back to the office and announced that a girl singing on the session sounded just like he would sound—if he was a girl singer. He invited her to stop by the office and he invited me to hang out in the kitchen with them. That hang in the kitchen would change a lot for me and even more for Garth. The demo singer was Trisha Yearwood, future superstar.

Mainly, I was upstairs in my writing room with windows and white wicker furniture upholstered in fabrics that reminded me of the house-dresses Dear wore on her porch in Detroit. There I started writing about Detroit as an outpost of Alabama, and the South as the abusive mother of Black culture but its mother nonetheless. I wrote "Detroit, Alabama" with one of the songwriters hanging round the new house, Buddy Mondlock, but mainly I had to find the co-writers for these new songs out of the house.

Four of the best co-writers I found—Bobby Braddock, Ray Kennedy, Pam Tillis, and Kevin Welch, with whom I wrote "Mammy's Song"—were all writing for Tree. The new songs we created were radically different than anything on Country radio. "Mammy's Song" co-written with Kevin includes the lines: *I brought you into this world / Now you want to touch my little girl / just for the brown of it / I'll take you out of it / I brought you into this world.* It concludes with the words *I love you boy / You've been like a son / Don't make Mammy use this gun.*

Verse by verse it became clearer that nobody in the new building wanted to work with these songs. They wanted from me more "Girls Ride Horses, Too," "Reckless Night," "Many Mansions." They wanted me to write with Garth. I tried it once, and he is brilliant, one of the best, so I knew after I tried it and didn't like it that I didn't want to be with an old-school, male-dominated boutique publishing company. I wanted back in my original game, putting trouble on the Country radio, and working with women.

I started plotting an exit. I talked with Edith about the need to stop being management.

And I started talking to Pat Halper, who got me my first cut, then at Hayes Street, about creating a new intersection between political Black Music, Country, and Art music. Think Talking Heads. She and I even flew out to Los Angeles together and met with a Black and female executive at an A&M Records publishing division to see if we three were "a fit" to collaborate. That wasn't it. Close but not it.

I started thinking about Tree. The whole town was talking about Buddy, my host to that big "Country goes to Washington to show off to the whole world via television" DAR concert where I got to hear Ray Charles sing and Charley Pride sing. I was thinking about a woman I will call BS.

Buddy Killen had just sold Tree to CBS for thirty million dollars, leaving Tree to be run by a big, 'Bama-born blonde. She who now ran Tree was clearly the most powerful woman in Country publishing. I bothered a receptionist till I got a meeting with the woman.

The Tree building was at the north end of Music Row. Three stories high, with a red clay tiled Spanish or Mexican roof, and cream stucco, it wanted to look like a hacienda. The second and third story featured a fully enclosed balcony boasting five arches. There were two big, fabulous offices on that floor.

In my day, one belonged to BS and one belonged to the creative head of Tree, Paul Worley. The guitar-playing son of a Vanderbilt economics professor, Paul had sold harmonicas to DeFord Bailey, had a brother-in-law who had played guitar in the Kossi Gardner, and his father was from where my father was from, Alabama. The man who would eventually produce the Dixie Chicks got everything about the collection of songs I was calling Mother Dixie.

I sold my share of Midsummer Music to Edith, probably officially to Edith and her husband, Michael, and then founded my second publishing company, Mother Dixie Music, which was wholly owned by me. Concurrently, I signed a co-pub deal for a significant chunk of change, with the woman who now helmed Tree, thrilled that Tree had some great female writers on the roster, Pam Tillis, Mary Chapin Carpenter, and that a cool new A&R woman, Tracy Gershon, sister of Gina, was hired or about to be.

We all agreed it would be hard to get my Black Country songs into the world via radio. I imagined two ways to make the impossible possible: find a great Black female singer who wanted to sing Country; or work through film and television to establish an audience for the songs.

Paul envisioned a third strategy, have me sing the songs. I wanted to stay focused on writing songs and screenplays and songs for screenplays. With the help of my friend Reggie Hudlin, I had already sold a screenplay to Paramount. With Paul's vision and BS's money, Tree was ready to pull the trigger on *Mother Dixie* as an album project in search of a film deal. BS and Paul and I were going after some movie and TV money.

I doubled down on screenplays that could include music. Not just for *Mother Dixie*, I also had a Black Western I wanted to co-write: *The Cosmic Colored Cowboy*. Yes. But. Paul made records. BS dealt in reality. If the

Mother Dixie album performed by me wasn't the fallback, something was missing. Until it wasn't. Quincy Jones.

QUINCY JONES AND *THE COSMIC COLORED COWBOY*

I was wearing banjo earrings, custom made with real steel strings. They had been molded out of colored modeling clay and baked in a toaster oven in a nearly dilapidated second-floor walk-up apartment just off Music Row by Heidi Hyatt, the redheaded wife of the songwriter with whom I wrote "Get the Hell Out of Dodge" and "Baby's Blue Lullabye," Walter Hyatt.

The earrings reminded me of objects that I had made out of playdough as a girl. The rolling, punching, and layering out of colored shapes on colored shapes. They reminded me of brown schoolteachers and Sunday school teachers mixing up batches of playdough with food color, flour, and salt, and I don't remember what else. I wanted to go to Los Angeles with banjos on my ears. A banjo on my knee would be a lie. I can't play any instrument. Banjos on my ears signed the music I was listening for, bringing with me. Heidi got it. She made banjos for me and only me. I appreciated that.

Back then I loved flying as both an escape from responsibility and as danger and as a closer-my-woman-God-to-thee space. The flight out to Los Angeles was a thrill. Along with the strange earrings, I was wearing a black denim skirt and a button-down white shirt and black loafers. I know this because it was pretty much what I always wore. It was about 1990. After the baby was born, I stopped wearing color and took to wearing uniforms. I would have five pairs of the same leggings. Or three of the same skirt. To Los Angeles, I typically wore black and white, not just black. Danny Glover asked me about the black loafers. He didn't get it. I said they were comfortable and classic.

Anyway, I was on the flight, and I was so excited to be going to a meeting with Quincy Jones. It was a quick trip, one of those there-and-back things. I was in the middle of writing my first movie for a major studio, and I wanted to sell my second one before I turned it in—in case everyone hated my first movie and I didn't get a second one. It was a strange time in my life. Every day my daughter's father asked me to quit working on screenplays. He hated the idea of me having a career, and every day I kept working on it. I had had too much of not having a career. I had booked myself for a month at a spartan hiking-based spa in Utah with the idea that I would walk my way into knowing whether or not I should get divorced. The plan was to sell the second movie and go to the spa almost as soon as I turned in the first movie. Nothing worked out according to that plan.

Everything started auspicious. I wanted to do a Black Western and I knew that would be a hard sell. It occurred to me the person who could get that done was Quincy Jones. I told everyone I knew that I wanted a meeting with him. A development executive I knew said she was able to set up a meeting with Quincy. This woman was very young, very smart, quite beautiful. She ran Danny Glover's production company. As Danny had been one of the stars of Quincy's *The Color Purple*, it made sense to me that she was able to get me the meeting with Quincy.

I bought the plane ticket. I clipped on my banjo earrings. I boarded the plane with high hopes and no fear. I was working on the principle if you're going through hell and keep on marching you might get out before the devil even knows you're there. The audacious executive picked me up at the Los Angeles airport. I had no luggage, just an oversized black leather Coach bag. We went over my pitch in the car. She expressed how excited Danny was about the project. We were rolling into Bel Air, which was very beautiful. It was the first time I had seen it. Beverly Hills had been disappointing. Bel Air had a bit of jaw-dropping grandeur.

"This is amazing!" I said referring to both the opportunity to meet Quincy and the surroundings. The young executive frowned. "We haven't addressed the big challenge." I thought the big challenge was making a Black frontier story relevant to modern audiences and that the pitch addressed that. "What do you see as the big challenge?" I asked. "You don't actually have an appointment with Quincy Jones." I thought she was joking. Her demeanor suggested she wasn't.

"I don't have an appointment?"

"Right."

"I spent money on a ticket for nothing?"

"No."

"Why are we in Bel Air if we're not going to his house?"

"You don't have an appointment, but I've arranged for you to be let into the house. Once you're in it's up to you. And it's up to you if you want to go in without an appointment."

"Is this legal?"

"The guard is letting you in. It's not breaking and entering."

"Are you going in, too?"

"No."

"Where will you be?"

"Waiting in the car down the street."

"This sounds crazy."

"You said Quincy is our best chance. I'm getting you into Quincy's house. You can make this happen."

"Do we even know if he's home?"

"He's home."

"You're friends with the guard?"

My father always told me there were two ways to get things done. Know the person at the very top or know the person at the bottom. The janitor and the president both have keys to the building. One might be to the back door and one to the front, but they both can let you in. The young executive's move was so Motown I couldn't resist accepting the challenge to see if I could improvise. I was let into the house and led into a room that was something like a library. And left there.

Alone in the room, the first thing I did was laugh out loud at my costume. Quincy's house was more than semi-fancy. It was a cutting-edge yet comfortable mix of contemporary and classic furnishings. And here I was sitting on his elegant library sofa with kitchen-made banjos clipped to my ears and preppie black loafers on my feet, looking a whole lot like the weird Country cousin.

So, I was sitting there frozen to Mr. Jones's upholstery. A part of me is a rule follower. As far as I knew, the only part of his house I had been "invited" into, under what pretenses I did not know, was the room where I was sitting. I wasn't moving from that room. It was hard to see how the pitch was going to happen. It was hard to imagine how I was getting out of the house. Or how long I should wait. Fortunately, I wasn't there long when Quincy Jones briskly walked through the room, passing a few feet away from me. I said nothing. I didn't know what to say. Minutes later he walked back across the room, seemingly oblivious to my presence.

Once again, I was alone in my strange clothes in the lovely room that connected to the other room. Just as I was thinking, *I have missed my chance*, the man I had come to see walked back in, looked at me, and asked, "Why are you here?"

He didn't ask me who I was or what I was doing, he asked, "Why are you here?" And I said, "How would you like to make a movie about a Black cowboy whose wife is kidnapped and gang raped and who goes on a successful epic journey to find, rescue, and love her—despite the fact the white community says she and the other women taken are now worthless and soiled? I'm here to ask you to produce that movie for me and to sell that movie with me."

And that's exactly what we did. But first, Quincy sat down on the couch right beside me and said, "Let's start all over again. What's your name? Who are you?" "Mari-Alice Randall from Detroit City and Harvard and Nashville," I said.

"Motown and Music City. Now, tell me some more about this movie you want me to make?"

When I was done with the telling, maybe ten minutes later, Quincy said, "I'm going to sell that story to a major studio. We will go together. But you need to come back in a few weeks. Can you do that?"

I said, "Yes," though I was supposed to be in Utah in two weeks hiking through the red rocks while trying to decide if I should stay married. Quincy stood. The non-meeting meeting was over. "I've got to go lay down a velvet carpet for my pearl." He was headed to Montreux to record his dear friend Miles Davis at the Montreux Jazz Festival, or maybe he was headed to engineer the recording he had made. I don't remember that detail clearly. What I know for sure is he said, "I've got to go lay down a velvet carpet for my pearl." And he was gone. Four months after that Miles Davis was gone. But not before Quincy laid down that carpet.

Short weeks later we sold *The Cosmic Colored Cowboy* to Warner Bros. I was shocked. I shouldn't have been. In Los Angeles Black Country is victorious.

THE CAPITAL OF BLACK COUNTRY, LOS ANGELES

Lil Hardin played piano on the genre-defining "Blue Yodel #9" session in Los Angeles in 1930. Herb Jeffries starred in four movies filmed on a Black dude ranch just outside of Los Angeles, creating images and sounds of a Black singing cowboy that delighted and intrigued Black audiences from coast to coast. Bill Withers recorded *Just as I Am*, the unheralded-as-a-Country-classic-yet-Country-classic album, in 1971 in Los Angeles. Ray Charles cut a contender for greatest Country song of all time, "I Can't Stop Loving You," in Los Angeles at United Western. We can debate whether it is "Grandma's Hands" penned and sung by Bill Withers or Ray Charles covering Don Gibson as the greatest Black Country cut of all time, but for my money it's one of those two. Either way, the greatest Black Country song of all time was recorded in Los Angeles. Lionel Richie was living in Los Angeles when he penned Kenny Rogers's mega Country hit "Lady" and when he recorded his own Country album *Tuskegee* in 2012. Richie's twenty-eight-room house in Beverly Hills, one of the most envied mansions in the city, is a physical manifestation of Black Country victory.

Originally built in 1929, for Carrie Guggenheim, Richie's home has been reimagined, renovated, and decorated to reflect the desires, dreams, and needs of a Black man born in Tuskegee, Alabama. Landscaped for Richie with cypress and magnolia trees, the house is the place where Richie talks to God—about money. As he explained to *Architectural Digest* reporter Nancy Collins, "If I can't find a lyric, I walk to the end of the garden and say, 'OK, God . . . I need a second verse.'" Why does he need a second verse? Things are getting delivered for the house! "Deep River Woman," a hit for Alabama, and "Lady," a hit for Kenny Rogers, are but two of the Country songs still sending mailbox money to a prince of Black Country living in a Black Country palace.

Lionel is a historian. In his house in Holmby Hills are framed copies of letters Booker T. Washington and George Washington Carver wrote to Margaret Washington, Lionel's grandmother and Booker T.'s third wife. In honor of Lie-on-el, I'm going to tell you some way back things about Black Country in California.

This is all to say, L.A. is the seat of Black Country. The story starts when a Black cowboy, or a Mexican vaquero who had some African and Indigenous ancestors, sang on the Avila Ranch or on one of the Catholic church-owned missions.

Or maybe it starts even earlier than that. Maybe it starts with the *pobladores* arriving from Mexico in 1781 to what we now call greater Los Angeles. Six of those original eleven founding families *had African ancestry*. What did they sing?

If we limit ourselves to recorded music, it starts in the thirties with Lil playing on the iconic Jimmie Rodgers session and the release in 1937 of *Harlem on the Prairie*, the "all-colored Western musical" starring Herb Jeffries that will be followed by more bronze buckaroo horse operas.

Herb Jeffries, Bill Withers, Ray Charles, and Lionel Richie. Two members of the founding family of Black Country (Jeffries and Charles) and two of their shiniest descendants (Withers and Richie) set up roots in the City of Angels, anchoring their recorded performances to the unrecorded performances of Black and brown cowboys who went before them and unrecorded Black church performances.

These artists transformed the audio-scape and the hard-scape of the city as they styled themselves, their homes, and their graves. Images of these artists (in Western wear, in blue-collar work clothes, in suits, and tuxedos) and their related artifacts and architecture-troubled attempts to regulate and redline Black presence in these United States, troubled attempts to contain Blacks within assigned spaces that did not include a mansion on the hill, bedroll on the prairie, or hardworking man in the factory; that did not include rooms with spectacular views, or autonomous lives lived free-breathing beneath a welcoming sky. To anchor the case that Los Angeles is the capital of Black Country, I'm spilling a few facts and taking you on a tour. I will start with a fact. Los Angeles–based pioneers of Black Country (Hardin, Jeffries, Charles, Withers, and Richie) spent more than 210 years living and working in Los Angeles, creating a mappable legacy. I'm starting the tour with the studios because that's where the money to buy the mansions is made—and it lets us start the tour with Mama Lil.

Los Angeles is home to five studios particularly important in the history of Black Country. Victor Hollywood Studio where Lil played on "Blue Yodel #9"; United Western Recorders where Ray Charles recorded some of the most important songs on *Modern Sounds in Country and Western Music*; Sunset Sound Recorders and Wally Heider Recording Studio where Bill Withers recorded his first album *Just as I Am*; and Bolic Sound Studio in the section of Los Angeles County called Inglewood where Tina Turner recorded *Tina Turns the Country On!*

Leaving the studios, heading to the mansions. First stop: 4863 Southridge Avenue, View Park. This is the 8,000-square-foot, six-bedroom, nine bath, contemporary mansion Ray Charles built in 1956 to live in with his wife, Della, and their three sons, Ray, Jr., Robert, and David. Photos of their first dream home were widely circulated in the Black press. At the bottom of the pool? A portrait of a piano. The view from his window? Downtown Los Angeles all the way to South Bay.

Who can beat that view? Bill Withers. And you can rent his longtime West Hollywood Hills home (purchased with money earned by unacknowledged as Country classics "Grandma's Hands," "Railroad Man," and "Lean on Me"), currently for $250 an hour. Decorated with a white-on-white clean-mod-cool that celebrates highly styled intelligent design, the house is situated to be in conversation with nature. Built in 1990, purchased by Withers in 1998, it is a three-story Mediterranean dream with views of the Sunset Strip and views from the balconies of the Pasadena Hills and the Pacific Ocean.

Third stop is Lionel Richie's estate at 145 Copley Place in Holmby Hills. It is that 18,000-square-foot Venetian palace built in the early twentieth century in America by a woman born in the nineteenth century.

Fourth stop, 2801 Edgehill Drive. Herb Jeffries, with his wife, Elizabeth, and his daughter, Fern, lived in this two-bedroom, one-bath bungalow in 1950 after his first *Bronze Buckaroo* heyday when Jefferson Park was known as little New Orleans.

The final two stops take us back to Lil and DeFord's genius child, Ray Charles.

THE MAYOR OF BLACK COUNTRY, RAY CHARLES

In 1998, Terry Gross asked Ray Charles a simple, significant question: "Why did you first want to record Country Music?" And Ray responds, "Truthfully, because I love it. I've always loved it as a kid. That was the only time my mom would let me stay up past nine p.m. on a Saturday night to listen to the *Grand Ole Opry*. It's strange, and I know it's quite unusual, but that was the way it was."

Aretha Robinson would let Ray stay up late to hear the *Grand Ole Opry* on Saturday nights. And who was playing on the Opry when Ray was first listening to it? DeFord Bailey.

And so, the man who appreciated a fictive kin relationship, the man who preferred to be called "Brother Ray" by other musicians, wasn't just listening to the *Opry*—he was loving on it hard and still talking about that love as the twentieth century drew to a close.

And he was listening to Lil. Ray recorded her "Just for a Thrill" before he recorded *Modern Sounds in Country and Western Music*. Her playing, her work with King Oliver (cornet virtuoso and bandleader whose 1924 sessions are often named as the greatest recorded jazz sessions to that date), and with Louis Armstrong (whom King Oliver mentored and Lil married), was in Ray Charles's head from before his first recording. Her Country piano was in his ears before he played his first bar of a Country song.

On October 12, 1983, Ray Charles made his *Grand Ole Opry* debut stepping into the very circle that DeFord had stepped into to perform.

What did Opry mainstay Roy Acuff think when he saw Ray make his way to stand in the limelight on the Opry stage, to stand in the circle of flooring that had been carved from the wood of the Ryman floor? I saw Acuff driving around town in a dark blue Cadillac with a vanity plate that read WALTZ, but I don't know what he thought. I even exchanged a few words with him in the Opryland theme park, but I don't know what he thought. I do know what my daddy would suspect Roy was thinking:

> *When I went out with DeFord, he was bigger than me; and now comes Ray Charles, bigger than all of us. We kept him off the charts in the early sixties. Can we keep him off now?*
>
> My favorite haint, Lil, be telling me this, *DeFord in heaven, bouncing on a cloud, blowing on a harp, Foxchase and angel-halo hollering, "Get 'em, Son! Get 'em, Ray!"*

Ray Charles got it done. He released a lot of Country singles. Starting with "I'm Moving On" in 1959, the list of some of the most significant include: "Georgia on My Mind," "Carry Me Back to Old Virginny," "I Can't Stop Loving You," "Born to Lose," "Your Cheatin' Heart," "Busted," "Crying Time," and ends in 1987 when "A Little Bit of Heaven" entered the Billboard Hot Country chart.

There was a Country album, *Wish You Were Here Tonight*, that only charted Country singles: "Born to Love Me," "Ain't Your Memory Got No Pride at All," and "3/4 Time." In 1985, Ray Charles reached the top of the Country Charts with "Seven Spanish Angels."

Yep, forty years after the first Billboard Chart to rank Country singles or albums debuted in 1944, twenty-one years after the debut of the Country Hot 100, Ray Charles stood at the top of the ladder DeFord had done much to build but had not been allowed to climb.

My daddy believed Black people invented Country Music and kept reinventing it. Ray Charles on the cover of *Modern Sounds in Country and Western* looking as elegant as Lil and playing as virtuoso as DeFord, embodied all the proof I needed for what Daddy said was true.

So that's why our second to last stop on our Los Angeles mansions of Black Country tour is 3910 Hepburn Avenue, Ray's first house in Los Angeles. Located in Leimert Park where I have loved giving book readings, it's a two-story stuccoed California classic with a pretty porch and maybe three bedrooms.

Close out the day of your Houses of the Black Country Stars tour in Beverly Hills proper. The home where Ray Charles Robinson was living when he died. It's still owned by his foundation: 349 South Linden is an immense modernist and many-windowed fort with an oval pool on the roof holding down the corner where South Linden intersects West Olympic Boulevard.

Each of these homes is a vision of prosperity, a sign of Black power and Black thrive, an emblem of improbable success in Los Angeles.

In mainstream white Country and white Americana, Los Angeles is often a location of failure. In white Country you go out to Los Angeles and discover, according to the Gatlin Brothers, "All the gold in California is in a bank in the middle of Beverly Hills in somebody else's name." Or you discover, "You're sweeping up a warehouse in east L.A., and opportunity sure comes slow." Or you're trying to pack up and escape L.A. and its freeways "without getting killed or caught," haunted by concrete living in rental houses filling up on vanilla wafers.

Ray Charles, Lionel Richie, Bill Withers, Herb Jeffries got some of the gold and kept it. That's got Lil smiling down from on high, whispering, *Brown Gal, that tickles the hell out of me and don't you think about giving out Quincy's address.*

With Lil whispering in my ear after the mansions, head to a church I associate with Ray Charles. One he never attended. When I was thinking about taking this stop off the tour, I almost thought I heard Ray Charles saying, *Mari-Alice Randall* and not in a nice way. Lil's ghost did say, *Don't make me go upside your head, gal. Tell them about Arizona!*

LOS ANGELES BLACK GOSPEL, A TAPROOT OF BLACK COUNTRY

The Apostolic Mission Church located at 312 Azusa Street was the first home of what came to be known as the Azusa Street Revival that took place in the Little Tokyo section of Los Angeles between 1906 and 1909. The leader of the revival was a Black preacher named William J. Seymour who well understood the power of mixing Black gospel lyrics with rich instrumentation and was able to persuasively make the case for inclusion of instruments in worship services.

At the time of the revival, many Black churches nixed instruments. Much traditional gospel, as exemplified by Nashville's famed Fisk Jubilee Singers, leaned heavily toward a cappella singing, a habit born of necessity that had become tradition. Instruments were central to the Azusa Street Revival and Seymour's theology. Quoting Psalm 150: 3–6, which reads:

> *Praise Him with the sound of the trumpet; praise Him with the psaltery and harp! Praise Him with the timbrel and dance; praise Him with stringed instruments and organs!*
>
> *Praise Him upon the loud cymbals, praise Him upon the high-sounding cymbals.*

Seymour radically altered Black gospel music. I imagine him thundering those words from a Los Angeles pulpit. Music of the Los Angeles–based Azusa Street Revival would evolve into what became known as the "Holy Blues." The Holy Blues is a rarely recognized, Los Angeles–born, and powerful influence on all Country Music.

What piano player related to the Azusa Street Revival sounds a lot like Lil and a whole lot like she may have influenced Ray Charles? Arizona Dranes.

Seymour's theology made possible the rise of Arizona Dranes, the piano-playing missionary who first started getting noticed by COGIC ministers in 1923. COGIC stands for Church of God in Christ. It is a denomination that claims the slogan "COGIC history is Black history" to boast its deep aesthetic and theological roots in the Black community. COGIC churches are known for expressive and ecstatic worship often driven by music. Arizona, a presenter at the national COGIC convocation of 1945, was a co-creator of Country. Consider Arizona to be Lil's Texas-born, piano-rolling, blind, older half sister who recorded more than a dozen Country influencing gospel tunes *before 1930*.

Arizona Dranes recorded Holy Blues in the 1920s. She sang with a nasal voice, with a danceable beat, with a gospel influence, an African influence, and with her own kind of what I will call a yodel. That gets her part of the way to Country. This gets her the rest of the way: she sang about God and trains; she played with words; and drumbeat; she crossed paths with Lil Hardin in Chicago in June of 1926 *before* Lil recorded "Blue Yodel #9" with Jimmie Rodgers in Los Angeles.

Yep! The Hot Five recorded three tracks in the very same studio and with the very same producer as Arizona Dranes a day apart from each other.

Michael Corcoran writing about the recordings of Arizona Dranes states:

> *The standout track is "He Is My Story," a rewriting of "Blessed Assurance" by blind hymn writer Fanny Crosby. Where the Crosby version has a chorus of "This is my story / This is my song," Dranes makes it all about God. "He is my story / He is my song," she sang with a voice quivering like an arrow at impact. If not for Dranes's exuberant presentation, the song* could almost be considered Country music.

But it is, Country Music, Black Country Music.

As the city of Los Angeles begins to examine its role as a center of Black gospel (it is home to the Crouch Family, to the Edwin Hawkins Singers, and other legacy groups), it's time for folks to start thinking about the ways L.A. gospel influenced Country. It ain't just white Southern gospel, and Black Southern gospel influencing Country. Black Western gospel is a huge influence on Country. Arizona Dranes is a founder of Country and Black Country. The way she pounded the keys influenced Lil Hardin, Jerry Lee Lewis, and Ray Charles.

There's an event and a final recording studio that clinches the "Los Angeles is the capital of Black Country" deal for me. Check out 1416 North La Brea Avenue.

When I was slipping into Quincy's house, A&M records, A&M publishing, and A&M recording studio were all located at that address in a complex built in 1917 to house Charlie Chaplin's film studio. In 1985, "We Are the World," a single recorded to raise money to fight famine in Africa, was recorded in the faux English village/studio.

Quincy spearheaded "We Are the World," the only 1985 single that sold more than twenty-million copies. It features three stars of Black Country: the Pointer Sisters, Ray Charles, and Lionel Richie, who co-wrote the song with Michael Jackson. There were other Country singers on the recording: Kenny Rogers, Willie Nelson, Kenny Loggins. And two more Black artists, Tina Turner and Diana Ross, who had recorded Country albums.

The lyric is streaked with Evangelical Christian references from the assertion that all listening are a part of God's "great big" family to direct reference to Luke 11:11 and Matthew 7:9 through the mention of "stones" and "bread." Lionel Richie, a veteran hit Country songwriter, maybe knows a little something about integrating the New Testament into a secular song. But that's not all he knows.

Country loves a patriotic anthem. Black Country loves reimagining global citizenship as human right. Ain't nothing more Black Country than calling a group USA for Africa. Quincy is a whole lot more Black Country and Black Country–adjacent than most folks realize.

Quincy pulled me to Los Angeles in the first place. His visible and audible tryptic of blockbuster success, "Thriller," *The Color Purple*, and "We Are the World," were each category destroying and category connecting in a way. To a degree, that made me know he was the *only* partner that could help me reinvent the Black Western.

But something bigger than that happened to me in Quincy house. That very first meeting he gave me a new and higher ambition—lay down a velvet carpet for my pearls, Lil Hardin, DeFord Bailey, Ray Charles, Charley Pride, and Herb Jeffries. And it reinforced a primary ambition: to do well, while doing good.

A thing Quincy Jones and Herb Jeffries had in common? They understood the relationship between music and film, in a manner that allowed them to anticipate a way Westerns and Country Music could be turned into a Black wealth engine.

Quincy, working with me on *The Cosmic Colored Cowboy*, Quincy optioning *Mother Dixie*, was drawing me deep into Herb Jeffries's economic playbook, supporting my desire to write new chapters.

To fully understand that we've got to get out of the Los Angeles city limits. And I've got to tell you a lot more about the Bronze Buckaroo.

HERB JEFFRIES, THE BRONZE BUCKAROO, RIDES, SINGS, AND FILMS APPLE VALLEY

The Bronze Buckaroo was not the only Black singing screen cowboy. He was, however, the only sepia star of the horse opera launched toward the silver screen by Louis Armstrong and Lil Hardin. The only sepia star of the horse opera born in Detroit. The only singing cowboy to have his portrait painted in full cowboy garb and hung in the Gotham Hotel, proclaimed by Langston Hughes as the best Negro hotel in the world. He's my favorite Black singing film cowboy and the only one who is in the First Family of Black Country.

How's that? In 1933, Lil Hardin, in the company of her then husband, Louis Armstrong, caught a set at the MDL (Michigan Democratic League) Club, a black and tan, in Detroit. (Black and tans were nightclubs that welcomed African-Americans and race mixing.) After the show, Jeffries, then just twenty years old, was invited to join Louis and Lil at their table.

Armstrong advised Jeffries to leave Detroit and head for Chicago, specifically the Savoy Ballroom. To seal the deal, Louis scribbled an "endorsement letter" which he signed *Pops* on a cloth napkin to be presented to Erskine Tate at the Savoy.

It took Jeffries a few months, but he eventually followed up on the advice he received at the MDL club. The introduction was his birth into the big time. Playing with Tate, Jeffries was discovered by Earl "Fatha" Hines.

Four years later, Jeffries had come up with the idea of a singing Black cowboy starring in all Black Westerns. He sold that idea to a producer with himself as the star, and with actress Artie Young, born in Pasadena, California, in 1915, as a variation on the beautiful bronze cowgirl.

With five feature films: 1937's *Harlem on the Prairie,* 1938's *Two-Gun Man from Harlem* and *Rodeo Rhythm,* and 1939's *The Bronze Buckaroo* and *Harlem Rides the Range*, Jeffries made such a vivid impact on his audience that Herbie Hancock's parents named their son, born in 1940, after the Bronze Buckaroo.

The Hancocks were not the only ones enthralled. A large Black audience all through the thirties sang Jeffries's Black Country cowboy songs and went to see his movies in Black theaters or in white theaters at midnight. They were seeing the stretch he was putting on a reality, his hero cowboys were a particularly loyal lot, and their spreads were picturesque. Some of what he was selling was aspirational. But some of the appeal, to some of his audience, was nostalgic.

Jeffries was provoking some of his audience to remember their own days cowboying, their grandparents or other relatives cowboying, friends cowboying. He provoked people into remembering Black history that was quickly being forgotten. And he was doing it with nostalgia. Nostalgia is as Country as cornbread.

But he wasn't just provoking his audience to be nostalgic. He was provoking his audience to be nostalgic *and eccentric*. The only Black singing cowboy I knew of in my childhood was the Black singing cowboy who most conspicuously prized and practiced eccentricity, Herb Jeffries.

In 1937, around the time *Harlem on the Prairie* was released, the *Michigan Chronicle*, one of America's most influential Black newspapers, ran a candid photograph of Herb Jeffries taken at the Utica Riding Academy (not far from Joe Louis's training camp) accompanied by a few words in support of Jeffries's first film. It noted a "substantial run in the larger cities" and that the "Native Detroiter" was an "expert horseman" with an "unusual singing voice" that "allowed" him to appear in Western movies.

What they call "unusual" I am calling a particular and individual Black twang. I'm calling it the granddaddy of Black Country eccentric. His horse opera voice was not like anyone else's.

His "happy on the range" was original, too. This is no "happy darky" working for the white man. This is a man who is happy because he has autonomy and because he is well equipped. He has a rope, a saddle, a horse, and a gun. He has a seamless engagement with nature independent of all engagement with other people.

This is an eccentric Black happy narrated by an eccentric Black voice, claiming a forgotten, once common, victorious Black life story. It is estimated that at least 30 percent of cowboys in the American West were Black or brown. Every bar of *The Bronze Buckaroo*'s theme song is an example of the wildly weird serving the everyday.

By refusing to be relegated to the spaces, roles, costumes, and genres being offered to Black people in film and on musical recordings in the Great Depression, Herb Jeffries created *unexpected* sights and sounds of Black liberation.

He invented himself as a person atop a horse, not behind a mule. He invented himself as a Black person surrounded by other Black people. He costumed himself in elegant western wear (part empowered Black dandy, part efficient frontier work togs) that conveyed serious eccentricity.

By claiming the rugged, wild, and staggeringly beautiful Western landscape as a territory where he belonged and could invent himself and reinvent himself through song, he exploded caricatures and stereotypes.

By employing Black people and collaborating with Black business in the making of his films, Jeffries broke radically and deliciously from established norms.

Which brings us to Apple Valley, California, where Murray's Dude Ranch was located. Herb Jeffries shot his films at Murray's.

There's not much left to see but what's left isn't geographically hard to get to. It's located off the Dale Evans Parkway (where's Herb's parkway?) just a little more than an hour and a half drive from Los Angeles. If you take the train, you get off at Victorville and then catch a car ride eight miles northeast. Getting there is easy. The hard part is all the imagining you must do after you get to Murray's.

Start with imagining Joe Louis riding on a horse through Apple Valley, fully decked out in western gear on November 17, 1937.

Murray's was founded by an extraordinary Black couple, Nolie and Lela Murray. When they married in Los Angeles on March 19, 1913, she was already the owner of a Los Angeles dry goods store and he was already a Los Angeles bail bondsman and the manager of at least one Los Angeles nightclub. Soon they opened Murray's.

The couple transformed a cattle ranch into America's first Black dude ranch and a motion picture set. The dude ranch was so swank that when the Murrays sold out and closed up shop, it—the pool, the tennis courts, the riding stables, the large and small houses—would become the estate of a Black superstar, Pearl Bailey.

Ultimately disaster struck. The people who bought the property after Bailey let it fall into disrepair. Eventually the Apple Valley Fire Department—in a craven act of evil, a destructive act of ignorance, or an intentional gesture of vicious but ultimately impotent destruction—burned down the last vestiges of Nolie and Lela's vision, burned down the last standing buildings, burned down proof of Black industry, proof of Black singing cowboy films, and proof of Black leisure. They called it a "training exercise." Training what? To save lives or to erase lives?

If I am to be a "Happy Cowboy," the theme song of the song that Herb sang on the pictures made on the place, I have to imagine that at least one fireperson, trained while burning down those buildings, saved at least one life. I have to hope that many people trained on those fires saved many lives or later taught people to save lives. I hope somebody reading this makes a movie about Murray's and the Murrays.

Who would know anything about them now if Herb Jeffries hadn't filmed his Westerns on their ranch? A great pleasure in the present of watching the Bronze Buckaroo films is seeing the ranch. It is our best documentary evidence of Murray's existence.

The genius of Jeffries is his ability to braid erased Black history to acts of his present self-invention. He connects fiction to history, and history to fiction. By advocating to have his films shot at the Black-owned Murray's Dude Ranch in Apple Valley, California, he invents himself as an activist with Marcus Garvey leanings. And he doubles down on self-respect. He signs that he is not *imitating* white cowboys. He is *echoing* Black cowboys past in the present, and anticipating by preparing a way for Black cowboys, Black cowboy singers, and Black eccentrics of all ilk in the future.

Me and Quincy Delight Jones were all about all of that from the get-go.

We never got a big Western made working together, but the work I did for and with Quincy, in terms of screenplays optioned or sold, was a significant small wealth engine for me. And it taught me a few things.

There would be no massive Country Music audience without Gene Autry, Roy Rogers, Tex Ritter, and Dale Evans. People who didn't listen to Country on the radio, people who preferred opera to Opry and never tuned in to WSM, people who would never play a honky-tonk jukebox, fell in love with Country songs by watching "horse operas" featuring singing cowboys and cowgirls and followed that love into record purchasing and radio listening. Movies impacted the development of Country as an art and as a business. Herb Jeffries, the first Black person to see and *successfully* exploit the synergy between movies and Country Music, had blazed a trail too few bronze buckaroos have followed.

But being a bronze buckaroo wasn't all, or even mainly, about the money. It was about refusing to be confined. It's about that thing Lil taught, "defying all conventions." It's about elevating that free-y feeling that comes atop a horse when sensual pleasure, nature, travel, and sound converge in a radical celebration of self as beautiful as sky. It's riding alone on a trail and singing out loud to yourself some song you have never heard before and will never hear again and letting your song take you off the trail.

Horse operas supplied Country Music with a visual grammar, an aesthetic, a style that was comprehensive and coercive. Herb Jeffries disrupted this by dismantling the grammar and reassembling it to suit his purposes.

The movies told the audience what a singing cowboy looked like, what a singing cowboy wore, how a singing cowboy fixed their hair, as well as influencing expectations of height, size, and skin tone. They established the norms. Individual entertainers worked with or against elements of norm. In the thirties the big studios told an international audience the American cowboy was white. Herb Jeffries disrupted that narrative. He was a twentieth-century disrupter. Lil Nas X, on stage and in his video, is visually descended from Herb Jeffries and a twenty-first-century disrupter.

Looking back on the day I think of as "the day I broke into Quincy Jones's house," I pray: "Please God, let there have been some kind of appointment." I hope I didn't actually go into my icon's house uninvited. I think I did. And I trusted two things, Quincy knew his history and Quincy appreciated a disrupter. I hope Quincy Jones was straight-up thinking when he met me, "This crazy-ass girl from Detroit City, with banjos clipped into her ears and black penny loafers on her feet has to be some kind of relation to crazy-ass, also from Detroit, Herb Jeffries." I am all kinds of quirky, no kind of kinky, but all kinds of quirk. I am proud to be called "the E word." Eccentric. It took a lot of eccentricity to walk into Quincy's house.

But the most eccentric, the most Herb Jeffries, grown-ass and eccentric, thing I ever did in Country: *The Mother Dixie Demo Tape.*

THE SECOND-BEST GIFT MY BAD MAMA GAVE ME: MOTHER DIXIE

The Wooten Brothers' first public performance occurred in Hawaii in 1966 and established their identity as prodigies. Regi, the eldest son of Elijah and Dorothy, was born in 1956. Victor, the youngest, was born in 1964. The first three sons arrived just a year apart—Roy in '57, Rudy in '58, Joe in '61, and three years later Victor came. Victor learned to talk and play music at the same time.

Under Regi's musical direction, they had formed their band the day before the performance. The eldest matched temperaments to available instruments. Regi played ukulele, Roy drums, Rudy a tonette, Joe a tambourine, and Victor, just two years old, strummed a mousegetar—on the beat without chording. Their plan was to entertain their neighbors with familiar and new tunes.

Growing up on, or near, a variety of military bases, with both of their parents listening to the *Opry* and the military radio (which played a whole lot of Country Music), the Wootens had an auspicious beginning if their intent was to change the face and sound of bluegrass music. These brown-eyed, brown-skinned, beautiful brothers listened to the *Opry* and wrote some of their own songs for their show.

Their first set started out with their version of "In the Midnight Hour," then they dived into an original song written by Regi intended to make his siblings laugh and inspire them to want to play, "I Head Butt a Man." It's about their favorite TV genre, wrestling. The melody was evolved from "Double Shot of My Baby's Love." Decades later both Joe and Regi can still recite the lyrics to me.

This is something often erased in the stories America tells about herself: Black children as intentional creatives. The Wootens were intentional and intensive creatives from childhood's hour.

THE WOOTEN BROTHERS, THE GREATEST BLACK COUNTRY BROTHER BAND OF ALL TIME

When Regi, still the leader of the family band, was sixteen, and Victor the youngest was eight, the Wootens opened a series of shows for WAR and Curtis Mayfield. Their father would travel with them, carrying a briefcase. In it was the "game changer"—his gun. Mama, who was so musical she had written her school alma mater, kept the home fires burning.

Years later, billed as the Good Time Family Band, the Wooten brothers were playing not far down the road from me in the same larger DMV (District of Columbia, Maryland, Virginia) area while I was in high school.

I've seen footage of four of the Wooten brothers playing at Busch Gardens. It's extraordinary to hear and watch. Standing behind two ersatz white Country singers (a redheaded poor imitation of Dottie West and a tall string bean of a Gary-from-the-Oak-Ridge-Boys imitator who had the grin but not the baritone) they burn down songs that were then burning up the charts: "Stranger in My House," "Wind Beneath My Wings." And they blaze their way through Country standards including "Your Cheatin' Heart," "I Fall to Pieces," "Coal Miner's Daughter," "It Wasn't God Who Made Honky Tonk Angels," and "Tennessee Waltz." They paint new beauty with the old melodies, taking apart and putting back together again, sometimes with wild additions including samples of other songs, older rhythms. They celebrate the classics while evolving them.

The Wootens don't copy the old records. They are in conversation with the old records: reframing what they love, deconstructing to reconstruct where they can see opportunities to bend a note or change a beat beyond what the original writers and interpreters could imagine or perform themselves. Signing the African roots of Country in every bar they play.

The climax of the show is their version of "Country Boy," a song made famous by Ricky Skaggs. With Joe on piano, Roy on drums, Victor playing bass and fiddle, and Regi playing steel guitar and guitar, things get most interesting when Victor, with bow hair flying, uses his fiddle to battle Regi. The brothers produce a performance of "Country Boy" that eclipses the legendary performance by Ricky Skaggs captured in the "Country Boy" video that co-stars Bill Monroe—who toured with DeFord Bailey in the forties. Monroe, perhaps the closest thing DeFord had to a friend at the Opry, openly acknowledged he was inspired by DeFord's playing and enriched by DeFord's audience. So, when Monroe props up Skaggs, lifts him high in the Opry fold, the debt Monroe owes to DeFord becomes Scaggs's debt, too. The Wootens' performance wrests thunderous applause from the Busch Gardens audience.

When the Wootens sing "Country Boy," it dismantles expectations. This is an amusement park. The expectation is that when you come to hear the Country Show, you have come to hear live covers of the songs you know from the radio performed by pretty people who look like younger versions of established stars. The expectation is the performers will be white and less talented than the stars. The Wootens defy all of that. These brown-skinned Black brothers wearing cowboy hats and cowboy shirts and jeans are singing, "You may think I'm a city slicker . . ." and then they go on to outplay Ricky Skaggs.

How stunned would you be to sit in that audience and discover that some "local Country colored boys" could outplay Ricky, could make the fiddle bow fly? Could bend the notes of the steel guitar? Could color within the lines of established forms with such innovation and vigor that the original lines become insignificant, and this becomes significant—you can't hear the Wootens play "Country Boy" and not know they play from the heart of the Country Music story.

The Wootens were performing a popular contemporary Country radio hit with Black bodies. This seemed to cause some in their audience to wonder if they could carry a Country tune in a bucket. The applause that follows their performance indicates an audience that is aware that the Wootens are fully mature musical men, Country capable, and Black. For the price of an amusement park ticket, some folks got a revelation.

In 1988, Victor and Roy would play with banjo great Béla Fleck on an episode of the PBS series called *Lonesome Pine Special* and begin the process of radically and rapidly transforming America's understanding of bluegrass. Playing as the Flecktones, they exploded the notion that bluegrass is white and always looks back to the past. The Wootens use their instruments to carve future from present moment sound. As of this writing, Roy Wooten has five Grammy wins and eleven Grammy nominations. Victor Wooten has five Grammy wins and twelve Grammy nominations and was voted by *Rolling Stone* readers as one of the top ten bassists of all time. That's who I invited to join me in the studio.

If I had to pick three high points for my forty years in Country, one would have to be recording demos with three members of the most Grammy-awarded Black Country family band in history.

It is the spring of 1990. We're in a basement studio owned by Biff Watson, a white boy who went to prep school whose first Nashville gig was playing with Kossi Gardner. It was not his last. Biff has performed with Dolly Parton, Crystal Gayle, Don Williams, and other Country stars.

On the first day of recording for *Mother Dixie*, April 9, the session leader is bassist Willie Weeks. Willie was one of the few people other than Stevie Wonder to play on Wonder's album *Innervisions.* He's played on eight Vince Gill albums, six Wynonna Judd albums, too many Country albums to count, likely more than any other Black sideman in Country history.

I requested Willie. Born in Salemburg, North Carolina, Willie is just over a decade older than I am, so he's just over forty, whip slim, and whip smart. I want his taste, his Country experience, all up in *The Mother Dixie* mix.

We got off to a bit of a rocky start. One of the female singers was offended by the title "Mammy's Song" until she read the lyric. Scat Springs, who was supposed to sing the title song "Mother Dixie," dropped by, sang out a bit of his interpretation, and we both agreed he would be a better fit for "The Ballad of Nat Love." On a break I talked to Victor and Roy Wooten about the concept for the larger project and about playing as sidemen on "Mother Dixie." They suggested their brother Joe for the vocalist gig. They said he had the voice and the attitude the songs needed. I asked them to get Joe to the studio as quick as they could so I could hear for myself. I had already made a big mistake casting Scat, I didn't want to make another. Joe was in Virginia. Roy and Victor convinced me to audition him on the phone. He was perfect. Joe got the job, then he got on the bus.

In the studio he effortlessly nailed the performance. That's what preparation will do. He got what I was talking about between the lines, the South as the abusive mother of Black culture but the mother nonetheless. When Joe sings "Mother Dixie," it sounds just like how I imagined my words would sound: confrontational and chilling, bruised and defiant.

He carved this into it: this is the moment when love for the abuser vanishes and love for the self begins. Joe sounded like who I wanted to be. Who I wasn't yet. These are the words he poured self-love and world reckoning into:

I was rocked in the cradle of the confederacy,
In my soul I can't forget you gave life to me
But when I was young, you showed me things a child should never see
Mother Dixie, I'm coming home.

You taught me to call him mister,
You taught me to call you ma'am
You hardly ever touched me except with the back of your hand
You held me down until the day I finally broke and ran

I grew up hungry
I grew up wild
I grew up strong enough to be your child
Let us make amends now
Let us atone

So gather up all your children
Sing a bittersweet harmony
A song of true freedom
Learned from my slavery
There would be no you without me
Mother Dixie, I'm coming home

The Wootens helped me change wound into sound. They put the hands they had taught to perform superiorly to other people's hands to my service. It's not innate Wooten dexterity, precision, delicacy of touch, power of press; it was developed in the family's Regi-led insular, arduous, and migrating conservatory. And generosity is as distinctly Wooten-ish as virtuosity. The Wootens carried me up to a mountaintop I could not have reached without them. They carried me high as they had carried each other.

Like DeFord Bailey, the Wootens (Regi, Roy, Rudy, Joe, and Victor) are instrumentalists who sometimes sing but typically conduct complex and nuanced conversations with their audience without the use of words. Like Lil, they came to the attention of the mainstream Country public as Black sidemen supporting a known white star. But those familiar with music beyond mainstream Country are aware they had a storied history playing with Black stars long before they stepped onto a stage in support of a white one.

Like Ray Charles, they used pure musical virtuosity to redefine and challenge the bounds of genre and played through ignorant questions. Is *Modern Sounds* a Country album? Are the Flecktones bluegrass? They stand on stage like athletes; this is an essence of Charley Pride; their bodies demand respect for evident kinetic intelligence. Pride's was rooted in his historic success on a baseball field, the Wootens' in their ability to play two saxophones at once, to toss a guitar such that it double flips and sails back into hands. They are like Herb Jeffries in their embrace of eccentricity and dandyism crystalized in a nickname. Jeffries was the "Bronze Buckaroo." Roy Wooten becomes known as "Future Man." As Future Man, he will invent instruments, the drumitar and the RoyEl. He wears a tricornered hat that makes him look like a pirate to me. Over time I have come to understand that he wears the hat to disrupt notions of who is and isn't a founding father, what is and isn't classical music. He has become equally interested in the Chevalier de Saint-Georges, an eighteenth-century classical composer sometimes referred to as the Black Mozart, and his RoyEl instrument that plays sounds not in the Western scale. The tricornered hat was George Washington's hat, the Black Mozart's hat, and now Roy's hat.

When Future Man walked into Biff's basement wearing his black tricornered hat, Victor walked in wearing a serene smile, and Joe walked in talking with a warm Newport News, Virginia, accent that marks him as having spent a lot of time in the vicinity where the first Africans enslaved in America landed, I wanted to be their sister.

MAYA ANGELOU'S COUNTRY CAMEOS

I remember Maya Angelou singing a cappella in a ballroom of the Opryland Hotel.

It was at a cocktail party hosted by the Links Incorporated, and Maya Angelou was the guest of honor. She was in town to address the 1986

National Assembly of the Links, a service organization founded in Philadelphia by Black women "who strive to do some good each day for those who need our aid." Forty years after its founding in 1946, the Links had grown to be one of the largest and influential service organizations in the nation. A great fan of *I Know Why the Caged Bird Sings*, the first of Angelou's many autobiographical works, I made my way to stand as close as I could to the woman. I wasn't expecting we would actually speak. I just wanted to hear what she was saying. I was one of the younger people in the room. She asked me if I was in school. I said I was a "Country songwriter." She let out a laugh, sang a few lines from a current tune, confessed that she loved Country Music, and demanded to know where I was from and how I became a Country songwriter, then sang a bit of some old Country song. I was in shock. I was in thrill. Maya Angelou loved and knew Country Music. The whole conversation was short, rapid fire, and intense. And then it was abruptly over. One of the hostesses was giving me a you-are-monopolizing-the-guest-of-honor look, so I moved on.

But I didn't move away from the explicit affirmation I received from Maya Angelou that writing Country songs was a worthy enterprise and that to be a Black woman writing Country songs was to make the invisible, a Black audience's connection to Country, visible. And I didn't move away from my desire to visibly connect Maya Angelou to Country.

The opportunity arose when I was invited to develop a treatment and write a screenplay for a Reba McEntire video. This job had the added advantage of being something "small" I could do in film and television with music while looking for something big I could do, like my projects with the Wootens or Quincy Jones.

Susan Longacre's song "Is There Life Out There" has nothing to do with child abuse or Maya Angelou, but I used it as a vehicle to talk about both. The storyline is a diluted fairytale version of my experience with my mother. A stressed mother seeking to better herself ends up inflicting verbal and physical violence on her daughter—before coming into her maternal senses and consoling her child by reading her to sleep with Maya Angelou's *I Know Why the Caged Bird Sings*.

Angelou's book cover is fully visible in the video, which becomes a kind of coded work through its existence: it connects Angelou to Country; it puts a real-life Black child's experience of domestic violence in conversation with a fictional white child's experience of domestic violence; and it hides my own troubles in plain sight. Why else would a memoir of childhood rape be so important to me that I needed to include it in a Country Music video?

One answer was that it was written by an extraordinary Black author who loved Country Music, and the memoir itself was a kind of Country Music.

In 1992, my memorial to Angelou was named ACM Video of the Year. Accepting the award, Reba called my first name, "Alice," and thanked me. Anticipating that some people would doubt I, a Black woman, wrote a Reba video, I signed my work with a cameo. I put a scene into the script where I walked through Hillsboro village, one of the neighborhoods in which I would eventually raise my daughter, following behind Reba and the young actress playing her daughter. The exact things they are doing in fiction, Caroline and I did in real life.

In the twenty-first century, Angelou would become much more vocal about her love of Country and start writing Country songs herself. She will claim "I Hope You Dance," written by Midsummer Music's former writer Mark Sanders and my daughter Caroline's once Saturday-night babysitter Tia Sillers, as her favorite Country song. When I read reports of Lee Ann Womack singing the Country mega hit at Angelou's memorial service, it took me back thirty years to Angelou singing Country to me at the Opryland Hotel.

THE THING CALLED LOVE: A WHITE COUNTRY MOVIE WITH BLACK COUNTRY DENOUEMENTS

My brief close encounters with Quincy Jones began to bear some fruit in the form of friends made in Hollywood, notably G. Marq Roswell, who was getting songs in movies that were making their way to the screen.

Shortly after I met Marq, he signed on to be the music supervisor for *The Thing Called Love.*

The Thing Called Love wanted to be the first big movie about people in the Country Music industry that conveyed the edge, grit, and brilliance of what we who were a part of it called "Babylon on the Cumberland." The strategy for achieving this was to focus more on songwriting than singing, and to focus on the ways singers and writers formed a circle of love, sex, competition, and artistic influence comparable to Paris in the time of Hemingway and Fitzgerald and Harlem in the time of Hughes and Bontemps. They stumbled over that part.

If you were me or Kossi and you were in Nashville in the eighties you said, "This is like Harlem in the twenties." Black folk in Nashville knew a whole lot about Harlem in the twenties because so much of it migrated down to Nashville in the thirties and the forties. James Weldon Johnson arriving in 1930, Arna Bontemps in 1943, Aaron "Doug" Douglas also in 1943.

The Thing Called Love starred River Phoenix and Samantha Mathis and featured Sandra Bullock, who would have stolen the show—if Samantha hadn't stolen it back with her Marilyn Monroe–like breathy performance of "Big Dream," also known as "God's a Woman, Too."

Sam Ingles, in an article for the *London Economic*, calls *The Thing Called Love* one of 1993's genuine "unsung gems." And it is that. It is also so much less than it woulda-coulda-shoulda been. What kills *The Thing Called Love*? It's lying whiteness. The filmmaking team hid the Blackness too deep in the mix. It depicts Nashville and sound-sculpts Country as lily-white music created by a lily-white community. To echo Elvis Presley, echoing Big Mama Thornton in "Hound Dog," *that was just a lie.*

It could have gone another way. The original director of the picture, Brian Gibson, the man who initially came to scout locations and invited me to move around town with him, bolted from the project, literally left from location scouting to go to prep and direct *What's Love Got to Do with It*, the Tina Turner biopic. Had Gibson been at the helm we might have seen and heard Blackness higher in the mix.

Gibson was a fan of the Rolling Stones and had paid attention to their Country side. He understood everything Country in the Stones was Black Country. He understood that the Beatles are not Country—because they eschewed Black aesthetics. That's the kind of thing we talked about a mile a minute while looking for locations. All of that and how wonderful his wife, Lynn Whitfield, was. Years to come his daughter with Lynn Whitfield, Grace Gibson, would include some Country tunes when she emerged as a singer songwriter.

Peter Bogdanovich, of *The Last Picture Show* and *Come Back to the Five and Dime, Jimmy Dean* fame, chose me to write the songs for the main character, Miranda Presley, and it's a running joke in the film that she is no relation to Elvis—the inclusion of the name Presley is a nod to race.

This is more than a nod: The song that is the climax of *The Thing Called Love* is a Black Country song. "Big Dream" or "God's a Woman, Too" was written by a Black woman, a Black girl, and a white man. Lots and lots of big songwriters vied for the job of writing Miranda Presley's songs. Me and Ralph Murphy got the job.

We built on work I had done collaborating with my young daughter. Caroline and I liked to hum-sing back and forth to each other, throwing words like a ball between us. Caroline started it off . . . *love goes around . . . you give it to me . . . I give it to you . . . love goes around . . .* This turned to, *love is a circle, you give it to me, I give it to you, you give it to me, love is a circle.* And finally, *love is a ball.* Listening to my daughter, riffing with her, clapping hands with her, acting out the gestures of throwing love and catching it with our fingers and with our eyes and tucking it into our pockets, I came to a significant conclusion: one dream I had with my ex-husband came true. Caroline. I wrote "One Dream We Had Came True" with Bob DiPiero, one of the most successful of Country songwriters who was for a while married to my friend Pam Tillis.

I told Caroline she was my dream come true and she hum-sang at me, *I had a big dream last night, big enough to share.* And soon she was miming, tossing me her big dream and I was miming tossing it back to her. We were having a big time. Big was our word for "good."

My girl stopped hum-singing and miming. She asked me a question, "Can a dream be a friend?" It was a good question, a big question. We were onto a conversation that wasn't a song lyric.

I toted Caroline's questions into the co-writing session with Ralph Murphy when we set out to write the songs for the female lead in *The Thing Called Love.* I also toted some of her "Love Is a Circle" variations.

Soon we had an answer to Caroline's friend-dream question. *I have a dream of my own, and it's mine and mine alone, it's been my friend since I was just a girl, it has a life, it has a heart, it has a soul, and it's a part of everything this woman gives the world, and it's a big dream big enough to share, like a rainbow hanging in the air.* Those last lines were pure Caroline, *it's a big dream, big enough to share, like a rainbow hanging in the air.*

Ralph and I stole from my daughter, but he told me it wasn't stealing because I was going to spend anything I made on her, and I half let myself believe him. Then I started wondering how I could steal from somebody who truly believed God put rainbows in the air as a promise. Finally, my Lutheran Sunday school, crossed with Baptist Vacation Bible school, theology kicked in with a rush. I was thinking about being made in the perfect image of God; about how little girls were so creative, and God created the world and the words, and how all of that *makes me think maybe God's a woman, too.* Those words popped out loud from my mouth and Ralph said, "That's the hook of this song." "I thought the hook was 'Big Dream,'" I said. "Two hooks are always better than one," said Ralph.

Much of *The Thing Called Love* was filmed on location in Nashville. But some was filmed in Los Angeles on a soundstage where a more camera-friendly version of the Bluebird was erected. By the end of the shoot, I was one of the few people Peter was still talking to and on good terms with involved with the film. The climax of the pic was to be shot in the re-creation of the Bluebird to maximize sound quality of these two most important minutes of the film. Peter flew me out in case any last-minute rewrites of the lyrics were needed. The producers were not sure my presence was a necessary expense. They relented but they didn't put me in the best hotel they were using, they put me in the Hollywood Roosevelt Hotel instead.

Thank God for that. Otherwise, I wouldn't have met Ruth Brown. She was coming out of an elevator in the Roosevelt, dripping furs, and she wasn't even going outside. She was making her way from her room or suite to the Cinegrill, the bar off the hotel lobby. She was a stunningly beautiful woman, every inch a diva. She looked something like Weezy in the Jeffersons, which is probably to say that Weezy was styled to look something like Ruth Brown. She had milk-chocolate skin, a helmet of fluffy black hair, dark cat eyes rimmed top and bottom with kohl, significant eyebrows, red lips, regular teeth. I recognized her immediately.

This was the woman who sang "(Mama) He Treats Your Daughter Mean," "5-10-15 Hours," and "If I Can't Sell It, I'll Keep Sittin' on It." Whatever I was supposed to be doing in Los Angeles I was making it to her last set, every night if I could.

When we sat together after her show at the Cinegrill, she declared over drinks that Atlantic Records *was* the house that Ruth built.

You can't be old Ruth and young Alice and drink in the Roosevelt Hotel (especially with Alice in L.A. to work on a movie) and not get to talking about how the Roosevelt Hotel was reputed to be the site of an early Oscar ceremony. And if you are Alice and Ruth, Oscar talk moves straight to Hattie McDaniel—about what she achieved that was not fully acknowledged even as she was in flashes dramatically acknowledged. Reflections on McDaniel and *Gone with the Wind* inspired "Mammy's Song."

The song starts with an instrumental riff on Rock-a-Bye Baby.

This song is the rest of the story of all those "maid" performances. It's my coda that reveals Mammy as a woman with agency, as a life bringer, as a sexual person, as a mother with ambitions for her daughter to marry a fine colored doctor, as a woman who loves the little white boy she raised to be a man, a man she is willing to *kill* should he attempt to date-rape her Black daughter, *just for the brown of it.*

Ruth Brown could have sung the bejesus out of that song.

Ruth Brown was a reckoning bell who got results and was recognized. Ms. Brown was inducted by Bonnie Raitt into the Rock & Roll Hall of Fame, class of 1993, a class that included Van Morrison, Etta James, Creedence Clearwater Revival, the Doors, and Black Bottom Saint Dinah Washington. Morrison, James, and Creedence all have significant connections to Country—as did Bonnie Raitt and Ruth Brown.

Ruth listened to Country Music as a girl growing up in Portsmouth, Virginia. And at least one white Country singer, Janis Martin, who is sometimes known as the female Elvis, cops to stealing, or shall we call it borrowing, or copying Brown's work.

Both her status as a victim of artistic theft and her calling as a protector of other creatives intrigued me about Ruth. Specifically, her work advocating for creatives of color. This woman who worked as a school bus driver, a domestic worker, and a Head Start teacher. And she rang the reckoning bell with Atlantic Records and got herself paid hard-earned, well-overdue monies, and she got a lot of other folks paid, too, including the Coasters, the Drifters, and Big Joe Turner.

Sometimes the first step of doing something about being a victim, is to see that you are one. And the last step is to see that's not your whole story. It's what you make, not what they take that counts. That's what I figured out watching Ruth Brown perform. Ruth Brown hipped me to all that with her words and her actions. That big old tall fancy building is the house that Ruth built!

When I checked into the Hollywood Roosevelt Hotel, I felt like I was checking into a defunct place. It was not the newer and shinier hotel where they put the stars in the cast. I discovered it was the better hotel—Ruth Brown was in residence.

Ruth Brown recorded one Country song that I've been able to find, "I Burned Your Letter." Though it breaks into a few bars of "C. C. Rider," Ruth's song exists in a territory far from the blues. This song is about working through wildness to return to consoling domesticity, *Pull up a chair and we'll sit by the fire.*

With one cut, and shameless artists advocacy, Ruth Brown earned a place in my Black Country canon.

But I was in Los Angeles to work on *The Thing Called Love*, so I found myself in a small space sequestered with Samantha Mathis, who was being coached through playing and singing "Big Dream" by T Bone Burnett. Peter Bogdanovich had sent me in to talk with Mathis so that she might gain, might borrow, some of my lived experience of having been almost exactly her age and moving to Nashville to make it in Country Music. I didn't stay long. Mathis didn't seem interested in my experience as a source of inspiration. Or maybe she was just nervous about learning the song and pulling off a performance compelling enough to be the climax of the film.

She succeeded to a significant degree. When we started working on *The Alice Randall Songbook* project, Rissi Palmer shared that on a vacation trip to Mexico as a teen, while staying in a hotel with limited cable she had stumbled on *The Thing Called Love* and fallen in love with "Big Dream."

This was a complete surprise to me. I had no idea there were Black teen girls who had watched *The Thing Called Love* and fallen in love with "Big Dream" let alone a Black teen girl who grew up to sing on the *Opry*, get mentored in Country by Prince, and land a top forty Country hit. When Rissi watched that movie, did she imagine moving to Nashville and trying to play the Bluebird and finally succeeding in playing the Bluebird? If the film provided her with any tangible steps to take on her journey up the Country charts it was worth it. How much easier would Rissi's journey have been if they had put a few conspicuous Black people in their fictional Bluebird?

I didn't fall in love with Samantha Mathis's performance of "Big Dream." I liked it, but I didn't love it. It sounded more folk, to me, than Country. I didn't hear the Black in it. Or the South. I didn't hear me in it.

The performance bruised me, but there is balm to come for this specific bruise. One day I will meet, backstage at Nashville's War Memorial

Auditorium, a young Black woman with multicolored dreads atop her head who (though living in New York City the day we met) was born in 1982, in Jackson, Tennessee, then raised in Humboldt, a small Tennessee town with a steadily declining population. Growing up, this daughter of the small-town South would assist her father in both his concert promotion business (posting flyers) and his demolition business (sort through brick). She would sing in church on Sunday and become intrigued and inspired by the variety of voices that rose from the congregation in praise. Eventually, she will teach herself to play guitar, and banjo, and ukulele. When she starts songwriting (songs that are at once universal and rooted in her Humboldt, ethereal and gritty) she will report hearing literal voices, like the voices she heard in church she will explain and tell how they dictate lyrics and fragments of lyrics. Singing her own kind of Country (she is a fan of Dolly Parton and Hank, Sr., and Prince) she will release albums and gain a degree of fame and a higher degree of respect. The world will know her as Valerie June.

When *The Alice Randall Songbook* project starts to come together and pairing songs with artists begins, Ebonie Smith pairs Valerie June with "Big Dream."

Valerie June performs "Big Dream" with a voice sweet as Tennessee wildflower honey. That's a Southern sweet that can trill like a bird and growl like a bear, but it's also an accent, an inflection, a way of phrasing, that many of us who identify as Black, female, and Southern, recognize as reflecting us, signifying us, universalizing us. In 2021, she will release an album called *The Moon and Stars: Prescriptions for Dreamers.* I receive it as a prescription for me and her performance of "Big Dream" as a benediction.

Dozens of major writers independently pitched their songs to be in the movie, dozens of major publishers pitched their writers; and the music supervisor put writing teams together to submit songs. Guy Clark was flown out to Los Angeles to participate and never got called from his hotel. A

Harlan Howard song was chosen for the male lead, River Phoenix. Because Miranda's song is the climax of the film, the fight was even tighter. When it got down to a choice between three songs, one was "Big Dream" and others in the running were Hall of Famers or on their way to the Hall of Fame. Our song was chosen.

I co-wrote "Big Dream" with Ralph, but he told anyone who cared to hear that I came to that session with most of that song written and with a melody I couldn't sing. He would emphasize the "she can't sing" part. What we didn't tell? I was writing my life with someone who knew my life.

Ralph Murphy, a lanky Englishman, who wrote an iconic hit for Crystal Gayle, "(Don't Take Me) Half the Way," was one of the people I met that first scouting trip to Nashville. Our lives braided in powerful ways.

Ralph got sick in 1987 and missed an in-the-round at the Bluebird. Garth Brooks replaced him—that launched Garth and helped Midsummer make money. Ralph co-owned Pic-a-lic Publishing with his business partner, Roger Cook, who wrote, "I'd Like to Teach the World to Sing." Ralph was one of only two people on Music Row who knew I had been raped as a teen. I told him after he told me he had been abused by his stepfather.

For all these reasons, Ralph was thrilled for me, one of his "songwriting babies," when I was recognized. And because he had a systematic mind, he would go on to write a book about songwriting and coach songwriters in navigating the industry. He settled down with me in a back booth behind the bar at the Sunset Grill not far from Music Row and asked me some hard questions, starting with, "What got you into the room?" And ending with, "What's going to keep you there."

I didn't have a complete answer the first long lunch when he posed the question. And when I did figure it out, I didn't tell him my answer. I just told him I had one.

Working my original plan, writing songs that were about something other than love, writing from a decidedly female, Black, and bookish perspective, troubling the water in ways that mattered to rural Black people, and to the descendants of rural Black people—that got me into the room.

I was haunted by lynching and healed by witnessing my grandparents' sweet and loyal Black marriage, so both of those coexist in "The Ballad of Sally Anne." I was in love with Black preaching and alarmed by environmental racism, so I came to co-write "Who's Minding the Garden?" with a title that could be loaned to a Black Baptist preacher as both theme and line of a Sunday sermon. Drug wars were reshaping America nowhere more dramatically than in my hometown of Detroit. "Girls Ride Horses, Too" was about the reality that women were being drawn into the game and drug running required rural places and rural complicity. "Reckless Night" calls out slut-shaming before it was called that. "My Hometown Boy," the pain of invisible identity.

I was born and young raised in an all-Black small Alabama town located in the state of Michigan where a watermelon truck rolled through the neighborhood on summer days and a kid sitting atop a big green melon hollered "Juicy fruit!" and I would step into the street and buy a nickel slice. And the father who gave the nickel to me was an ardent follower of Malcolm X.

"Your participation in that movie gave it something it couldn't find any other way . . . Peter at a deeper level knew Miranda had to be you, was you, young, gifted and female," said Marq Roswell, the music supervisor of *The Thing Called Love*.

I had broken through the boys' club. And the club took notice. The top writers in Nashville had fought for the spot and I got it. "Big Dream" was a big dream come true.

XXX'S AND OOO'S

Rissi Palmer wasn't the only person who heard "Big Dream." Brandon Tartikoff, the president of Paramount who green-lit *The Thing Called*

Love, heard it, too. Tartikoff was the fan who changed the trajectory of my career on Music Row.

A near fatal car crash on New Year's Day 1991 had left Brandon and his eight-year-old daughter severely injured and in intensive care. Brandon rapidly mended. Seeking intensive and innovative intervention for their daughter, the Tartikoffs had relocated to New Orleans. Focused on his daughter's healing, Brandon stepped away from head honcho positions and into the land of Southern music.

The "XXX's and OOO's" story starts in 1993 at a Country Music celebrity bowling event hosted by BMI's legendary Frances Preston to raise funds for cancer research.

Between frames, I met a Hollywood agent who knew that Brandon Tartikoff, the former president of NBC and Paramount Pictures, was looking for a writer to develop a TV series about the ex-wives of Country stars that he wanted to call *XXX's and OOO's*. Only he didn't tell me that. He told Brandon about me.

When Tartikoff's office called and left a message on my answering machine, I didn't return the call because I thought it was a prank. Eventually they got through. I sent an initial treatment and got invited to interview with Brandon in New Orleans on April 5, 1993. There were no available commercial flights to New Orleans. So, the agent rented a tour bus. We were off. I freshened up on the bus and took the meeting. I got the job. Brandon invited me to join him that evening to watch the national college basketball championship with an A-list star. I said, I would go if not going was a deal-breaker. He announced, "You have no starfucker in you whatsoever." We both laughed at that truth. It was the start of a very profitable relationship.

We got the job. Tartikoff set a deal at CBS for a movie of the week that would be a backdoor pilot for a series. Soon, in addition to co-writing the script (I named one of the Country star characters George Randall after my father) and co-producing the pilot, I was writing the theme song. My publisher was thrilled. I invited Matraca Berg to co-write. We worked hard and got nothing. Eventually, I made the call to my publisher to break the bad news. I would not have the theme song in the new CBS pilot. They would use a Country classic.

The next day, demoralized, I slapped a smile on my face, clipped a bow in my daughter's hair, and drove her to school. I was jumping into the shower when my bedroom phone started ringing. A permission slip that my first grader "had to have" wasn't in her backpack. I stepped into the shower cussing at myself for being a failure as a mother and a money-maker. Hot water was spraying on my head when these words came to me, *You got a picture of your mama in heels and pearls, and you're trying to make it in your daddy's world.*

I rushed to my daughter's school with the permission slip, then over to Matraca's. When she opened her door, I spat out new lines before even saying hello. She waved me in. The lines to the second verse came to Matraca almost as fast as the lines to the first verse had come to me. We told the truth we were living, how hard it was to make money, make love, and care for family all in the same day. The whole song was written in less than ninety minutes.

Fast-forward. Wynonna Judd records the song but doesn't show up for overdubs. We're back to using a Country classic. Except I knew a singer, a woman who had years before sung demos for me, who had the vocal control and voice required to sing on Wy's tracks and eclipse Wy's performance, and she was at a nearby studio working on her own album. Nashville was still a very small town. I raced to where Trisha Yearwood was recording. I blasted past the receptionist and into Trisha's session. I blurted out the truth starting with, "We have known each other since our first marriages . . ." I entreated her to help me save my last best chance to have a big hit. Trisha said, "Yes." That generous woman left her own session to save mine.

On Independence Day of 1994, it seemed every time I got in my car and turned on the radio, I heard "XXX's and OOO's." A few days later when the Billboard Country Chart was released, the song was listed as the No. 1 Country single. The second week at number one was sweeter than the first. Rumor had it the label wasn't pushing for a second week.

That they had another song they wanted at the top. That second week was pure audience, girls and women, seizing our tune as their summer anthem that celebrated all the mamas trying to keep the balance up between love and money, and all the girls and women writing letters and writing songs, recorded and unrecorded, as they completed chores, sought sex, and yes, got paid. And I didn't just hear the song on the radio, there was a cassette version of the single that I heard played in bedrooms and living rooms, there was a vinyl 45 disc single that I heard played in family rooms, and there was, eventually, a cut on a long playing album that some friends would throw on the stereo to celebrate with me every time I came to their house for a while.

It was a new pinnacle. Even now I get excited when I am traveling someplace, driving down the highway so many times, stepping onto a boat in the marina in St. Augustine, Florida, once, when "XXX's and OOO's" comes on. And it was sweet and bitter to have my portrait made and hung on the walls of Sony with the other writers who have hit number one. It was good to be up there and hard to be the only Black woman. All of those were "I've made it" moments.

What gave me the biggest chills? Hearing the song sung in Opryland theme park on the Opryland campus. That, for me, was the "I'm here to stay" moment.

For a quarter century (1972–1997) you knew you had arrived as a force in the world of Country Music when a soundalike was singing your song at *the* theme park that was home to the Grand Ole Opry House.

When that moment came for me in 1994, I was licking Dippin' Dots in the company of sweet Caroline, seven, while shaking my head looking straight in the direction of the place where Roy Acuff used to sit and wave at the drenched folk on the Grizzly River Rampage.

UNEXPECTED CONSEQUENCES

The extraordinary success of "XXX's and OOO's" put a target on my back. Anyone reading the Billboard Charts knew big money was soon to be rolling in. New opportunities in the form of publishing deals with big draws came my way. I wasn't greedy. I was on a roll. I just wanted to stay where I was and keep writing songs and see if I could get to the next hit. I wanted to be fair. My publisher had supported me in so many ways, sending me on scouting trips to California, taking me to parties where I danced with Harry Connick, Jr., had Brooks & Dunn play songs at a dinner party in Tartikoff's and my honor at the publisher's house, let me use the publisher's pool to teach my daughter to swim, and borrow the writer's room to give a children's Christmas party. We were all good and the future was bright.

My publisher, who I then thought of as a big blonde bombshell fighting on my side, invited me to lunch at Amerigo's, a mid-price Italian restaurant. I should maybe have taken that as a sign. I should have wondered why we were not on our way to Mario's or Sunset Grill, one of the places we usually went to celebrate important things.

Looking back, I think maybe she didn't want to betray me in a restaurant she loved or maybe she didn't want to spend a lot of money on someone who wouldn't be with her long. At the time I was thinking maybe she just wants to try the new place.

So, I met her in her office on Music Row and we were supposed to just jump in the car and head to the restaurant to celebrate the success of "XXX's and OOO's," and she says something like: *My contract is coming up and your contract is coming up. It will help me a lot if I can show folks that you are staying with Tree. You've had this big hit. Folks think you may be leaving, or that you're going to shake us down for more money. If I can show that you're extending your deal for three more years, at the same rate, that's a win for me. And I will make it a win for you by funding the expenses for more of the things you want to do in Hollywood. Can you do that?*

I said, "Yes," easily. A draw is an advance against future earnings; if I'm going to earn a lot I will get my money. And my advance, as I understood it, was just recoupable against my publisher's share, not against my writer's share. So, all was fine. And I said something like, *Fine, just send the paperwork to my lawyers.* And the rest of the conversation went something like this: *That's the thing. My meeting is coming up. This is just extending the exact deal you already had, it doesn't change anything. Your lawyer has already seen this deal*, she said. *Still, he needs to look at it*, I told her. She had a question: *Why? It's just going to cost you money. I promise this just extends it and changes nothing.* Pause. I ask, *Nothing?* She responds, *I need you to show a commitment to me like I showed to you before you had this hit. I need you to sign this before we go to lunch. Sign so we can celebrate.*

And I did. I signed without reviewing the large stack of papers, without having a lawyer review them. Emotionally ambushed, I signed.

The Blonde Shark was just about three years younger than my mother and a whole lot like her. She was from Alabama just like my daddy and his people. And she was arguably the most successful woman in the history of Music Row. For a deluded, broken moment, with the Blonde Shark having hung, or promising to hang, a picture of me on the wall of Tree, it was like Buddy Killen was my daddy and the Blonde Shark was my mama and I owed them something. In that broken moment, I was the furthest I would ever get from Detroit City and good sense. I was exhausted by being a single mama and I signed those papers that more or less signed away much of the writer's share of the profit to "XXX's and OOO's." This is something I would not have knowingly done. Something so stupid nobody would believe I had done it. I let BS rob me. I know you're not supposed to sign papers without a lawyer, but I did it. And when I asked BS about it directly, she said to my face, "It's my job to cheat you if I can." She said that. We were alone in a room and some folks believe she said it to me, and some folks don't, but I know she said it to me. And I said, and it always seemed crazy to me that I said this, "But you let me swim in your pool."

I couldn't fight the great blonde shark because she reminded me so much of the brown-eyed bitch who had so frequently and completely defeated me. I couldn't fight the shark because she was like a mama, and much as I hated the woman who birthed me, I didn't fight her out of some kind of gratitude for being born.

That same crazy gratitude didn't allow me to fight the shark. It was all mixed up in a daughter's belief that I was tiny and puny, and they were big and strong and I was floating breathing their water as air. I feared, if something happened to the mother, I would die.

I could not fight them. I had to flee them. So "XXX's and OOO's" made it to the top of the charts, the shark stole almost all the original money, except about forty thousand which I spent, in part, on a trip to France to visit my best friend, Mimi, in the company of my daughter. And even that the shark tried to claw back. Eventually, I got a little brilliant Black law firm to try to dispute the contract on my behalf, the lawyer would eventually represent Rosa Parks, but I didn't have the funds to mount the necessary fight, they said. I told myself that the money I lost was my graduate degree in business school. And I blamed and blamed myself for getting robbed.

Only one thing related to the music business didn't get polluted by the BS robbery: the pleasure of hearing my song sung by some unknown Trisha Yearwood wannabe at Opryland USA with the original American girl in all her ribbons-and-bows glory seated beside me.

REVIVED THE RAILS: COWBOYS, PULLMAN PORTERS, AND SOILED DOVES

I was a match made to my second husband, David Steele Ewing, by my first husband's aunt and uncle.

Our first date did not start off auspiciously. I had to cancel it because Marq Roswell was in town and had invited me to a business dinner. I thought I told my then assistant to cancel/reschedule the dinner with David. I had a lot of work trouble and a hard workweek. I was stressed. I needed Marq's advice. I told my daughter I was taking a bath and not to interrupt me "unless the world was coming to an end." Twenty minutes later she was knocking on the bathroom door. "Did the world come to an end?"

"No, but David Ewing is downstairs on the living room couch looking like he's dressed to go on a date." I put on my frumpiest robe and went down, dripping wet with no makeup, and told him I had messed up. We rescheduled for early the next week. I assumed he would cancel. He didn't.

In December of 1996, he took me to dinner at Sunset Grill, a music industry hang spot, then out to see Christmas lights, making a stop at the home of Mr. and Mrs. George Jones.

I told him I wasn't writing Country songs anymore, that I had moved on after getting to number one on the charts. That I was doubling down on getting a *successful* television series or film made (*XXX's and OOO's* was a CBS movie of the week and backdoor series pilot, but it was not successful) or I was finally getting on to writing a novel. I didn't tell him about the music business stress I was in.

David proposed to me in Washington, D.C., on January 20, 1997, as Jessye Norman sang "Oh, Freedom" during President Clinton's second inauguration. He dropped to his knees on the Capitol's ground, and I thought he had been shot. In late April, we had an engagement party. Marcus Hummon sat at the piano and sang "God Bless the Broken Road (That Led Me Straight to You)." Written by Hummon, Bobby Boyd, and Jeff Hanna, "Broken Road" seemed a perfect theme song for my second wedding. In 2005, "Broken Road" would reach number one on the Country charts, allowing our guests a classic Nashville "I heard in a friend's house before it got on the radio" moment.

Jeff Hanna was the husband of Matraca Berg, with whom I had written "XXX's and OOO's." Marcus was the husband of the Episcopal priest who would marry David and I at 2:00 a.m. on the Vanderbilt campus. Nashville is a very small town.

David was a ninth generation Black Nashvillian and an attorney with ties to Country Music. His first job was cleaning the print blocks that had been used to make posters for artists including DeFord Bailey, Charley Pride, and Louis Armstrong. His African-American stepfather, Weldon Kidd, had for a time owned Hatch Show Print, the Nashville-based company founded in 1879 that has printed posters and showbills for generations of musical artists, Black and white, including a lot of legends and icons. After we married, David signed on to become one of the lawyers working for Gaylord Opryland Resort in community affairs and strategic initiatives, which meant we had behind-the-scenes access to the hotel, the Ryman, and the *General Jackson*. I got to see up-close the skill of Arthur

Keith, a graduate of the hospitality program at the Cornell University Business School who was the first Black general manager of the Opryland Hotel and the American Hotel and Lodging Association's Outstanding General Manager of the Year, because his tenure overlapped with David's.

My mother-in-law referred to us as her "vintage" couple because we both so loved Black history. We celebrated our first Valentine's Day in a tiny Italian restaurant that was more of a catering shop, but the chef could truly cook.

The next day I headed off to Charleston to meet my best friend, Mimi Oka, for our annual besties trip, leaving David to hold the fort that was our little pink townhouse that sheltered Caroline. I had barely settled into the Wentworth Mansion when I got a call from someone who identified themselves as a psychiatrist. My mother was dying and wanted me to call her. We had not spoken in a decade.

I made the call. Bettie told me she had four to eight months to live. Against the advice of many, including clergy, psychiatrist, friends, and with the support of others, I decided to walk Bettie, dubbed by a few of my friends who knew her as Bad Bitch Bettie, to her death. One friend said, "When you have a bitch for a mother she should expect to die alone." Another reminded me not to let her know when I was coming for a visit. "Why?" I asked. "She could plan. She could . . . get armed? Best to let visits be a surprise."

My mother had bold and calm people warning caution. Reggie Hudlin, a Black man who is as close as I have ever come to having a brother, the man who sat to my left at my daughter's wedding, pronounced, "Mama ain't always right, and your mama's almost always wrong."

But I was doing it, facing death with her so she didn't have to face it alone. Next hurdle? Bettie wanted to meet her granddaughter, and her granddaughter wanted to meet Bettie. We flew together to D.C. In my mother's comfortable Dupont Circle apartment, she asked my daughter a lot of questions then pronounced her judgment, "I prefer you to Alice, you do math and you're not fat," then sent me off on an errand to the kitchen. I let myself be amused by that banter. At least she was complimenting Caroline. Caroline was only ten years old, but she stood up for me when my mother sent me out of the room on an errand. Caroline said, "If you insult my mother again, we're leaving." I know this because my mother told me. Bettie never saw, or asked to see, her granddaughter again. She refused to meet my new husband. She claimed all of her friends and all the doormen thought I was still married to my first husband, and it would be inconvenient to update them.

By the summer of 1999, we had traveled together far longer than either of us anticipated. And all of it had me raggedy. I was broke. Picked pockets, jangled mind.

I wanted to run away from my bad mother. I wanted to run to my good mother. I needed to be home with my daughter—but I was too tired to cook, clean, or entertain. I wanted to stay in bed and not get dressed; and I wanted a thrilling adventure to distract me and mine from the death march. I wanted my people close, and I needed hours alone. I was trying not to be a songwriter, but I was exactly doing that songwriter thing of being "a walking contradiction."

Churning that litany of contradictory desires over and over in my mind, I soothed myself by listening to my favorite death is coming song, "Desperados Waiting for a Train," and I knew what I had to do, ride the rails—stop waiting for a metaphorical train and get on a real one.

CALIFORNIA ZEPHYR, RUNNING WITH LIL FROM BETTIE

I was on a quest to suppress old memories that involved my mother and Lil Hardin, while making new memories that involved my daughter and Lil Hardin.

Lil was beautiful in face and body like my mother but didn't hurt me; Lil was creative in three arts—singing, songwriting, and sewing. Lil wasn't just the mother I wanted for me, she was the grandmother I wanted for Caroline: creative, independent, glamorous, truth telling, and traveling.

Traveling was no small part of it. I can be a little static. I am curious and I love to be a long way from home, so I have gone on adventures, to Chile, to St. Petersburg, to Tokyo, but mainly I like to build a nest/fortress and burrow down in it, sequestered. Having been assaulted in my home, I have persisted in feeling I need to hold the fort.

This train trip was a chance to be more like Lil, to honor Lil, to chase after Lil, and to connect my daughter to Lil by giving her an experience Lil had had.

And the train trip was a break from being a dutiful daughter. I, who had once believed being a motherless child a long, long way from home was the safest thing to be, was past tired of being a dutiful daughter. Lighting out for the territory, escaping Bettie and convention, felt free-y (a word I coined in *The Wind Done Gone*), felt Black cowboy, felt exactly right.

Jumping on the train (wearing an oversized white button-down, white pearls, black leggings, and flats) accompanied by my second husband, my only daughter, and her best friend, Margaret, we are following in the footsteps of Lil Hardin.

We are traveling from Chicago to San Francisco as she had traveled from Chicago to San Francisco in 1921 to play with King Oliver, traveling to Los Angeles as she had traveled to Los Angeles to record with Jimmie Rodgers. We were crisscrossing the country by train once as she had crisscrossed it over decades. I wished to see what she saw. I wanted the girls to see it, too. I stared out the train window searching for anything and everything that might look in 1999 how it had looked in 1921. I believed her break for the coast had been the making of Lil; I hoped a break for the coast would be the remaking of me.

It's big steps to board the train. It's tight quarters to navigate our way to the roomettes, but when we arrive at our roomette, I am pleasantly surprised that my little compartment has a toilet, a sink but no shower, two facing chairs when set for daylight, and two large windows.

As we leave out of Chicago, we pull through the guts of the train yard and the guts of the city. The racks are like swirling intestines moving cattle, moving stuff. Mechanical detritus, abandoned machines, half-loaded pallets, the rusting container buildings, and containers appear randomly like ulcers or polyps on the landscape. So many things to look at that are real and no kind of pretty. This train yard view of heading west is an abrupt pivot from the grand lobby of the Union Station that promised adventure without danger and romance without trouble.

I lock the door. I wash my hands and the familiar odor of Dial soap rises to swirl into the odor of the sanitizer they have used to wipe down everything—the walls, the doors, the sink. I wonder for the first time in my life if a space can be too clean.

I packed to segregate what I will need in the cities from what I will need in the roomette. My larger suitcase is down the hall. In the roomette with me are my toiletries (Dial soap bar, disposable contacts, tiny travel bottles of shampoo and conditioner, makeup base, mascara, lipstick, and a plastic bottle of blood pressure pills), a white cotton nightgown, two changes of underwear, two clean white shirts, one change of leggings, a shower dress, thick black cotton pullover, plastic shower shoes, a battery-operated cassette player, cassettes, and earphones. All of this fits into a quilted black Vera Bradley tote bag smaller than a large purse. It can sit on the toilet lid. David keeps his things in the hall. He's too fastidious to put his stuff on the toilet lid. The train whistle hoots, and we begin our westward roll.

David is in the observation car. The girls are locked into their roomette. When I pull my door open, I can hear the sounds of talk and laughter but not what they are saying. I close my door and pull out the cassette tapes that Margaret's father, a Florida-born lawyer, has made me as a thank-you for taking Margaret on the trip.

I expect a lot of it could be songs about dying; it could be songs about mamas. He knows mine worries me. It could have a lot of rock, hip-hop, or R & B—these are Cliffie's favorite genres. I'm surprised by a bouquet of travel songs, about three dozen. Three cassettes full. A quarter of a century later I remember only six: Charley Pride's "Is Anybody Goin' to

San Antone," "Return of the Grievous Angel" by Gram Parsons, "Take It Easy" by the Eagles, Simon and Garfunkel's "(We've All Gone to Look for) America," "Me and Paul" by Willie Nelson, and multiple versions of "By the Time I Get to Phoenix," including the stone Black Country O. C. Smith version.

The conductor calls, "Galesburg," and I am startled into action. Galesburg is the last stop in Illinois. We are less than an hour to Iowa and one of the big sights of the trip. Soon enough, I stand and walk the two short steps needed to lean forward and knock on the thin wall of the girls' door. When they unlock it and press it open, I announce, "We're about to cross the Mississippi River. If we keep the doors open, we can see it from both windows."

They are not so very interested. They remind me this will not be their first view of the Mississippi. This will not be the first time they crossed the river on a bridge. "We already saw it in Memphis on Double King Day," they chime. That was David and my first road trip with these two girls. We took them to Memphis to visit the National Civil Rights Museum, then Graceland.

"This is different," I say. "This time we will fly above the river on the magic carpet John Henry and Polly Ann built." They keep the doors open. They accommodate crazy.

With the twentieth century rolling out, the musicians from Memphis they need to know are Lil Hardin Armstrong and Alberta Hunter. On this train ride the most important thing about Memphis and the Mississippi River will come to be Alberta Hunter was born near it in 1895 and Lil Hardin was born near its banks three years later in 1898. I want Caroline and Margaret to imagine Lil and Alberta, fishing on the banks of the Mississippi entertaining themselves and each other by making up little songs.

I must let them know song making, the tradition of putting words together in air, is often a colored girl's first inheritance. Sometimes it's the only inheritance. Song making is an elemental art. Around the globe, people sooth newborns with sounds and words; around the globe, some people harmonically wail their grief in sound alone or with ragged words in melody. Around the world, bored children make up tunes and add words to them to amuse themselves. I imagine Lil with some of her little friends who also attended the Hooks School of Music near the banks of the Mississippi River making up tunes.

The river I see is the same dark ribbon Lil saw. The girls have thirty minutes to peer into their books, their journals, into the reflections of their own eyes in the quickly darkening mirror the windows are becoming into each other's eyes before night falls, and they seize them.

My first night on a long train, a westbound *California Zephyr*, is one of the last hot summer nights of the twentieth century. I was comfortable; my cabin was air-conditioned. When Lil rode unair-conditioned trains in the 1920s, with dust and cinders, sometimes flaming cinders, blowing in through windows kept open by necessity, summer nights could be hellishly hot. The distance from Chicago to San Francisco was far greater in the first quarter of the twentieth century than it was in the last.

When Lil set off for the first time to the West Coast, leaving family behind in Chicago, maybe a quarter of Black families had a telephone and long-distance calls and telegrams were expensive. Maps and guides were expensive, too. And the ones that existed were not written for a solo, Black, female, traveling musician who had been educated at Fisk University and likely not worth the price.

To get on the train, she had to have what she called in her most enigmatic song, "vim." An essential element of vim, for Lil, is to "break all conventions" to be an independent path blazer who is the antithesis of Polly Ann and John Henry.

With Lil's vim, you don't *work* yourself to death. You art yourself to life. When she exuberantly labels herself "lazy," she explodes the caricature of the "lazy negro." So evident is the work of her melody making and phrasemaking. "Too dark for trouble to find a way in." Darkness is safety and beauty in this song, and Black identity is sweet. She exclaims, "Chocolate gal" like it is the best thing in the world you can be, like she can be tasted but never devoured. She is in community with other brown gals, the joke is on those who laugh at Lil and the brown gals. This is Lil's cakewalk. The song seems to confirm to an established order that it in fact disrupts. For the brown gal to be seen in the bubble and remain safe in the bubble, not laboring, not dressing, for the benefit of others but for the pleasure of self is fundamentally disruptive and fundamentally nurturing to brown gal me. What is vim if not vital curiosity and bold courage, a willingness to be a path-blazer. But the blazed path needs followers. I am following Lil's path.

I am renewing my willingness to be surprised. Lil had seen the big river in Memphis, and the big lake in Chicago. And she had likely seen maps and pictures and postcards of San Francisco and possibly even the route to San Francisco. No postcard, no picture, no painting, no returned traveler's tale could have prepared her for the vastness of the Pacific. And yet she roared toward it.

One of the small surprises of the train? I am surprised to see so many automobiles from my window, surprised we see so much road from the train. Will I pass a car made by someone I once knew in Detroit?

I first met Lil in Detroit city in Mary Frances's living room. All the First Family had Detroit connections. When DeFord Bailey was in his teen years, his uncle Clark Odom went to work in Detroit and sent money back to Nashville that helped all the family he left behind, DeFord included, survive. Lil discovered Herb Jeffries in Detroit and Jeffries himself was from Detroit. His portrait hung in the Gotham Hotel. Charley Pride came out as Black to the Country audience in Detroit. Ray Charles played Detroit's famed Flame Show bar over and over again and a lot of clubs in Detroit, but it was in that living room on Parkside that I first heard about Lil, heard Ray sing, and learned that Lil not only designed for the great Louis Armstrong, she designed for Count Basie, Lucky Millinder, and Fletcher Henderson, according to my aunt Mary Frances.

I wouldn't tell my daughter that I had long imagined away Bettie, as my mother. That I'd given Lil that place in my mind. I wouldn't tell her that Ray Charles's recording of Lil Hardin's "Just for a Thrill" was proof to me that at least two other people, Lil who wrote the song, and Ray

Charles who sang the song, knew as I knew that some people hurt other people "Just for a Thrill." That's the hardest truth I know.

I've seen Bettie smile as I cried. Saw it when I was just starting to walk and fell, saw it when I was learning to ride a bike. I think my father's mother, Dear, saw it, too. For sure she took over my bike riding instruction. Saw it when I was sixteen years old and threw myself crying on the kitchen floor and banged my fist into the clean linoleum and begged her to make him stop. And she laughed and said, "Stop what?" I couldn't say the words. She repeated the question. I heard her words as a taunt. I stopped pounding, kept crying, kept looking up at her from the floor and she kept smiling. Eventually I closed my eyes and heard the tapping of her heels. When that faded out and I was alone in the kitchen I heard the loud sound of blood pounding in my ears. Ray Charles's voice came to me. Some people treated other people like toys it pleasured them to hurt, "Just for a Thrill." Lil knew this. When I had no words of my own I had Lil's, "I was . . . a toy . . . toss around . . . filled . . . with pain." What I understood for sure from that? Mama Lil was telling me and everyone listening, it was better to be Ray than the person who hurt Ray, it was better to be me than Bettie.

I was lying on a kitchen floor crying when I decided in earnest to be a professional songwriter. One day I wanted to do for somebody what Lil did for me: write a song that seemed to be about one thing, that was heard by someone else just exactly as they needed to hear it.

IOWA: MORE TRAINS, PLANES, AND AUTOMOBILES

The train makes five stops in Iowa. For our little expedition party, Iowa demands contemplation of George Washington Carver and Tuskegee Airmen. David grew up spending summers with his grandmother in Tuskegee, Alabama, spending time in the little museum, exploring the town, learning everything there is to know about George Washington Carver, and so much about the Tuskegee Airmen. Some say so many of the Tuskegee Airmen came from Iowa because farmers used small planes to tend their crops, and this gave Black people opportunities to learn to fly.

The girls are almost ready to go back to their roomette when we hit Ottumwa, Iowa. David and I are eating dessert. We try to turn the conversation back to Carver. George Washington Carver, born enslaved, earned his PhD at Iowa State. Carver left Iowa for Alabama in 1896, where he famously promoted sweet potatoes and peanuts. In 1904, Iowa State launched an initiative called "Seed Corn Gospel Trains." The idea was the train would be ridden by teachers who would give lectures to farmers gathered at railroad stations. We veer to Ottumwa. It was the hometown of two Tuskegee Airmen, William V. Bibbs and Robert W. Williams. Ottumwa is home of Black architect Archibald Alphonso Alexander, born in 1888 and who died in 1958. There's a whole lot of Black history in Ottumwa. But the girls are not that interested in it. They have never been to Tuskegee and farming is not their thing. They are into Fisk. Fisk is art. Fisk is books. Fisk is family. Black and white, Caroline and Margaret made a small film called *Road to Jubilee* about the history of Fisk. Fisk's colors are blue and yellow. They wore matching dresses in Fisk's complementary colors to perform the narration. Margaret wore yellow and white and Caroline wore blue and white.

The girls go back to their roomette. David picks up his book. I go back to the roomette. It has been transformed from a sitting room into a two-bed sleeper.

It's eleven when we hit Nebraska, Omaha. I am alone in the roomette peering into the night sky. Nat King Cole, who put out an entire Country album in 1962, *Ramblin' Rose*, wrote "Straighten Up and Fly Right" in Omaha, Nebraska. I hear "Straightin' Up and Fly Right" different beneath the wide Western sky than I hear it in the city.

In Nebraska, the song is not only an allegory for addiction—of the importance of getting the monkey off the back. Here it hides a cartoonish portrait of Black barnstorming. Looking up at the Nebraska sky I hear the monkey and the buzzard are Black folk competently flying through the air—with appropriate coaching—to straighten up and fly right. Coaching the present beating of addiction by flashing past Black agency is pure Nat King Cole Black Country genius. Nat roots the ability to kick the fly-high of cocaine or the fly-low of heroin to a different and earlier kind of Black flying and competence, to the rare but real Black aviators who wowed the brown farm children of the West and who, starting in 1941, were wowing Southern brown children. From 1941 to 1946, about one thousand Black airmen were trained in Tuskegee, Alabama, less than forty miles from where Nat King Cole was born in Montgomery, Alabama. He wrote "Straighten Up and Fly Right" all by himself in an Omaha, Nebraska, hotel in 1943.

But "Straighten Up and Fly Right" is not the Nat King Cole song I am humming as I lay in my bunk stiff as a board in a roomette that feels in the sheltering dark like a welcoming-tomb. I'm humming "Twilight on the Trail," a song from Nat's Country album that celebrates approaching death being as beautiful as approaching night. The end of a life as natural as the end of the day. On Nat's Country album, he delivers a salute to rural Black women's independence, "Ramblin' Rose," a transgressive "Wolverton Mountain," and a heartbreaking "He'll Have to Go." He puts the Black cowboy in jeans, on a horse, by a stream, meditating on a contented solitary rural death and burial. Nat's cowboy anticipates, with languid joy, being buried beneath a lonesome pine after a time of sky as ceiling and earth as floor.

I wiggle in my bed no longer stiff. The train is rocking me to sleep like Mary Frances rocked me to sleep. I wake up in the middle of the night in the middle of the dark. Me and Nat let ourselves get robbed. I am almost as bad about money as I am good about bodies.

I am not financially insolvent, I still have some little money in the bank, and some little money coming in, but I had let myself get big-time robbed. The "let myself" part was the killing kick that was breaking me as my mother lay dying.

REDEMPTION REMEMBERED IN THE BLACK NORTHWEST

We're still rolling through Nebraska. So many acres, so much news not told. News of Black fathers and mothers who audaciously sought their

160 acres of land, though people tried to convince them it would be impossible for them to homestead. People who read a Black newspaper published in Nebraska, sometimes arriving by train. People who got the news slow that the first world war had come but sent sons to fight in it. People who heard the second world war had come, fast, on the radio, and sent sons to fight in that while their daughters marched in Black Nebraska beauty pageants, and other lovely young Black women gracefully danced with brown soldiers. All these people knew John Henry songs. So many of them or their grandchildren listened to DeFord Bailey on the radio, listened to Lil Hardin on the radio. On this train we are riding through a Black, Western, and often invisible audience.

Waking up when the train stops and stays stopped in Denver, I hear the chattering of girls just outside my door. They are on their way to breakfast. They are not joining David on a quick jaunt into the station.

I face the public shower. It's tiny and clean. I am in a cloud of jasmine and almond steam. It's a good thing I wanted to wash my hair. The shower is so small there is no way, as short as I am, not to be hair-soaked. Soon I am thinking about another shower.

The shower in the little pink townhouse. The glass-doored, quick-to-fog shower at 3047 Woodlawn was my gold mine. It had some kind of magical power to launch me toward new ideas and new feelings.

I was in that shower when the words that would be the seeds of "XXX's and OOO's" came to me, "You've got a picture of your mama in heels and pearls and you're trying to make it in your daddy's world, that won't work kid, that won't work." It was in the shower where I realized that my favorite Country songwriter, a man who was trying to woo me with his sound, was what happened to his ruin of a brilliant wife. We were at the Bluebird, sitting in the pews and listening to Townes Van Zandt. We were holding hands. And I leaned in to take a sip from his glass, and he pulled the glass in closer to his heart and shook his head to indicate *No.* "I don't want what happened to her to happen to you." I stared at him and debated, sober, whether I should tell him what I had already figured out in the shower. I remembered that he often told me, "Love is largely a matter of paying attention." I was paying attention. "You're what happened to her." And he said to me, "I'm not counting on you not to tell this, I'm counting on you to tell it true." He desperately wanted a witness, a third chance, a bite of feminine strength that didn't rage, a chance to repay old debts, a way to restore to me what was stolen. It was a cocktail of arrogance, insight, and innovation that led him to love me as I wanted to be loved, with all my boundaries respected—passionately present yet withholding what he wanted, the only thing he would *call* making love, the man's sex in the woman's sex. But he embodied other silent and profound engagements. He washed me clean with his tongue. Every inch of me. With courage and curiosity, he claimed every inch of me, every humor that could rise from me in me. He told me with touch everything feminine, everything human, everything living spoke to all his senses. Nothing about a woman he loved disgusted him. That is how I knew I was a woman he loved. My shit didn't stink. My rejection didn't sting. He treated my rigidities, my fears, my rules, and the ghosts in my body like elements of an art form. Your flesh is unsoiled and un-soilable was his main idea—you are worth more than rubies was the volta of our visceral song, and so it was, in his office, in my shower on Woodlawn, in the shower on the train in memory.

In the dark, when Music Row was quiet, and there was a demilune window with a moon rising in it, he took all the rules that emerged from my fears for my body and my reputation—my history of violence and violation—and he found an honest way to be mother and lover for me all at once, that transformed me all at once and forever.

My father had promised I could always come home. My troubadour sang me into the twinned discovery that I was ready for adventuring into the wide and wild world. If I was in my grown woman body, I was in my grown woman home. And I got to decide who entered it.

Now, I knew about home invasion robberies of the literal and metaphoric sort. This discovery was of the everyday metaphorical truth—I got to decide who entered the house of me. Invitations were required. Invitations were not inevitable. Invitations were sought after. Invitations were not likely to be forthcoming.

As I had once told my father, I don't want to talk about it, and eventually made my father the person with whom I could talk about anything. I had told my Texas poet, after the death of my first marriage, I didn't want to fuck, and he turned to what he liked to think of as a vast vocabulary of acts of love and recalled, then performed one I had not previously imagined. It involved no pain. It was at once infantile and adult, it was at once self and other and self exactly like other. All it required of me was a willingness to be found, noticed, adored, respected, pleasured, and attended to with care, curiosity, and creativity. He knew this. He had a righteously wicked grown-ass smile. After he licked me clean. He delighted me. He swallowed all of our sin. He washed his mouth clean with hard liquor and water and allowed himself to be delighted by my appreciation of his respect for my phobias, which he eclipsed with gestures of most imaginative eros. I allowed myself to be surprised by joy. With bold sensuality he made a safe poem of pleasure. My body as a taste on his tongue was the story of my flesh unsoiled and un-soilable. Unwilling as I was to rock him like my back had no bone, to spread my thighs and invite him to push into me, he made a feast for us both out of featherlight flickers that caught a kind of star-fire that illumines but does not consume. That is what his loving taught me. The fire that reveals but does not destroy. The heat that brings bloom but not dust. I wrote a song for him that he loved that he made me promise not to share. All I recall of it is a fragment, "altar of desire." Desire unrequited in the expected ways became love reunited in unexpected ways. There was a moment when each of us saw ourselves wholly new and grown in the other's eyes and saw next that the other was wholly different and foreign and strange—was simply the place for one moment. We saw across the greatest distance and clearly. Life is lived among people with whom you share common sins and common strengths. Heaven on earth is made, sometimes, by uniting across the great divide.

I washed away all the traces of my favorite baptism, that is what I came to think of that night as. I was the Afro and he was the Celtic, and there was definitely some Evangelical Christianity all mixed up in our fishing in the dark.

I got out of the train shower. Dried my body and dried my hair and went looking for coffee, my one addiction.

The train climbs into the foothills of the Rocky Mountains and stretching out before us is a patchwork of various greens—grass green, evergreen green, leafy tree green, shrub green. Outcrops of rock appear in no discernable patterns, all irregularly placed and spaced, without rhyme or reason, a massive and majestic chaos. Undulating curves. Spatters of shadow. Patches of lusher soil. This is not pretty. This is shocking beauty. My brain breaks. My brain turns off and on, stops and starts, and each time it turns back on it is slightly different. This is what Lil saw.

It's six and a half hours from Denver to Glenwood Springs. We move from the foothills to the front range of the Rocky Mountains. We go through the Rockies, not around them. Twenty-six tunnels in twenty-five miles. Twenty-six chances to learn the mouth of a tunnel is a violated orifice of an inviolable mountain. Blasted and pierced, the Rockies rise with all their beauty.

I note the hiss of brakes. That hissing worries me. Will the brakes hold? But the train flashes daylight and then dark, flashes, now and then, and both beckon me. The hardest memories contain discarded pieces of me. The white water of the Colorado reminds me of a white-water rafting trip in West Virginia where a man raped me the morning of the most dramatic falls. I abandoned my love of paddling on that trip and retrieved it on this. I will paddle again, I promise myself rolling beside the Colorado. Deer. Elk. The river. And people on it. Shiny white asses mooning us. Salmon over Caesar salad for lunch and again for dinner. A tree growing in a rock. And another. They shock and awe. I spend most of the second day in the observation car. But not all of it.

I sequestered myself in my roomette for the Moffat Tunnel. The conductor had issued a warning. You will not be able to travel between cars in the tunnel. Chinese railroad workers built fifteen train tunnels using handheld hammer drills, pickaxes, and explosives through the Sierra Nevada mountains. The air is noxious now. What must it have been then?

We enter the Moffat Tunnel and ride almost a quarter hour through the belly of the mountain. It is a kind of death. It is a kind of walking through hell. It is a kind of waking, blank rest.

VINDICATION, PLAIN BUT NOT SIMPLE

Nobody ever had to tell me I didn't let myself get raped. When I was just fifteen years old, I knew how hard I fought back. With words: screaming "No!" whimpering, "I don't want this," with gestures, vomiting on his stomach; with acts, refusing to speak, escaping to study in London, and with invisible imaginings.

I have laughed out loud and let the monster think he had delighted me, when I was laughing about imagining he was collapsing on my young breast dead not spent. Imagining a female God who exploded his heart sometime, burst an aneurism, as he burst my hymen.

Half a century ago, back in 1974, every move I made had the intention of shaming and eclipsing every move he made. On the anniversary of my rape, I gave him a literal cake I purchased at the bakery. I don't know exactly how the gesture worked, but I know the gesture worked.

He was terrified. Bewildered. Confused. Repulsed. By me and by himself. For a week he didn't come near me. When I handed him the cake, he understood I was rewarding a performance I found comical. This was the first devastation. And this was the second: the cake told him I was still a girl, eager for a simple sweet sixteen party, hungry for frosted cake, over-sweetened punch, and gentle generous kisses. This reinforced the first devastation. I was not a woman wanting an edgy cocktail of domination and submission, of pleasure and pain. The menu he had offered.

I wanted kind and good and pretty and he wasn't any of that. The cake told him that. And it told him this final thing—I had a dangerous imagination. I had imagined an event he had not anticipated. Imagination allowed me to evade and confound them. I had not allowed myself to be raped. And no one has ever been able to convince me otherwise.

I did not allow myself to be raped but I allowed myself to be robbed because I had been raped. Because I had to work my way through an immense theft, I didn't even begin to know how to deal with a large theft.

We emerge from the tunnel. The bright makes me squint. The thing I wanted to be over, I want to do again. This is new for me. The trip has a trippy way of decentering familiar habits of my mind. For the first few seconds after I emerge, light is something I taste, feel, smell, touch, and see. Breathe and watch are a single braided act, air and light, a single swirl of energy.

Green Canyons. Pale Gray Canyons. Red rock canyons. Slate green river with white froth. Evergreens. So much curve. We are on the train and see the train ahead of us. Near Helper there's a swirling dark foothill. Open plain.

At a time when so much of my reality is so impossibly hard, I want to die or lose myself completely in alienated imaginings; the view outside my window shouts: staggering beauty is reality, too. Colorado into Utah, staggering beauty.

We reached Green River, Utah, in the afternoon, and we are due to reach Salt Lake City about midnight. Utah is the only state in the nation that over half the people belong to the same religion, Mormonism. Green Flake, Hark Lay, and Oscar Crosby, enslaved Black men traveling with Brigham Young, were the forward scouts who, alone, blazed the path for Mormons to make their way through the canyons. And there were free Blacks who came with Young as well, the James Family, the Abel Family, and the Sion family. Sion was a shoemaker. Early in the life of the church Blacks were not denied priesthood. Not all Blacks who came to Utah came with the Mormon church. Some were drawn to Utah by the railroad, to be porters or waiters, or created businesses that served the

Black railroad folk with their steady paychecks. In Ogden, Utah, Velma McHenry, a Black woman, opened the Wonder Coffee Shop on what was called Two Bit Street in the late 1930s. She served steaks and what she called "Southern-style fried chicken." In Salt Lake City there was a Black trapper, James P. Beckwourth, who worked Salt Lake City. These Black people lived, loved, worked, danced, and sang on the Western frontier, in the shadows of snowcapped mountains.

On our third day we hit Reno, Nevada, at breakfast. I had the French toast. I think they called it Railroad Toast. It's our third stop in Nevada. I have slept through the first two but have eyes wide open in the berth about the time we hit Winnemucca just after sunrise, which in early August comes just before 6:00 a.m. in this part of Nevada. An hour out of Reno we roll by Truckee, a picturesque gold rush town with a one- and two-story main street. The porter tells us that Truckee means "everything is alright" and I think to myself that is the strangest possible name for a town so near the Donner Pass, where people ate other people when they were isolated in a blizzard. But Lake Donner is seal-sleek in the shadow of the Sierra Nevada. Behind it are mountains where people ski in the winter. Donner Pass in August is an immense blue lake ringed by tall Jeffrey pines and gnarly Sierra junipers. Everything green. Nothing shrouded in cold white snow. Mercy rises with the tall pines. Later that day we will roll beside the Pacific River. Lake. Ocean. Everything is alright. River. Lake. Ocean. *Copacetic.* That would be Lil's word for that. Copacetic.

We disembarked the *California Zephyr* at Emeryville in the late afternoon and took a taxi into San Francisco. When we arrive at our destination, the Fairmont Hotel, it is in scaffolding.

THE POINTERS, THE PANTHERS, THE BARBARY COAST

I had debated staying at the St. Francis and chosen the Fairmont. Had to. It was the first old-line San Francisco hotel to welcome, starting in 1947, Black guests. The first to say anyone good enough to perform in the hotel was good enough to stay in the hotel. We eat in the Tonga Room surrounded by bamboo and steamed dumplings. I drink a strong sweet tiki drink, still wondering if we should have stayed at the St. Francis. In the early sixties, when Louis Armstrong was in San Francisco trying to make an opera about the civil rights movement, he stayed at the St. Francis, even if all the work was done at the Fairmont. But that's not the full reason, the full reason is the Tonga Room celebrates Buffalo soldiers who went all the way to Hawaii and played music there. And the steel guitar that puts some of the African-bent into Country was invented in Hawaii by a man who started playing his guitar with a railroad spike. It took me three of those drinks to get to that, but I did. Lil wasn't invited when Louis came to San Fran to make that big opera. But Lil had gotten there first.

There is a dazzling photograph of Lil surrounded by members of King Oliver's Band in San Francisco. It's from 1921. Lil's wearing a light-colored dress, bobbed hair, and dark stockings. A hand is held to her ear or cheek. She doesn't have an instrument. It is almost as if she is being serenaded by the horns, the stand-up bass, and the fiddle. She looks fresh, clean, and young. Almost too young to have come to San Francisco to play with King Oliver in the ocean-front neighborhood known as the Barbary Coast.

Established in the mid-nineteenth century, the Barbary Coast was known as a "Sin City" providing the live music, dance halls, pool halls, gambling dens, and brothels known for having a raw, wild-West edge. When Lil arrived, the glory days of the coast were coming to an end. The Barbary Coast survived the 1906 earthquake, barely missing a day of servicing customers. It shut down a decade later, when a minister and a newspaper colluded to destroy the neighborhood by waging a war on pleasure that included a prohibition on dancing that led to the silencing of live music.

When Lil arrived, Sid LeProtti was *the* Black piano player in the Barbary Coast. Lil and Sid had a lot in common besides playing piano. I have wondered if he was an inspiration for Lil. LeProtti worked every kind of side hustle, from piano demonstrator to shoe shiner, to keep the music going. Lil would work side hustles from demonstrating sheet music to sewing stage costumes for others.

When King Oliver sat in with LeProtti, Lil would have been there. LeProtti performed at a club on Pacific Avenue called the So Different Café. His spot was Lil's introduction to the coast. The joint was established in 1907 by Lou Purcell and Sam King, two former Pullman porters. Pullman porters were uniformed valets who worked on overnight trains and organized one of America's first and most powerful Black labor unions. So much Black musical culture springs from the train.

I don't want to tell the girls about the Barbary Coast. I want to tell them about the Pointer Sisters. Margaret's father has put a hippy-rock classic, "San Francisco," on the cassette he made for me. That song and just being in the Bay Area puts the Pointers on my mind.

The Pointer Sisters—Anita, Bonnie, Ruth, and June—are arguably the first most publicly visible embodiments of Hippy Black Country. They sang with big silk yellow and pink roses in their hair that nodded to the counter-culture revolutionaries who headed the instruction, "If you go to San Francisco, be sure to wear some flowers in your hair," and Black church lady roses. One also wore a giant Afro, a crown of Black power.

When Pointers traveled to San Francisco it was a quick trip across the water. They hail from Oakland, where their father and mother pastored a church, where the Black Panther Party was born in 1966. All the Pointers were born in the Bay Area, Anita in 1948, Bonnie in 1950, Ruth in 1946, and June in 1953.

Anita Pointer typically introduced "Fairytale"—the hit Country song she co-wrote with her sister Bonnie, the song that became a smash hit for both the Pointer Sisters and later for Elvis Presley—with the confession: she liked Country Music.

Over the many years the Pointers performed "Fairytale," they converted others who looked like them to an appreciation of Country Music that might compel them to make the same confession. And they shocked thousands who didn't believe that anyone who looked like the beautiful and brown Pointers could appreciate Country Music, let alone write Country and perform it magnificently.

But they could. After the Pointer Sisters performed "Fairytale" wearing their trademark silk roses in their hair and vintage thrift store dresses on their tall, lean, brown bodies, they were typically met with applause from their audience.

Before their performance was different. When they showed up to play the Opry they saw ignorant signs reading "Keep Country, Country!" Like Black wasn't Country. They had shows that started with audience members cursing in disbelief when they realized the women who sang "Fairytale" were Black.

In 1974, the Pointer Sisters won a Grammy for Best Country Performance by a Duo or a Group for their performance of "Fairytale." To win the category, they beat out Kris Kristofferson and Rita Coolidge, Bobby Bare, and Willie Nelson and Tracy Nelson. No small achievement. Yet in the highlights of the year that appear on the Grammy website, as I write these words, no mention is made of the Pointers' historic win.

I, Mari-Alice Randall, sang along to "Fairytale" on the radio before Elvis covered it. Anita Pointer would have made a great character to dress up as for Halloween, pin a big silk flower in the hair, don a cut-down vintage dress, hold up a spray-painted Grammy. That's something I want little girls to know.

Every second of "Fairytale," starting with that recitation that claims Black affection for Country and Black ability to create Country, strikes me strong. It was the song in my mind when I left Country Music. My theme song. Strongest in the moment of disillusionment. To quote Ms. Pointer, "something's wrong . . . nothing . . . get better if I stayed . . ." After being "used" and "deceived" it's time to "move on." Time to wake up, after being "lost in a dream." Time to grow up past the "fairytale" of believing the twentieth-century Country Music industry cared anything about any Black female creatives.

A few years after we ride the trains, David and I will dance at the Swan Ball in Nashville to the Pointer Sisters.

THE *COAST STARLIGHT*, RIDING A SPINE OF THE PACIFIC, TO THE CITY OF ANGELS

We boarded the *Coast Starlight* at about 9:00 a.m. in Oakland and notice that it is a fancier train, serving fancier people, fancier wine, in fancier chairs than the *California Zephyr.*

The scenery is different, in rapid turns tamed, exotic, mildly alarming, and wild. Agricultural fields. Rows of cultivated green are followed by flats of mud and water that give way to our first palm trees. We pass through an edge of Vandenberg Air Force Base, now home of America's Space Force, and there are signs that read "No photography" and "Controlled Area." But all we see are sweeping dunes and shoreline and wild horses. The base, so wild, so empty, has a surreal dawn-of-creation beauty, and a surreal beginning-of-the-apocalypse feel—people on the train are whispering, "If space aliens attack, our counterattack will launch above these dunes."

With the Pacific Ocean on our right and the Santa Ynez Mountains in the distance on our left, closer to us we see familiar-to-Southern eyes: live oak, pines, and cypresses, and we are thrilled by the unfamiliar eucalyptus trees, the dunes, the wild horses.

Just for the thrill of it, I will show you beauty. I have rewritten Lil's song.

Over the best train dinner we will have on this trip, I regale the girls with stories of climbing under, over, and between barb wire near and in Palo Duro Canyon, researching the life of Britt Johnson, with J. C. Crowley collaborator on my almost-got-made Black western.

This story gives an answer to something that has been puzzling my daughter, "So that's why there are cow skull bones in our living room!" The bones are signs of life, not death. We laugh in shared knowledge and relief.

We disembark the *Coast Starlight* about 9:00 p.m. In the dark that veils Los Angeles Union Station, we walk as quickly as we can, rolling and toting luggage toward the bright lights of the big city.

The day brings a strut down the Santa Monica Pier followed by lunch at my favorite shabby chic Black Hollywood power hang, Ivy at the Shore.

For Caroline, Los Angeles is where I went when I left her. She drew a picture of me entitled *Miss Black Is Back from Hollywood.* The title screamed how often I was away. I wanted that portrait to be called *Mama Home in Nashville.* It wasn't. Once when she was mad at me she threw her little backpack on one little shoulder like I would throw on a purse and she opened the door and said, "I'm going to work!" She said it like she heard it, as "I hate you," not like I meant it, "I am so sorry to be leaving you, but I need to make money for us and I am going to try to sound extra cheerful, even if I end up sounding extra brittle, so you won't be sad."

Running from my daughter's sad, I made her angry. Then she projected her anger on me. And so, we remember the moment completely differently, completely honestly. Multiple meanings of a singular text. The best thing, for me, about Los Angeles is Lil, and in this moment even Lil is not enough.

I am ready to start heading eastbound back to Chicago.

And I am starting to think of myself as a railroad woman. It's not all the hours on the train. It's the shape shifting, identity shifting, and code switching. It's the embrace of multiple realities.

Listening to "Railroad Man," written and performed by the great Bill Withers, hundreds of times helped me get to that. I come over time to appreciate Withers as a psychologist who explained something important about life to me, as a critic who makes real to me DeFord Bailey's genius, and as a major Country artist, the Black son of a Black West Virginia coal miner, who was never publicly lauded when he slipped into Country identity.

"Railroad Man" begins with a question within a recitation. Bill Withers enquires if the listener ever lived near a train. Then he describes growing up in West Virginia living by the railroad track. He would stand alone by the train tracks. Listening to the music the train made he would start improvising by rhythmically throwing gravel to add to the train music. I guess next he added melody and lyrics because he says in the recitation he started making up songs. I learned to write Country songs in a Motown cherry tree; Withers learned to write them standing by the Slab Fork, West Virginia, train tracks.

Withers, by narrating his own lived proximity to a train, affirms Big Avon's truth that DeFord's audience wasn't interested in an imitation of a train's sound. He didn't need an imitation train sound, he had a real one. They wanted the effect of a train in sound. They wanted music that transported them away from their present confinement. But Withers also noticed something bigger. Trains allow us to shift identities ". . . change . . . name . . . every place he came . . ."

I hear the ghost of King Oliver, walking through "Railroad Man." The reference to "hauling bananas to Savannah" gets me there. Oliver was the man who led the band that got Lil to San Francisco for the first time. A man who recorded "Frisco Train Blues." His birth name was Joseph Nathan Oliver but jazz greats called him King. Sometime after the stock market crashed in 1929 and King Oliver's bank closed taking his entire life savings, sometime after he had lost all of his teeth, sometime after his bus broke down in Spartanburg, South Carolina, in 1937, King Oliver found himself living in Savannah selling fruit and cleaning a pool hall. He had come to believe the world had come to see his jazz as "old-fashioned, not sophisticated. Not where it was at." He had bad luck with busses, they blew up on him. He was a railroad man.

Louis Armstrong and some of his band members ran into King Oliver outside of a Savannah pharmacy. Louis came across the broke King and he sprang to action: "Got his suits out of the pawnshop . . . He was sharp like Joe of 1915 . . . He looked beautiful." He looked like the man who strode through San Francisco's Barbary Coast with Lil. And he looked like someone who was destroyed by what created him. Looked like someone who might want to step in front of the train like the railroad man does at the end of Withers's song and go out back on top.

We're back in the Los Angeles train station. We are walking through a train station where all the First Family of Black Country has been present walking or their voice or their sounds pouring through the radio. Lil, Ray, Charley, Herb, they walked through this train station.

A TRAIN WHOSE NAME SHOULD BE CHANGED

The *Southwest Chief* that pulled out of L.A. about six in the evening is due to arrive in Albuquerque just before lunch the next day, but we're running late.

There's time before we leave the vicinity of Los Angeles to mention one last longtime Los Angeleno, Arna Bontemps—the poet, librarian, and Caroline's great-grandfather. I should have been talking about him all the while we were in L.A. Arna was born in Louisiana in 1902 but he lived for good little while growing up in rural Los Angeles. He captured his now largely forgotten rural Black Los Angeles neighborhood in his novel *God Sends Sunday*, describing it as a place of cows, guinea hens, dusty tracks and wagons. If it wasn't for Arna, I wouldn't know about Nat Love. And boarding that eastbound *Southwest Chief*, I am thinking about Nat Love, a Black cowboy who evolved into a Pullman porter, then wrote and published the story of his transformation as a book-length memoir, *The Life and Adventures of Nat Love Better Known in the Cattle Country as "Deadwood Dick."*

There is a close and abiding connection between the cowboy and the entertainment community, and that connection was the Pullman porter. Many Black cowboys including Nat Love became Pullman porters when they stopped riding the rails. Because show people, singers, dancers, actors, spent so much time traveling on trains from place to place, they got to know lots of former Black cowboys, hear old Black cowboy stories, and hear old Black cowboy songs. Oscar Micheaux, the Black director known for *Within Our Gates* and *The Homesteader,* was another luminary who got his start as a Pullman porter. I let the girls know: the attendants working this train work as part of a long line of Black audacity all dressed up to look like something else. They get it. And the train gets underway.

NAT LOVE, COWBOY, PORTER, MEMOIRIST

After the *California Zephyr* and the *Coast Starlight*, the first miles of the *Southwest Chief* disappoint. The industrial detritus of train yard after train yard no longer excites. Containers, warehouses waiting to be loaded are less interesting each time you see another one. We get to Fullerton Station, and it is a pretty adobe building, and that is pleasant. Our new roomettes are comfortably familiar and fresh to us—another pleasance. We will move across California, into Arizona, and from Arizona into New Mexico.

I'm jonesing for a jolt of beauty and more train coffee. Seated in the chair that will fold into my bed, the view out my window is flashes of half grim, followed by more half grim. I sip on a bottle of water.

The setting changes, the land stretches, not quite flat, but almost flat and gently undulating. The flick-past power lines start looking like crosses in the stark rising dark. Smokestacks puff dramatic plumes of smoke that become a welcoming feather in the sky. Plumes wave, beckon, greet. Yep, the trip is still trippy.

We hit Winslow, Arizona, at sunrise. The land is flat and golden, vast: it is green and shrubby. There are mesas, and buttes, and the red rock rises, trumpeting color, a visual hymn. This red rock land satisfies and challenges. This is the thick of it. Red-striped buttes and mesas juxtaposed to industrial plants. There is a choice to be made. Focus on the ruby, blood, poppy, earth, red, rock, or be distracted by chemical storage tanks at their base? I focus on the rock. Naked rock face. Roof tops. People live near these train tracks. Billboards. More scary tanks, this time gleaming white and bulbous. And more of the streaked rock beauty. Now, fields brown from hot summer.

The porter knocks. He brings coffee. He wants to know what time we want to eat dinner. I don't tell him I'm on my way to Albuquerque chasing a Pullman porter. He closes the door. I settle back into listening to my cassettes and gazing out the window. I am now chasing a Pullman porter, Nat Love.

While I am working on this book, I will spend time with Joe Wooten, who has been traveling the world as "hands of soul" in the Steve Miller Band, since shortly after he arrived in Nashville to sing demos for me.

He tells me after the *Mother Dixie* sessions, whenever he would run into the singer Scat Springs, Scat would sing out loud, "Back before law and order he rode the western range . . ." And Joe would sing back, "Now he's a Pullman porter on an eastbound train."

They were trading lines from "The Ballad of Nat Love" recorded as part of the never released *Mother Dixie* project.

"We did that for the thirty plus years we knew each other . . . before and after Scat was sick," Joe said. "The last time we saw each other, we sang at it, even when his voice could no longer reach the old notes."

I was intrigued. Scat had sung on hundreds of demos and dozens upon dozens of master sessions. I had handed Scat a typed lyric sheet of "The Ballad of Nat Love" when he had arrived at the session and seized it back to maintain confidentiality of the project at the end of the session. Scat was never given a tape of the recording—yet he remembered *all* the words to the song about a Black man born enslaved in Tennessee who grew up to be a Black cowboy. And he pushed those words out into the air of the Nashville music world time after time, decade after decade. I didn't know that Scat and Joe had that ritual, but maybe I knew, "Why?"

On a farm that rolled right to the edge of the Cumberland River, we had a conversation that gave me a clue. We had both been invited to the same Christmas party. It was December, I think of 2017. Scat leaned his head toward mine and sang *all the lyrics* of "The Ballad of Nat Love" a cappella quietly into my ear. Then he told me how much it meant to him "*to sing proof*" that many cowboys were Black. He thanked me for writing a song that translated the autobiography Nat Love had written into a biography Scat could sing and share with a wide world that needed to know about the existence of Black cowboys.

Scatt's day job and other calling was educator. As an educator, working in public schools and Sunday schools, he understood the importance of role models, As a son, a father, and a musician himself, the song was more intimately useful. He needed the Country Music world to know about the existence of Black cowboys.

Scat had a lot of Black skin in the Country Music game. Not only did he come from the region the mainstream Country Music industry claims as Country's birthplace, East Tennessee, Scat's father, Kenny Springs, was a Black man who had left a significant but ignored mark on Country Music. Kenny had ventured to Nashville and cut two remarkable Country sides, "Just Walkin'," and "Please Tell Me Now," when Scat was small. In his turn and time, Scat would perform and record with Country greats including Faith Hill, Hank Williams, Jr., Vince Gill, and Garth Brooks.

Scat and his daddy both had connection to my First Family of Black Country. Scat followed in DeFord's footsteps and record a political jingle for Avon N. Williams.

His daddy shared a stage with the most brilliant Black Country performer of all time—Ray Charles. And this is the kicker about why Nat Love meant so much to Scat. His daddy opened for Ray Charles in Knoxville July 28, 1963. That was just a year after the release of *Modern Sounds in Country and Western Music.*

"The Ballad of Nat Love" was important to Scat, a second generation Black Country musician, because it announces in rhythm and rhyme the debt Country owes to a specific group of Black men: the Black cowboys of Texas and New Mexico—including Nat Love—who put the ". . . and Western" in the original name of the genre.

When you realize just how many cowboys of the nineteenth-century American West were Black you come to a new understanding of how essential Black people have been to the evolution of the genre. Scat wanted Nashville to have that new understanding in no small part because he thought it would improve working conditions for his daughters who were emerging as musicians in Nashville. Kandace had released her first album in 2016. Kimber and Kenya would soon be coming along.

It was past time, Scat conveyed at that Christmas party, for some of the walls his father had faced, he had faced, I had faced, to come tumbling down. The way Scat sang "The Ballad of Nat Love" around Nashville reminds me of Joshua walking around Jericho blowing that horn.

When I was pregnant with Caroline, after being medically evacuated from the Philippines, I lived in Nashville with my husband's grandmother. Sleeping in Bontemps's library I discovered his copy of the book *Negro Cowboys* that led me to writing "The Ballad of Nat Love" and other grounded in specific history cowboy songs in the late eighties and early nineties. And there were some more mythic, less specific, cowboy song co-writes before that.

By the time I got on the train, I had completed, with the support of various collaborators, a five-suite Black Country horse opera featuring Nat Love and other Black cowpokes, female and male, "Girls Ride Horses, Too," "Went for a Ride," "Get the Hell Out of Dodge," "Solitary Hero," and "The Ballad of Nat Love."

THE ORIGINAL SINGING COWBOYS WERE BLACK

The *Southwest Chief* rolls right through the city of Albuquerque. We glide past modest but tall chain hotels. The Albuquerque train station is designed in the Spanish mission style, a nod to the founding of the town of Albuquerque in 1706. Caroline wants a souvenir. When the train pulls into the station she gets off. She comes back with a necklace with a bear made of turquoise and other local stone. It has been decades since she last wore it, but it's still in her jewelry box.

Santa Fe is sixty-four miles north and east of Albuquerque. A pang of guilt strikes me rolling near Santa Fe. About a year after I divorced her father we celebrated Christmas in Santa Fe with friends. She went sledding and skinned her nose and strangers teased her about looking like Rudolph. I had passionate negative feelings about any failure to protect my child. She handled the red nose well. I was distracted to the point I took it as a sign it was time for me to start some intensive therapy. If Caroline had not gotten hurt on the sled I might have found my way to the archive in Santa Fe two decades earlier. But I needed to be near her, more than

I needed the proof. And, ironically, it was wanting to be near her again, and traveling with the same friends we had traveled with that Christmas in the 1990s that finally got me to the archive.

I return to Santa Fe in 2022 to see Caroline and Rhiannon perform in a ballet they have collaborated in co-creating. This time I made a pilgrimage to the Fray Angélico Chávez History Library. There is a book I have heard about and read about, even perused edited versions of, but never touched. A book it is time for me to see. The Monday morning after a Sunday night performance of *Lucy Negro, Redux* (a kind of global Black Country ballet), I held a small leather-bound red booklet embossed with gold, *Songs of the Cowboys.*

Privately published in 1907, in a limited edition of two thousand copies, *Songs of the Cowboys* by Jack Thorp is widely acknowledged as the first-known collection of cowboy songs. In 1921, Houghton-Mifflin published an expanded version of Thorp's original book.

With both the 1907 and 1921 edition of *Songs of the Cowboys* now in the public domain, reprinting and expanding *Songs of the Cowboys* has become a cottage industry. There are dozens of versions of the work. Many of the versions have illustrated covers including versions with one cowboy on a horse and versions with two cowboys holding instruments. There are photographs of cowboys and paintings of cowboys. All the versions depict white cowboys.

If this could not be further than Jack Thorp's truth, blame it on Thorp's pejorative and vicious namings—and the movies. The first feature length American Western, *The Great Train Robbery,* was released in 1903, six years before Thorp's original fragile red volume that did not include illustrations. All the cowboys in the film are white. Singing cowboy films, also known as horse operas, in the entertainment press, became a mainstay of Hollywood in the 1930s. On the silver screen the cowboys were all white.

Inside the red covers of Thorp's book we find a different West.

Blackness (creativity, spirituality, and pain) was present in the little red volume: in the word "Nig"; in the name Nig Add; in the phrase "Old

Nigger"; in the word "Nigger"; in the word "hoodoo." In the observation, and the music started "windin' and wailin' like . . . haints had come to cast their hoodoo on the cowboy New Year's dance." Black musical influence was present in the described instrumentation of fiddle, guitar, and banjo.

The songs of Thorp's cowboys were the songs of Black, brown, and white cowboys and they were streaked through with the colors of Africa, the British Isles, and the wide Western skies.

I have found online the *Atlantic* magazine article where Thorp told his version of the whole story of his first close encounter with "Nigger Add" in March of 1889. It included this description:

> *Add . . . was the L.F.D. outfit's range boss, and worked South Texas colored hands almost entirely. Black though he was, Add was one of the best hands on the Pecos River, well, well liked, and in due time the hero of a cowboy song himself.*

In another place in the same article (published in August of 1940) Thorp reported asking one of the cowboys for the name of the singer who had been singing. He was told it was "Lasses, a Negro cowboy."

Lasses, according to Thorp, only knew two verses of the song he was singing. Thorp states that one of the challenges he had collecting cowboy songs was he would pick up two verses one place and two verses another, that the cowboys who could sing never remembered them all.

Or perhaps these Black Texas men didn't want to share their songs with an unfamiliar and unknown white man who grew up in Newport and New York City, the son of a wealthy banker, and learned to ride horses playing polo?

Something about Scat remembering every word of my song about Nat Love makes me wonder if the Black cowboys were not holding out on the interloper with so little skin in the cowboy game and none of it looking like theirs.

Thorp showed up, unexpected and uninvited. He asked a cowboy who was very likely to be exhausted (the men were out working) to sing *again* the song he had just sung. Thorp was lucky he heard any verses at all. I'll give the polo player this, he sang his Black cowboy hosts a song. In Nashville songwriters sit in a circle passing a single guitar that is pulled around the circle. The thing about a guitar pull is not the guitar. It's about taking turns being performer and audience. Back in 1899 on the Pecos River, Jack Thorp and Addison Jones and a few of his men had a guitar pull.

Addison Jones was the full name of the person Thorp referred to as "Nig Add." Jones worked the Littlefield Ranch and was considered to be one of the best "toppers"—people who could ride a wild bucking bronco in the West—and a fine cowboy singer and song collector.

Jack wasn't the very best audience. In the *Atlantic* article he mentions a song about a "colored girl named Mamie." But he didn't take care to remember the rest of the lyrics. The song about "the colored girl named Mamie" gets lost. Some cowboy songs celebrated colored girls, Black girls, Negro girls. That's the kind of thing that Scat wanted Music Row to know.

More importantly, I believe it is a thing he would have wanted Black women to know, would want his mama and his daughters to know. And the preacher in him, Scat was an ordained Baptist preacher, would have wanted everybody to know this.

Cowboy songs existed in a world that is not secular. Thorp explains this in that article that got published in the *Atlantic* posthumously so we don't know if he knew it got titled "Banjo in the Cow Camps," "I had started my travels toward Red River because an old cowman once told me that they did nothing much in that district but sing, cuss, and go to camp meetin'."

Some of the "church" in Country is Texas and New Mexico Black Cowboy church. And some of the cussing in Country may have its origins in Black Texas and New Mexico, too.

I particularly appreciated the cussing part. My daddy claimed to have won cussing contests when he was a boy. In my Black Country, cussing is important language play. Unfortunately, these traces of Blackness and of ribald Rabelaisian whiteness were sanitized out the published texts by Thorp who boasts, "many of the songs had to be dry-cleaned for unprintable word before they went to press." The dry-cleaning was often followed with a layer of whitewash.

That said, Red River, New Mexico, functions as a quintessential Black Country place as described by Thorp. It's embedded with religion, Celtic and African melodies, and white and Black vernacular language.

And there is Blackness both evident and embedded in these cowboy songs. Titles like "Educated Feller," "The Zebra Dun," and "Cowboys Victimize" include lyrics that can be heard as trickster tales (rooted in African narrative tradition) that encourage the challenging of accepted hierarchies and equalizing inequitable power balances.

And I will give Thorp this kudo: he documents "Mexican" cowboy singing. He witnessed "El Rio Rey" being sung after he stumbled into what he described as "a strange assemblage of wagons, all manned by Mexicans." He described the song as a ballad about a palomino stud who would not be tamed and translated the title to "The River King." The songs sung by Mexican cowboys Thorp met near Juno, Texas, camped out on the Devil's River, are precious examples of the few *found* examples of Indigenous people's presence in Country and Western. The people he called Mexican were likely descended from Indigenous, African, and European people.

Cowboy singing is a special kind of bumping uglies. In Thorp's essay he observes: "the cowboys didn't have good voices, they sang alone." To sing without the good voice is to sing as something other than entertainment, to sing for self, not other. To sing naked, to sing unashamed and ugly. Think of an old, sun wrinkled, time expanded, barroom brawl–cauliflowered ear on a lonesome prairie around a campfire. Ugly the sound, ugly the ear, beautify the connection, the emotion, the thought, the feeling conveyed.

Alone in my berth I am that cowboy singer who sings with poorly pitched voice.

And I am singing, "The Ballad of Nat Love."

FRESH HORSES

"The Ballad of Nat Love" begins where Nat's memoir begins, enslaved in Tennessee. Nat Love lures his readers in with a namby-pamby sop thrown to the man who owned him, "he was in his way in comparison with many other slaver owners of those days a kind and indulgent master." Then he goes on to be unstinting in his portrayal of the viciousness of slave owners and overseers.

Every time I reread Nat's words, I realize my early readings of Nat Love informed my hatred of *Gone with the Wind.* They reinforced my understanding that the pages of that book contained lie after lie. Nat was but one example of the child excluded from the pages of the book, the mammy's child. Love depicted the everyday cruelty, the everyday sadism, of the planters and their ladies. He depicted the entrapment of a particular enslaved child, a Black person with desires and wishes, with observations and ambitions, with love they wished to receive and love they wished to give, a person like no Black person in *Gone with the Wind.*

Nat Love educated himself. But he didn't just educate himself. One of his first acts as a free child was to buy books for other Black children. In freedom at the age of about ten, he was earning about three dollars a month. This is how he spent his money and thought about this money: "With so many at home to provide for, my wages did not last long, but out of my three dollars I bought each of the children a book. The rest went for provisions and clothing."

Long after his death, with these words, he educated me. One of the lessons: To write one's autobiography is to weave a kind of immortality, is to continue making ripples in the world, long after you have turned to ashes.

We see horses on the train. And I am remembering this: In my Detroit, horses were a Black thing. Charles Diggs, Sr., the funeral home millionaire whose congressman son would co-found the Congressional Black

Caucus, rode on the bridle paths at Belle Isle, a center city park in Motown. Anna Gordy, sister of Motown Records founder Berry Gordy, started a Black woman's riding club. Black folk from the city come summertime flocked to the lake town, Idlewild, where there would be horseback lessons for kids led by a man called Sarge. Last but not least, Joe Louis had a legendary training camp not far from Detroit and that camp had stables and a horse ring, and there was even a nearby riding academy, Utica Riding Academy, that had welcomed Black people. People I knew who worked in automobile plants bragged about riding. I only had a few lessons as a girl in Detroit, but it was something we did, and the approach was decidedly Western, Western saddle, Western jeans, Western bare head. We noticed and applauded Sammy Davis, Jr., playing Tip Correy, a fast gun, avenging the state-sanctioned murder of his father when we saw him on TV in *The Rifleman*.

We pull out of Dodge City, Kansas, somewhere around midnight. *One thing I do well, get the hell out of Dodge.* Walter Hyatt and me, we, didn't send the lyrics to the cleaners.

KANSAS CITY, CHARLEY PRIDE, AND BASEBALL

We blow into Kansas City on the *Southwest Chief,* and I am settling into my chair alone in the roomette. On this train David and the girls seem to spend more time in the observation car. I grab the ends of my curls and press them to my nose.

I was the only one who packed shampoo. Now the scent of jasmine and almond reminds me of my traveling companions. We are all beginning to smell like a perfume with a top note of disinfectant, base notes of Amtrak kitchen, with hints of organic shampoo, deodorizer, and floor cleaner. In my head I'm calling it Train Grease.

If we had time to stop in Kansas City, I would take them to the Negro Leagues Baseball Museum so they can better appreciate Charley Pride.

Pride, a Negro League player, was often described as an "extended family member" of the Negro Leagues Baseball Museum. A board member who showed up, he became a "mainstay" of the museum. To the delight of both other visitors and other board members, he often ended up with a guitar in his hand, which led to impromptu and unforgettable performances.

Nowhere is it easier to see that Charley Pride stands at an almost unique intersection of sport, music, and patriotism than in the vicinity of the Negro Leagues Baseball Museum. His two Black Country performances for the ages, one happened before we got on the train and one after, are both connected to sports.

On January 13, 1974, Pride sang "America the Beautiful" and "The National Anthem" at Super Bowl VIII. This shocked the shit out of a lot of white folks and Black folks. It was Country and Black. Both vividly. I've listened to a recording. He is so twangy and so rural Black in that performance. And he sang "The National Anthem" before game five of the 2010 Baseball World Series. Along the way he became a part owner of a major league baseball team, the Texas Rangers. That was a Pride signature move. He wasn't owned, he owned.

I didn't know that on the train. It hadn't happened yet. I did know an ugly story of back when he was playing in the Negro leagues one team traded him—for a bus. I am writing that down as a lie that tells the truth. Working at the intersections Pride worked, he had to do a lot of negotiating with the reality he was a human being that some others considered a commodity.

DeFord Bailey knew a whole lot about that. In 1947, DeFord came on the Opry, sat down with his guitar, and sang "Kansas City Blues." I wonder why? I wonder how? It was during the time he was supporting himself almost exclusively with a shoeshine parlor. When folks want to disparage DeFord because of that or are embarrassed by DeFord because of that I remind them of something Charley Pride would have known. Some powerful Black men started off as shoeshine boys. I don't know what names he would call but I will call Lloyd George Richards, dean of the

Yale School of Drama, and Marc Stepp, vice president of the United Auto Workers and head of the UAW at Chrysler. Pride following DeFord onto the Opry would not let anybody shame DeFord. And maybe he would notice, like me, the performance was in December with Christmas coming on, maybe he needed extra money to make Christmas for his kids.

This trip we are only getting off the train in Kansas City to stretch our legs.

A thing David Ewing is good for—knowing all the Black history trivia of a place. So, he probably tells the girls about the legendary 18th and Vine neighborhood which gave rise to Charlie Parker, about the *Kansas City Call*, a Black newspaper founded in 1918. A paper treasured by Black cowboys and Pullman porters. That the Negro National League was founded in 1920 by Rube Foster in Kansas City and that's why the museum is in Kansas City. I hope he doesn't neglect to tell them that before Charley Pride, the man from Sledge, Mississippi, was a Country singer, he was a pitcher who played in the Negro American League for the Memphis Red Sox and for the Birmingham Black Barons. He may leave that out because he's not chasing the First Family of Black Country like I am. That's my private project that I share in flashes with the girls. I am not in the observation car so I don't know what was said, but David he would be good for saying all of that.

LIL, THE TERRITORY BANDS, AND LETTING GO

Because I've put Nat Love down and we're back to chasing Lil, I'm not loving that I don't know a story that connects her to Kansas City. Chasing that over time I discover a favorite scholar of mine, Dr. Tammy Kernodle of the University of Miami. Kernodle has described KC as "the de facto capital of the Southwestern jazz scene." She positions KC as the center of a musicverse, my word, that stretches outward from Kansas City "into Texas, Oklahoma, Kansas, and as far west as Denver, Colorado," so much of the same region Nat Love covered on horse and train. She writes of "territory bands" playing ragtime and boogie-woogie that "supported a vibrant musical scene that catered to Black and white listeners." I love her phrase "territory bands"—it sounds like you go out from urban space to play under the wide-open rural sky.

And I am wondering about those territory bands and who might have heard Lil in Kansas City and taken some of her back out into that Southwestern musicverse where what she was doing got all mixed up with some old Black cowboy songs and some polkas.

I don't know for sure if Lil Hardin performed in Kansas City, but most likely she did. We know Louis Armstrong played Kansas City. We know Mary Lou Williams and Julia Lee, Black and female and contemporaries of Lil, were stalwarts of the Kansas City jazz scene. It would be most unlikely that Julia Lee played for twenty years at the Tap Room and didn't play any of the standards Lil wrote, "Struttin' with Some Barbecue"; "Hotter than Hot"; "Brown Gal." And if they didn't play those tunes, someone else at 18th and Vine did. And some of those bands heading back out to the territories carried Lil into hidden corners of the Western and Midwestern world. I can't prove that, but I believe that. I feel Lil's presence in Kansas City.

More acutely because it was somewhere near Kansas City as I remember it looking back, that I started thinking about Lil's death.

Lil Hardin died on August 27, 1971, sitting on a piano bench in downtown Chicago. She was in the middle of playing "St. Louis Blues" in the broad daylight for students. Educating. Honoring Louis Armstrong, who had recently died, for sure, but maybe more than that using the moment as an opportunity to educate.

She played piano in legendary bands. Virtuoso players who could not read or write musical notation counted on Lil to translate for them. Sometimes it was taking their sounds and turning it to sheet music. Sometimes it was reading the sheet music they had been hired to play but could not read and singing it to them or picking out the melody on her piano. She wrote hit songs that became Louis Armstrong standards like "Struttin' with Some Barbecue" and "Brown Gal." She was the most significant manager Louis ever had, the one who changed the way he dressed, his position in the band, his understanding of his place in the horn pantheon. When Louis Armstrong, Jimmie Rodgers, and Lil Hardin came together to record "Blue Yodel #9" she was arguably the most experienced musician of the three geniuses in the room, and the only one who read and wrote music. She drove that session with her piano and knowledge of so many versions of the traditional blues song that is the skeleton of "Blue Yodel #9."

Lil's story starts in Memphis, but I never forget, and I don't want anybody in Music City to forget, Lil's story runs through Nashville. And it's not just that she studied at Fisk for three years. It's whenever I hear Bessie Smith's "Nashville Women Blues," and Bessie snarls "Nashville women the way they strut it ain't no bluff." I know Bessie's talking about Lil.

And I think Lil thought that, too. Bessie recorded "Nashville Women Blues" about 1925. A few years later Lil wrote, "Struttin' with Some Barbecue." Some folks think Louis wrote it. Wrong. Lil wrote it in 1928. In 1956, three years before Ray recorded "Just for a Thrill," six new versions of the song were recorded and released. Ray Charles would have known that. And out on the road he would have heard memories of other recordings of "Struttin' with Some Barbecue."

Between the day Ray Charles was born and the day he died, Lil got cuts on "Struttin'" in all these years: 1945, 1949, 1953, 1954, 1955, 1956, 1957, 1958, 1959, 1960, 1961, 1962, 1964, 1965, 1967, 1968, 1969, 1970, 1971, 1972, 1973, 1974, 1975, 1976, 1977, 1978, 1979, 1981, 1982, 1983, 1984, 1986, 1987, 1988, 1989, 1991, 1992, 1994, 1995, 1996, 1998, 1999, 2000, and 2001. She got cuts on the song in 2008 and 2011 after his death. After her own death. I don't know that on the train, but I know that now and it needs telling.

Two years after Ray Charles recorded Lil's tune "Just for the Thrill," two years after entering into the orbit of the woman who helped to define

Country, that's when Ray Charles embarked on recording *Modern Sounds in Country and Western Music*, an album that would redefine the Country sound and connect him to his past as a Black child listening to the Opry. Lil was all up in Ray's accomplishment.

We arrived at Chicago's Union Station a little more rumpled, a little awkward walking on solid ground, and distinctly more wide-eyed. In the round-up chatter in the cab we all claimed different highlights—but we all claimed a highlight. We had seen vistas that eclipsed paintings and dreams.

The people who disembarked the *Southwest Chief* in Chicago are not the people who boarded the *California Zephyr* a week before. The girls have spent 178 hours largely unsupervised. They awoke when they wanted and went to sleep when they wanted. They ate what they wanted and when they wanted. They learned without instruction, and they learned more than they learned with instruction. Which had been considerable. Caroline had gained a wildness she wouldn't lose. Margaret had enhanced her ability to keep her serene self-counsel.

Seven days in August have left me revived.

I step off the train in Chicago light. Dazzled by the sights of the great plains, of the vivid green trees rising from the gray-black hard stone of the Rocky Mountains, of the high golden Sierra Nevada desert, of the eucalyptus forest on the Pacific Ocean, and the buttes of the Southwest, I was wooed back into love with plain and simple beauty.

Red rocks. Green trees. Blue sky. White clouds. Brown skin, audible heartbeat, visible pulse, the womb that carried Caroline into a world, the skull my father thumped, the simple beauty of being an animal on the planet in the last days of the twentieth century. I made my way back to something I once found in a Motown cherry tree, the pleasure of being human inside and out.

I had hoped the trains would help me forget, the trains gave me a way to remember.

Seven days of chaste ecstasy, of magnificent awake, sober, now, wooed me back to reality. The ongoing shake, shoosh, and flash of the flickering panorama wooed me back to my memory. The sights, sounds, tasted scents, and touch of the journey. The roomette gave me a safe place for recall. The sights, sounds, tastes, scents, and touch of the train journey calmed me and consoled me. The roomette was a fine cocoon, then the roomette was a good womb, and in some minutes or hours, the roomette was a tomb, and the roomette was a birthing room.

I stepped on the train a daughter first. I stepped off the train a mother first. I would mother Caroline, I would mother me, and I would mother my Black Country First Family.

We returned to Nashville. Walking from the arrival gate to baggage claim, we pass pictures of Country Music stars, all of them white and I am thinking DeFord needs some of my mama love. All that love that had gone unspent on Bettie when little girl me had loved her and she wouldn't receive my love—well, some of it would be showered upon some ancestors who deserved veneration, and some of it would be showered down on all the communities and creatives who had cultivated the Black joy, the Black art, the Black song that had companioned me every step of the way in my walk through hell.

Surviving will give you the blues, grind you down, and make you want to die. The train reminded me the pleasure of a cherry warm from the tree, the sun a red ball in Mari-Alice's sky, the stars twinkling bright over Lil in Idlewild. Nature is a Black Country woman's very best friend, and a cowboy's.

I had followed twenty thousand miles of memory on five thousand miles of train track to reach a simple conclusion. I would no longer let someone's worst day define my best day. I was no longer most significantly a daughter. I was a mother. I was a lover. I was a guardian of a Black Country legacy.

THE ARCHIVE AND THE ACADEMY: CREATING A NEW COUNTRY CANON

I was some kind of finished with Country Music. I moved from writing Black Country, to writing *about* Black Country. I turned toward spotlighting Black Country past and imagining what I could do to catalyze a vibrant Black Country present and future. And I started writing novels.

I published a book, *The Wind Done Gone*, in 2001, that reclaimed stories obliterated by the pages of *Gone with the Wind*. The story of the intimate wound of being an enslaved Black child on a Georgia plantation; and the story of the intimate joys of being a Black woman in Washington, D.C., in an era of effective Black congressmen and Reconstruction anchored my first novel. The street proclaimed *The Wind Done Gone* the literary equivalent of Prissy slapping Scarlett back—and we made the *New York Times* Bestseller List, as well as mentions on *The Gilmore Girls*, *Jeopardy!*, and (I've been told) an AP English exam question. Black-owned independent bookstores showed up and showed out for the release. Marcus Books in Oakland hosted a talk that went on until almost midnight. Eso Won Books in

Los Angeles hosted a reading attended by a relative of Hattie McDaniel, the actor who played Mammy in the film *Gone with the Wind*. A chief librarian at the main library of a major Southern city library bought dozens of copies for her institution. After my public lecture, the librarian drove me the long way back to my hotel, past the house where her Black mother had cleaned toilets, floors, and linen for people who admired *Gone with the Wind*.

One day the mailman delivered a fan letter, dark ink on yellow legal pad, beautiful handwriting, beautiful sentence structure. The signature read "Harper Lee." We swapped letters. She said I changed things. The best proof that she was right? Hearing from Black women themselves who worked cleaning houses and who told me my book made them feel loved and *chosen*. After *The Wind Done Gone,* I would publish four more novels.

I wanted universities to start paying attention to the art and history of Black Country. I leaned into working my new Country agenda. I wanted to push the city of Nashville and the Country Music Association to champion Black Country as essential public history and to get Nashville archives and museums to start collecting material on the subject. I wanted to discuss Black Country in any national forums (magazine articles, interviews for someone else's book) that came my way. I wanted to change the larger Country conversation so that it finally included the Black Country history that had for too long been erased or ignored.

Nashville is home to four universities with which I have strong personal ties: Fisk, Tennessee State, Meharry, and Vanderbilt. Before getting on that train, I'd had informal discussions with individual faculty members on all of those campuses about Black Country. Leslie Collins at Fisk; Joan Elliot at TSU; Dr. Henry Foster at Meharry; and Ann Cook Calhoun at Vanderbilt were all interested in exploring ways a scholarly address of Black Country could enrich understanding of Black culture, Southern culture, and America.

Ann Cook Calhoun encouraged me to consider developing a course on Country Music based on my lived experience as a Country songwriter and my lived engagement with the culture of Music Row and the South. I thought she was joking. How could I do that without a PhD? She suggested a Writer-in-Residence path, only I would be a Songwriter-in-Residence. We both laughed. She might have been joking. But I put that idea in my back pocket and got on with novel writing and salon building as a way to further my cause.

Changing hearts, minds, and votes (for various Country awards, Country boards, historical plaques) can start with shaking up a cocktail and strutting with some barbecue. I wanted a house big enough to throw huge parties that featured live Country Music highlighting Black influences and presence, particularly. While still in the little pink townhouse, I stopped talking to people about my songs and started pitching everything interesting and Black Country I encountered, like its connections to other arts including soul food.

I moved into a house on Blair Boulevard in 2001 and the first big party came shortly after that. The money earned from *The Wind Done Gone* allowed us to often entertain large groups, with the best (and most seeped in Black Music Row history) bartender in town, Bill Forrester; with locally sourced food, and live music. The McCrary Sisters—daughters of one of the original Fairfield Four singers—sang live at one party. Adia Victoria sang an entire set once out in the backyard and wrote some poetry about the blues in the living room.

My daughter, Caroline, wrote poetry about the blues and Country in every single room of the house.

The house (which wasn't fancy, just big and cool) became a mission of common cause. I convinced a local artisan carpenter to make me a table for eighteen because I couldn't afford to purchase a ready-made one. And he had a friend in Texas who made cheap but sturdy restaurant chairs. I got sixteen of those, then drove around town one early November with Thanksgiving coming to find a restaurant that could be convinced to sell me two more. I found such a place on Elliston Place right across from where Kossi Gardner had a regular gig, the Exit/In. Rhiannon Giddens would sit in those chairs and eat at that table.

I wasn't settled into the house long when Vanderbilt approached me to be a Visiting Writer-in-Residence teaching a Beginning Creative Writing Workshop. I seized the chance to enter the Academy, very part-time at that point, while continuing to write my own novels and stirring the cultural pot with parties and projects.

When Caroline came home for Thanksgiving her senior year of high school, 2006, we couldn't have dinner in the house. I was in the middle of writing *My Country Roots,* in collaboration with Courtney and Carter Little of a band called Saddle Song. We'd covered the dining room table with about a thousand little note cards, each with the name of a Country song and the artist who had performed it. We grouped the songs by theme and placed the cards to visually display how those themes connected, interconnected, and conflicted. Thanksgiving dinner took place in a hotel that year. When the book came out months later, the Littles and I had a release party in Nashville's Bluebird Café on Hillsboro Pike, where Garth Brooks, Taylor Swift, Vince Gill, Keith Urban, and Lady Antebellum cut their teeth way back.

We hoped the book would be big, but many a slip takes place between cup and lip in the entertainment industry. That book was tipped-over glass on a white tablecloth; the press closed shortly after the book was released. Caroline graduated high school in the spring of 2006 and entered Harvard that fall. Thanks to G. Marq Roswell, she got an internship/job on the set of a movie about a Black debate team that was filming in Shreveport, Louisiana. On *The Great Debaters* set she met Rhiannon Giddens. Neither of us had an inkling how much Rhiannon and Caroline's set born alliance would impact all three of our lives. Time would tell that that meeting was the first essential step toward the Bomb Shelter studio, and an album created in collaboration with artists who reminded me of me—Black, female, and wild as they wanted to be. These women would show me a new way to hold the fort.

I have told you I didn't *see* the Bronze Buckaroo movies, in my childhood. I got told versions of them, by my father. I haven't told you this: he used the fragments of the shards that he remembered as a starting point to invent all Black and utterly heroic adventures for me. Ones involving riding with your friends to rescue a friend, that involved being true to your family, that required "holding the fort." Often his last words to me upon leaving, and a line that occurred in all his versions of the Bronze Buckaroo, was, "Hold the fort, till I get back."

To hold the fort was to take charge. Was to refuse to be invaded. It was to be capable of being alone, going solo, and protecting the family homestead. To hold the fort included being prepared to fight and think. Required courage. And according to my father it required great beauty. He was very clear that the sister in the Bronze Buckaroo was very, very beautiful, and not in a showgirl way, in an unadorned bright flash of nature on the wide Western range way. So, Daddy's versions of the stories involved miming the riding, the holding the reins, the bouncing in the saddle. And they involved crooning and yodeling in rhyme, involved fighting back, involved shooting, involved cussing. All my cowboy songs were about holding the fort, Black cowgirl style. And yet the songs, just like me, were invaded. Yes, sometimes the recordings themselves felt like invasions, like I hadn't managed to hold the fort.

About that same time Caroline met Rhiannon, I was offered a long-term position on the Vanderbilt faculty. When asked to name the course I would like to teach in addition to an Intro to Fiction workshop I immediately chimed, "Country Lyric in American Culture!" I had given up thinking anybody was ever going to lay down a velvet carpet for my cowboy songs, but I was determined to lay down some velvet for Black Country folks past and future by creating classes that attracted students who would go out in the world and find and document unheralded moments of Black genius, power, and connection to Country.

LIL NAS X ENTERS THE ACADEMY

Sometimes I describe the sweep of my course on Black Country as moving from Lil Hardin to Lil Nas X. Mickey Guyton, the first Black woman to win a Grammy in the Country category, came to class that very first year. When I taught the class in 2022 after I acquainted my students with Lil Hardin Armstrong, they acquainted me with Reyna Roberts. Gritty, glamorous, and transgressive, Roberts, one told me, weaponizes beauty and sexuality in a way that shakes the foundations of the patriarchy. One of my students presented a Swamp Dogg song about fishing that I had never heard. It was an interesting find because it documented Black leisure as an engagement with nature. This is rare in American literature; in Black Country it's characteristic.

In an earlier course one of my students documented a Southern city juvenile detention center that sought to punish Black teens by blaring Country Music. One of the young incarcerated "subjected" to this anguish, heard and latched on to "I Hope You Dance" as inspiration for turning their life around. Motivated by the same song that Maya Angelou claimed as her favorite Country recording, that unexpected Black Country fan is now a dentist serving poor people out in the West.

Things aren't always as stagnant and divided up, as some would have you believe. Radical Black uses of Country blaze into unexpected moments propelled by young people. On August 5, 2023, a group of white boaters, illegally parked, viciously assaulted the Black co-captain of a riverboat as he was going about his legal duties. Other Black workers joined the fight. The notable allies being, three Black men skipping toward the trouble; an older Black man wielding a folding chair; and a teen dubbed "Aquamayne" who jumped off a boat, swam across the river, climbed up on the dock, then entered the fray to protect the Black captain. Two songs have become widely associated with the event: "Lift Every Chair and Swing" (a sly reworking of "Lift Every Voice and Sing," often called the Black National Anthem) and "Try That in a Small Town."

A song and its video are used to fuel hate, fear, bigotry until that song is seized by justice-loving young people. The young people got that so right! New videos, lots of them, that are a celebration of Black resistance to white oppression are made. The song takes on entirely new meaning, even as its original bigotry and implied threats of lynching and other acts

of terror and killing violence are laid bare. Try the old ways in this new "small town" world and small-town Black people will fight back with joy and impunity and get justice. "Try That in a Small Town" became the unofficial anthem of the unofficial Alabama Sweet Tea Party Rebellion. I propose that August 5 become Black Country's first national holiday and that we have a huge Black Country hoedown in Montgomery, Alabama, in Hank, Sr.'s hometown every year to celebrate.

Sixteen-year-old Aquamayne got it so right, swimming to the fight to defend the outnumbered, the rebuked, the scorned. He had a far better understanding of small-town virtue, small-town courage, small-town values, than Jason Aldean.

In a small town, we know racism when we see it, and we saw it on the Montgomery boat dock. In a small town we take up for the underdog—and we don't lie and say we are the underdog when we are not.

The neighborly spirit, the justice spirit, the honest spirit, that got Aquamayne off the boat, in the water, up on the pier, that got three young men skipping down the pier, got an older man we're now calling the chairman swinging a folding chair, that's some heroic small-town shit. That's Black Country at its best.

Nobody got killed. Nobody got terrified. Particularly not the Black man the white folks set out to bully.

The event in Montgomery was its own brilliant and prophetic rebellion. But the repurposing of a racist Country song to become the soundtrack of small films made about the rebellion is another layer of rebellion. It says, "You don't scare me! I will ridicule you and I will resist you. I will swim to the fight." Swimming to the fight is as Southern and rural as sweet tea.

Lil Nas X, he's got some of that Aquamayne spirit. He jumps into the fray. He does Country and life his own way. If I didn't love Lil Nas X for anything else, I would love him for this: Black women are very rarely featured and celebrated in Country Music videos. Two and a half minutes into his "Old Town Road" video, we get an amazing sister dancing in red sweatpants, white shirt, and blue jacket, making a new place for her American, female, Country, and Black self—and her improvisations.

Country has a visual as well as an aural culture that Lil Nas X disrupts by circling back to Black cowboys past and circling out to Black dandies past, present, and future. Male, female, and gender nonbinary. He features and celebrates Black bodies and Black beauty that have been erased from the Country landscape—starting with his own, but not ending with his own.

Lil Nas X is, for me, the twenty-first-century Country star most directly descended from Herb Jeffries. Louis Armstrong, the dandy, gave rise to Herb Jeffries, another dandy, who gives rise to Lil Nas X, the personification of the Black Country dandy.

Dandies are not just about the clothes. But the clothes are important and when thinking about Lil Nas X and Herb Jeffries, the cowboy suits are a significant part of the connection.

At CMA Fest in 2019, the former was resplendent in an orange denim jacket and jeans and white boots and white T-shirt and white belt. Another of my favorite of his signature looks is that yellow and black-fringed cowboy parade suit costume. It features his name "Lil Nas X" emblazoned across the shoulders in the back and black stars across the top. He has been photographed wearing this suit without a shirt, his chocolate-brown chest exposed. When he wears the yellow parade suit, he wears yellow reptile-skin-patterned boots and he's stepping into a visual culture dominated by white men that he shifts forever with his presence and with a little help from a Black woman.

Lil Nas X is frequently styled by Hodo Musa, born in Somalia, raised as a refugee in Malmö, Sweden, and launched to her career through Los Angeles by way of Oslo. The last stop, in Black Country's capital, is where she would reimagine the cowboy in the twenty-first century.

Roy Rogers and Hank Williams had Nudie Cohn. George Jones, Marty Stuart, and Johnny Cash had the Rhinestone Rembrandt Manuel Cuevas. Lil Nas X has Hodo Musa, a Black woman.

Albert Camus said, "The dandy creates his own unity by aesthetic means." The Black dandy signifies an aesthetic that is at once loud and elegant, charming and disruptive, lavish and wholly original. I think of dandyism as self-appointed and deserved opulence. It requires the confidence to assert: I am stage, spotlight, and actor; and if you are fortunate, you are my audience. Lil Nas X has exactly that confidence. As Lil Nas X inhabits the show suit, he reminds his audience to be self-delighted as he subtly shifts the focus of self-presentation from the importance of being seen to the importance of being. This is work that Lil did first in "Brown Gal." There is a line to be drawn from Lil Hardin to Lil Nas X and it starts with Lil, zigs toward and through Herb Jeffries, bounces off Prince who had multiple close encounters with Country, before arriving at Lil Nas X, an artist well adept at asking interesting questions with every aspect of his being.

What is with, and in, his name? Allusions to hip-hop artists Lil' Kim and Nas (Nasir bin Olu Dara Jones), and politician Malcolm X? An allusion to Lil Hardin? Does his genius extend to that?

Where do we find the God in "Old Town Road"? No place obvious. Perhaps the finger pointed by Billy Ray Cyrus to the sky and in Lil Nas X's name? A cross earring when he first appears in the official video? Hiding in the word "valley" that the lyric juxtaposed to the droning mantra of the song that repeats, "I'm going to ride till I can't no more." "Old Town Road," a song about living until you die, works precisely because listeners understand it is a Country song and the Country audience anticipates the presence of God.

My favorite Lil Nas X performance is not on the BET Awards or on any of the big stages. It's in a school auditorium in the Midwest. Lil Nas X arrives not wearing some splendiferous Western-inspired stage costume but wearing a blue denim jacket and blue jeans. "Stagecoach" is stamped across the top of the jacket, and "Old Town Road" across his waist. There is brown suede fringe—but he is dressed to understate.

On this occasion, he is not the dandy. He is humble, he is audience. In the front row, *performing for him*, a little Black girl in a hot pink cowboy hat and hot pink T-shirt is singing, "Can't nobody tell me nothing."

She appears to be self-delighted, just like Lil Nas X. Surrounded by schoolmates, most of them white, all seeing her in a different frame, because she looks like the man on the stage, the brown cowgirl in the pink hat adopts a Western swagger and defiance that braids into her brown girl's swagger and defiance, and she becomes Country fierce—and utterly powerful and charming.

As I watch her, I can imagine and almost hear Nat Love, the iconic Black cowboy and rodeo entertainer of the nineteenth and early twentieth century, applauding for Little Nas X and for the little girl in hot pink. And I hear Herb Jeffries and Louis Armstrong applauding, too. But no one would applaud louder than DeFord, who I believe would appreciate this truth: Lil Nas X returns the Black body to the minstrel stage—then burns the stage down.

RISSI PALMER ENTERS THE ARCHIVE

Rissi Palmer named her radio show *Color Me Country Radio* as an homage to Linda Martell's brilliant 1970 album, *Color Me Country*. I knew that before I read Mac Hunt's thesis. What I didn't know until I read that thesis was that Rissi had been mentored by Prince; they worked together for several years. I knew a Country song is sampled in Prince's single "Kiss" and that he worked with Country artist Deborah Allen. I didn't know anything about Rissi and Prince and their long immersive involvement until my student Mac pored through hours of interviews and studied Rissi's papers in the Vanderbilt archive.

I donated my papers to the Schlesinger Library at Harvard, where they joined those of two of my greatest non-Black Country inspirations—Angela Davis and Julia Child. But Rissi got paid. I saw to that. I did it for Lil. I did it for me. I did it for scholars to come. I did it for Black women who want to see their lives represented in archives. I did it for Black Country. And last, but absolutely not least, I did it for Rissi Palmer—a history-making Black Country artist.

I worked with two very able white allies, librarians both, to secure the remuneration Rissi deserved. It felt good to see a Black woman get what the white boys get—paid with money for creative papers. Rissi's papers were a groundbreaking acquisition that put the Heard Library ahead of the Schlesinger, the Smithsonian, and the Schomburg in the area of documenting Black Country Music. It put Vanderbilt at the head of efforts to amend the reality that struggling musicians, people of limited means, single mothers, people of color, people shifting homes, people living peripatetic lives are not in a position to hold on to their papers long enough for them to be handed down after their death or when they reach a summit of their career. By the time they reach a summit, the papers are often lost.

Or, if the papers are not acquired *during* the career, during the life, they may pose an art-strangling burden on the artist as they struggle to pay for storage. I lived that. I wanted something better for Rissi.

The first time I met Rissi Palmer, I couldn't see her face. She entered the Special Collections Room, a wood-paneled, formal yet contemporary room, equipped with lighted display cases and large flat tables located within a huge modernist building on the perimeter of the Vanderbilt campus, masked. The pandemic was raging.

The librarians were playing her music when the tall, brown-skinned woman wearing camouflage pants and a huge sun-kissed Afro walked through the door with arms completely full.

"No Air," Rissi's highest charting single, was on my mind when she walked in the room. In the song's music video, she's a Black hippy girl on the beach. Almost no makeup, big curly hair, long flowy skirts, wild, natural. Getting close to nature is an element of the hippy authentic and it is an element of the rural Southern Black femme. A woman who is barefoot, not in someone's kitchen pregnant, but in a backyard, in a garden, or on a beach. She's a nonconformist who writes a song to a child she miscarried but believes in abortion rights. That's the Rissi persona. And the woman who walked in was all of that and more.

The Jean and Alexander Heard Library system houses eight million items throughout seven locations. Special Collections, where we met to add new items to the collection, is on the old Central Library campus.

Her forty-year-old brown eyes met my sixty-two-year-old brown eyes. I threw my bent arms up in the air as a gesture of welcome, celebration, and wonder. Soon her arms were empty, and sprawled across a gleaming library table just a shade darker than the walls was a garment bag, spiralbound notebooks, and clothbound journals. The exact same colorful notebooks and journals could be found on thousands of girls' desks, the exact same cheap gray garment bag in thousands of women's closets.

The contents were singular. Inside the journals were lyrics in every stage of development, including the evolving palimpsest of notes that became the lyrics to my favorite Rissi Palmer song, "Summerville." Inside the garment bag was the short black dress Palmer wore the first time she sang on the Opry stage.

Rissi's collection was a treasure trove of objects documenting decades in the life and interior life of a creative Black girl becoming a creative Black woman. A kind of a multimedia *Portrait of an Artist as a Young Black Woman*. Evidence that Prince mentored Rissi Palmer. That Deborah Allen, who wrote "Baby I Lied," produced tracks for Rissi Palmer. And Rissi was surrendering her artifacts to Vanderbilt University in exchange for enough money to pay off the mortgage on her house, enough money to buy herself enough peace to keep writing, to attempt to record again, to keep touring without agent, manager, or record label.

We are find-a-way *and* make-a-way women. It would have been nice had she earned enough from airplay, streams, and live performances to be able to hold on to these mementoes. She didn't find that way, so we made this way. Diversify the archive.

They took the stuff. She got the money. It was a fair exchange. There are lots of ways to roll out a red carpet. I was doing what Lil's love child, Quincy Jones, taught me to do, my way.

After she dropped off and Vanderbilt received the sacred papers, Rissi and I went to celebrate at City House. We ate our first shared meal in a plywood, three-wall room erected on a parking lot blacktop called a cabana. My favorite Nashville restaurant was taking an imaginative approach to managing Covid risks.

I was stunned by how many folks she knew that I didn't know. She was stunned by how much Black Country history I knew that she didn't know. In the cabana I started telling her about Lil Hardin and she started telling me all about Holly G of the Black Opry. We needed each other. And we had each other.

Rissi brought me Miko Marks, who I now think of as a Black Brenda Lee. She's tiny with a big voice. When Miko was coming onto the Country scene, Rissi Palmer was also emerging and at a time when the business seemed to think there was room for only one "Black girl in Country." Rissi got the nod. Now they often work together, and it was Rissi who suggested that Miko should be part of *The Alice Randall Songbook* project.

My favorite Rissi Palmer song is "Summerville." In the verse, a grandmother is quoted giving a loving and complex instruction, "Child, wash your feet before you come inside to eat." These ten words, like so much of the best Country lyric, is found poetry rooted in rural Black talk and the Bible.

Slavery did many things. One of them was steal childhoods. Black toddlers were put to work. Very young Black children labored in fields and kitchens beyond earshot of the voices of the women who loved them best. The grandmother in this song snatches childhood back from cotton-field history and gifts it to Rissi. The poor child is unshod because they have insufficient resources. Unshod in this song is to be closer to nature, play, adventure, and God.

The verse obliquely references Genesis 18: 4–5, where it is written that the Lord says, "Let a little water, I pray you, be fetched, and wash your feet, and rest yourselves under the tree; and I will fetch a morsel of bread and comfort ye your hearts." The Lord and the grandmother give similar instructions. This song is centered on sacred folk, a sacred child who self-anoints and a sacred grandmother who encourages the practice.

With ten words, the grandmother draws a portrait of her progeny as a barefoot child, unsexed, ungendered, with naked feet that she will self-anoint when she washes them. It is not just bare feet that get redeemed and repurposed in this song. It's also white sheets.

I remember running through sheets hung on a clothesline in my grandmother's backyard in Detroit. Above the green grass. Next to the rosebushes. I danced through those sheets as a girl, knowing nothing of the Ku Klux Klan riding around in sheets or that one day I would discover bedsheets could be a battlefield. When I made that bitter discovery, the memory of sheets floating above my grandmother's green lawn preserved my optimism. Then I forgot until "Summerville" reminded me. The song returns me to halcyon joys, four o'clock flowers planted near the street in the front. Green plants in pots on the porch, rose bushes and a goldfish pond in the back.

"Summerville" is a quintessential Country song.

The last time I gave the Black Country course midterm, in 2023, it included a live interaction with Rissi Palmer as a thirty-minute section of a three-hour exam. The students were invited to pose a significant question to Rissi. After she left, they were in turn posed a follow-up question: What surprised them most about Rissi's answers to their questions? The response was almost unanimous. How much direct racism she had experienced in the industry and at shows. My students didn't agree on who should be president, on gun rights, or on choice. They all agreed, though, that nobody should treat Rissi some of the ways she gave witness that she had been treated. And they all believed her. There is more than music on the syllabus in Black Country.

RHIANNON GIDDENS, CREATOR AND CURATOR

For years I would introduce my daughter to singers and songs that had become some of her very favorites, and then she started to reciprocate the gesture. This is not easy. We have very different musical tastes, my daughter and me. Our list of favorite artists would have little overlap. But at the center of the overlap is Rhiannon Giddens, the virtuoso Caroline met on the set of *The Great Debaters*, a 2007 film set in and filmed in the rural South, who had to fight to get some of the twang and Country into the soundtrack along with the blues and the jazz. Nobody knows Africa is in the cultural DNA of Country Music better or has taught it more than Rhiannon Giddens. Nobody.

Rhiannon Giddens is a Country quadruple threat: distinguished fiddler and banjo player; singer professionally trained for grand opera at Oberlin; phenomenal songwriter; and she's a charming, disarming, and mesmerizing beauty. Rhiannon has the caliber of voice that might win you a recording contract even if you were hard on the eyes; and she has the kind of beauty and stage presence that could win you a recording contract even if you could only carry a tune in a bucket.

I can only think of Dolly Parton when I experience Rhiannon's gifts. Both started out as part of a group: Dolly singing with Porter Wagoner; Rhiannon singing with the Carolina Chocolate Drops. And each went on to reach new heights as solo artists who continued to sing with others. Dolly notably as part of Trio with Linda Ronstadt and Emmylou Harris; Rhiannon as part of Our Native Daughters with Amythyst Kiah, Allison Russell, and Leyla McCalla.

Caroline played me Rhiannon's music the first time and I got this: She is the opry and the opera; she is global and local. She embodies and makes womenifest (not manifest) the grace and intellect, the agility and acuity, of Black string band music, of the African influences in and on Country Music. Rhiannon Giddens is the reigning queen of Black Country.

Her 2017 Freedom Highway Tour was a listening tour, a teaching tour; and a connecting worlds tour. It rolled into my town as art on a diplomatic mission. After she sang in Nashville's Symphony Hall, I found myself talking artmaking and world-building with Rhiannon Giddens in my apartment overlooking the Cumberland River till the early hours of morning. As I remember it, we talked a whole lot about land.

How do a people who were once owned as property, exploited as property, work to make the land their own? By living close to the land, living respectfully on the land, by living in a non-exploitive and symbiotic relationship with the land. And by singing the land.

Black Country is rooted in sung Black witness of rural beauty. It is sustained by connections to Indigenous peoples. It is a connection to nature and God forged beyond white gaze and affliction. Foraging, blackberry picking, understanding that you don't own the land, you live with the land, is practice and prayer. Singing along to a recording of Rhiannon singing the Carolina Chocolate Drops song called "Country Girl" I fall back in love with farming. Not the farming I did in Virginia, but the farming I can imagine in my Tennessee future, corn growing on a plot of shared land, on acres owned by the great and historically Black Tennessee State University. In "We Could Fly" I hear all of that and I hear the mother Lil was for me, "they held each other tight . . . flew away." I confess her song got me back to the soil, but I don't tell her what took me from it.

And she told me about a new project: Allison Russell, Leyla McCalla, Amythyst Kiah, and Rhiannon all play banjo, write, sing, and claim identity as daughters of this evolving American project that is Country. They will perform as Our Native Daughters. And when the album is released I will teach it.

That night we close talking about the nitty-gritty, about how to afford the babysitters that would allow her to take *Our Native Daughters* out on the road with instruments and kids.

In my Black Country we keep it all kinds of real. We dare to be mamas and musicians.

I thanked Rhiannon again for taking my daughter into her trailer in Louisiana to find refuge from the heat and the mosquitos so she could be swept into the private song catching conversation, so she could be there to be pulled forward by director Denzel Washington to peer through his picture finder to create his shot. "I see you peeping," he said. That doesn't happen without Rhiannon saying first, "Come on in."

This doesn't either.

Rhiannon introduced me to Leyla McCalla's artistry, then Leyla teams up with Ebonie to record "Small Towns."

When Leyla McCalla sings "Small Towns (Are Smaller for Girls)" she etches the sounds of the African diaspora into the tapestry of her performance. Her voice has a cosmopolitan lilt. We travel on it through time and space, from plunky banjo to Harlem horns, to quiet storm keyboard, to elegant strings, as she sings the story of a girl in some hamlet somewhere on the planet reading about New York City.

Leyla, born in Queens to parents who were born in Haiti, lived in Ghana for two years, before eventually settling in New Orleans.

The Holly Dunn recording of "Small Towns" released in 1987 on MTM records gives no indication any Black girl ever lived in a small town. Leyla's performance invites all girls living in places where they have fewer opportunities than the boys, are sexually confined by the patriarchy, to name then change that reality. When she sings we are invited to know that small towns and hamlets are outposts of the African Diaspora and power-speckle the planet.

ALLISON RUSSELL WRITES A CORNERSTONE FOR THE CANON

I first met Allison's work through Rhiannon, but the relationship established itself rapidly and independently when three things happened: we got introduced virtually by the Rock & Roll Hall of Fame, more on that later; she invited my daughter to perform with her at Newport on a concert show for the ages that was a full-on celebration of Black and female voices; and three, I fell head over heels in love with her song "Persephone." Allison Russell is a Lil Hardin fine songwriter—and Lil wrote standards. "Persephone" is a Black Country standard.

"Persephone" may be my favorite Country song. How could it not be? It's a wild retelling of a Greek myth about a girl who gets raped, and I am a protector of raped girls and a fan of twice-told tales. Allison's song captures an extraordinary victory. A young woman escapes a violent tormenter, a man, and lands in the bed of her beloved, a very young woman. Where she finds far more than escape. She finds joy, multiple sensual pleasures, and discovers, "my petals are bruised but I am still a flower."

It's a story I wish I had lived. So often the songs you can't get out of your head are exactly that.

My students fall in love with Persephone, the song and the character. Love is contagious and they catch it from me. Allison Russell is the person who knew and told me Ebonie Smith was the right and only person to produce my songbook. Rhiannon affirmed that project was worthy and, should it happen, she would participate. None of that happens without Caroline venturing to Shreveport, Louisiana.

Black Country travels sometimes just down the street, sometimes around the globe. We are familiar with every kind of salt and sweet water. We know travel as torture and travel as heal. In blues travel is escape. In Black Country travel is a place to heal. In blues we often travel alone. In Black Country we are fortunate when we travel together, and we are often fortunate.

FAR YONDER: BEYOND MOTOWN AND MUSIC CITY

I got three things out of the Ryman: a daughter, a reckoning, and a benediction. You already know how I got the daughter running from a chicken dressed in black. Let me tell you about the reckoning and the benediction.

LINDA MARTELL, A RECKONING

In the fall of 2009, I moved through a near empty Ryman to stand on the stage Linda Martell integrated in August of 1969, to attempt a kind of reckoning.

Linda Martell was the first Black woman to stand center stage in the Ryman Auditorium and perform on the Grand Ole Opry radio show. Twelve times she stood on the stage and stared out at the words painted across the Ryman balcony in large letters: Confederate Gallery.

That had to be all kinds of hard. That had to be one of the thousand cuts that sliced her till she left Nashville and quit attempting to pursue a national career in commercial Country Music. But before Martell left Music City she stood on the Ryman stage and sang with the best of the Country best, as a best of the Country best, on the most famous, most prestigious, most successful Country Radio show in the history of Country Music.

She fought "never" and won. Before Martell it had *never* been done. The silken-voiced subversive walked Black pride and Black beauty into the center of the Country stage and sang so sweet she wrested two standing ovations out of the audience.

Playing the Opry is an anointing. Linda Martell was anointed twelve times. It was widely agreed, she had the voice, she had the looks, she had a powerful producer, she had the goods to be a star. She didn't get to star. Didn't get to what her producer, Shelby Singleton, promised her, failed to achieve with her, then, some say, blocked her from: stardom.

Or maybe it was just her Black skin. She didn't go incognegro like Charley Pride when he was starting out. His team established his voice before they let the audience see his face. The audience saw Martell from the beginning.

Martell's biggest Country hit, "Color Him Father," reached #22 on the Country Chart. In the picture on her 1970 Plantation Records album cover, *Color Me Country*, Linda Martell looks chic and sexy in an orange minidress. She was pretty in a soft-as-Lynn-Anderson way—except her shining, long hair was brown, her shining eyes were brown, and her glowing skin was brown.

Her Countrypolitan voice was sweet of tone across a whole lot of piano keys. And she could bend notes and yodel. As Martell interprets the lyrics on her first and only album, *Color Me Country*, she captures, depicts, and explores a woman navigating a rapidly changing world armed with observant dark eyes, a large vocabulary of love, and an appreciation of both home and adventure.

Linda Martell contests racial divides while celebrating her own Black body, Black voice, Black face, Black identity. She was a new truth.

That truth got erased. She vanished from the national Country scene in the mid-seventies about the same time that the Grand Ole Opry quit downtown Nashville. But she left a trail for bold and observant women to follow. Never. Once. Again. These are very different sums.

In 2007, Rissi Palmer entered the Country chart with her song "Country Girl" and made her Opry debut at the Ryman. These were "again" moments. As I noted how hard it was for Rissi to walk on the stage I started to wonder how much harder it must have been for Martell. Soon the need to know felt urgent. And I wanted more people to know her. I started asking folks who might have information if Martell was still living, where she might be, and what her real name was. Rumor had it she was alive, living in South Carolina, and working as a bus driver.

In December of 2009, a video of "Color Him Father" was uploaded to YouTube. In 2010, I published an article about Linda Martell in the *Oxford American*. Together, the YouTube posting and the article generated a new audience for Martell while making visible the stalwart family and fan audience that had never ever quit her. A new audience joined the audience that had never stopped delighting in the sound, sight, and politics of her art a new awareness she was a pathbreaker. And that whole big audience started thinking about what it meant to be Black and singing for *Plantation Records*. Yes, Singleton named his label Plantation, while staring out at the bruising words *Confederate Gallery*. My article put a bright light on Martell's view from the Opry stage.

A few months after that article appeared in the *Oxford American* something subtly significant would happen at the Opry. It seems some other folks were thinking about how hard it would be to be Black and female and singing looking out at the words *Confederate Gallery*—and one of those somebodies did something about it.

ARETHA FRANKLIN, A BENEDICTION

Ryman Auditorium. Sunday, April 25, 2010. Aretha Franklin. Concert. Dorothy Height had died five days earlier. Aretha Franklin dedicated the concert to Height. She sat down to the piano and played some Black Country church piano for a lady who understood how much harder it was to be Black *and* female than Black *or* female and tirelessly worked to change that reality.

As soon as the concert was announced I knew I would get tickets for Aretha Franklin's Ryman debut, and I knew I wanted to do more than see the show. I wanted to speak with Ms. Franklin. We had met when I was a girl in Motown. I wasn't sure she would remember me. I didn't know if she had heard and liked, heard and hated, or never heard at all "XXX's and OOO's." But I wanted to know.

The head of the William Morris office in Nashville relayed that Franklin personally approved her backstage passes and meet-and-greet lists and that she didn't approve a lot of names. They would put my name forward, but there were no promises. She approved mine. Husband and I had all-access backstage passes and great seats for the show.

Because there was no opening act, the backstage was relatively empty. But it wasn't quiet. Even with mainly guards, ushers, and tech crew there was a loud expectant buzz. Some of the conversation was about what she might play. Would she do "Respect"? Would she play any of the Country songs she had recorded? Aretha recorded Hank Williams's "Cold, Cold Heart" in 1964; "You Are My Sunshine" in 1967; and "The Weight" in 1969.

Some of the conversation was about who was coming to be in her audience. How many big stars would come to see the biggest star? How many session men would scrape up the money to see the Queen they had once been paid to serve in a Muscle Shoals studio? And how had they treated her down in Alabama?

It got reported backstage that the audience was streaming in unusually early. I went out to take a peek and tears sprang to my eyes. The balcony of the Ryman had for years functioned as a billboard across which were emblazoned the words *1897 Confederate Gallery* in gold letters. This night you couldn't see those words.

Plain brown paper, something that looked like butcher paper, the paper you might wrap fish or meat in, had been securely taped to cover every letter spelling out those words. It wasn't a fancy job. It didn't look neat or pretty. It looked hastily and hand-done, but it looked sturdy.

I asked the guard working the main backstage staircase, a woman who usually knew everything going on, "How did that happen?"

"Somebody didn't want her to look up and see that," was the woman's explanation.

Somebody didn't want Miss Aretha Franklin to look up from the stage where she was performing and see a sign that should have been taken down long before. April 25, 2010, R-E-S-P-E-C-T looked like twenty dollars of butcher paper erasing ten thousand dollars of gold paint and plaster and a million dollars of apathetic injury.

A sign everybody working backstage had accepted for years as part of the history was finally a great big problem. Another guard I talked to was clearly in support of the act. "*She* didn't need to see that," the guard said.

The sign would come permanently down. But the first night Aretha played the Ryman, it was up but covered in a way that announced its shame and evil and her worth. With a gesture of covering, layers of wrong were acknowledged and denounced. Worker respect for the Queen created a triumph of good over evil. It was a benediction.

There was a steady stream of big names asking to be added to the list and receiving the same no. Eventually, Ms. Franklin arrived dressed head to toe in what looked like black Prada or St. John knits, dressed like an elegant traveling woman. She went almost straight into her dressing room, stopping briefly to warmly welcome all in her vicinity including me and a few family members. One of her people came out to explain there would be time to talk after the performance.

When she took to the stage, the show mesmerized in the way the old folks used to call—taking us to church. The performance went straight to that place where the music stops *entertaining* and starts *doing your spirit good.* Aretha played the piano with a brilliance that recalled to me Arizona Dranes and Lil Hardin but had roots way back to Africa—she made the piano a drum. She brought rhythms that told our African story, rhythms that held Black pain, Black joy, Black defiance, and Black creation and carried all of that into the Mother Church of Country Music.

It has been said that she uses the sustain pedal differently than many others do. For me, this is many things but mainly these two: she creates time passing, and time out of time; she creates the mesmerizing rhythms you can lose yourself in to find yourself.

She did all of that and she did these simple things: she sang with power and poise. In a bold scarlet full-length gown figured all over with sequined scarlet butterflies. A rope of stark white pearls dangled from her neck to graze her magnificent cleavage. A thin gold chain with a single pearl rested just at the base of her neck. A silver sequined jacket fell like a waterfall of light from her shoulders. Her lips and nails matched in a peachier shade of red. There were rings on her fingers. She spoke with elegiac urgency when she made the dedication to Dorothy Height.

She used the Ryman stage to say, "Dorothy Height is a star you should know." The strangers seated next to me had no idea who Height was. Now they wanted to know. Why? Aretha Franklin, a preacher's daughter, fully understood the power of calling a name in a sacred space.

The already mourning would find solace, some who had forgotten would remember, and a few who didn't know might be provoked to discover.

For forty years, Height served as president of the National Council of Negro Women. From that perch, she mobilized, always wearing a hat, often wearing pearls, thousands of women in strategically planned, stealthily shrouded in politesse, battles for rights. In 1986, she organized the first national Black Family Reunion, an effort to recognize the role loving community plays in sustaining frontline warriors and to recognize every member of every family is a frontline warrior in the battle for equality. In 2002, Height turned her ninetieth birthday into a five million dollar fundraiser for the NCNW.

Aretha understood the power of the purse. There was a huge purse, big as a small piece of luggage, under the piano. The quilted black bag with the thickest gold chain I have ever seen on a bag contained the money in cash for the performance. She insisted on getting paid. And she got paid. They didn't buy her art. They bought a sliver of her time—then she redefined time. With her piano. All of that added power to the performance.

After the encore and the applause, after she had had some time to herself, we spoke in an empty dressing room. She had changed out of her stage clothes and was wearing head to toe black just like me. Except her black was very expensive and chic and mine was frugal and frumpy Eileen Fisher. I praised her performance, and she praised the song "XXX's and OOO's." She liked being name-checked in a Country song classic and coming first before Patsy Cline.

It wasn't until Aretha Franklin called the song a *Country classic* that I realized that it was. She said, "You wrote a Country classic." Aretha spoke with the authority of being Aretha the songwriter, sister of Carolyn the songwriter. In our very brief encounter, she announced two judgments: I had done something big by co-writing a classic and done something big by putting her name in that Country classic. That was almost as good as career moments get.

This was better. I made her smile. She lingered in the doorway smiling when I left.

As a Black woman who had once been a colored girl in Detroit, it felt sweeter than sweet to celebrate Aretha in a Country song in such a way that it made her smile. We did it, Matraca and me, with eighteen words: "She's got her God and she's got good wine, Aretha Franklin and Patsy Cline, she's an American girl."

Those words opened the Queen's door for me.

Aretha was born in the city, Memphis, where Lil was born; and Aretha performed on the stage where DeFord performed, the stage DeFord's art helped purchase. She recorded in 1962 a song written by Lil Hardin, that was also recorded by Ray Charles. "Just for a Thrill." She shared with Herb Jeffries multiple song choices. He recorded "Say It Isn't So," in 1957; Aretha recorded it in 1962 on her album *The Tender, the Moving, the Swinging*, where she also recorded "I Apologize," which Jeffries released in 1978. When Aretha died in 2018, Charley Pride posted to Facebook: "Aretha Franklin was blessed with one of the most beautiful voices that God ever put in a human being. She leaves behind a wonderful musical legacy and will be remembered for her extraordinary impact on American culture. God bless the Queen of Soul."

Part of Aretha's "extraordinary impact" on American culture was her ability to infiltrate Country, infiltrate song lyrics, because she had already infiltrated set lists, because she had infiltrated the hearts and minds of Country artists. When she died, Wynona posted: "Aretha is THE shero who changed my life." Reba posted: "I've had so many influences in my life, and one of them is the Queen of Soul." Reba covered Aretha's version of "RESPECT" in 1988, released it as a single, and performed it on a Country awards show. Faith Hill sang "What a Friend We Have in Jesus" at Aretha Franklin's funeral.

Also at Aretha Franklin's funeral, Stevie Wonder played "The Lord's Prayer" on the harmonica. The performance is many things. One of them is the most extraordinary performance in a Celebration of Life that incorporated nineteen live performances. It is Wonder doing for Franklin what Franklin did for Dorothy Height: mourn, honor, and hope with blessed assurance and elemental beauty and music, utilizing African and European forms, telling a story without words. This is Black Country.

CIRCLING BACK, DEFORD BAILEY

I can't hear Wonder's harmonica and not think about DeFord. I can't be in the Ryman and not think about DeFord. Present or absent, he is a founder of the Opry feast. And he is absent a lot. As I come closer and closer to my life journey's end, I am thinking a lot about how DeFord carved meaning with his absence into his life and to his legacy.

DeFord was more absent than present at the Ryman. He sang "I'm Going to Kansas City" and picked guitar on a live Grand Ole Opry show recorded from the Ryman just before Christmas in 1947. And he played an Old Timer's Night at the Ryman in 1974 so he had stood in the stage I stood on when I first visited the boarded-up Opry in 1983 and looked out at the Confederate Gallery sign that Linda Martell looked at, but that humiliation was not DeFord's essential Opry experience.

He was spared that, and I am grateful for it. In my imagining he wouldn't have taken the job if he had had to look at that sign every Saturday night.

DeFord and the other early Opry stars sang in the National Life Building, a conspicuously clean-lined and corporate early twentieth-century edifice that signed prosperity and civic pride (where the WSM studios were located) from 1925 to 1934 on the fifth floor. In 1934, the Opry relocated to the Belcourt Theatre in Hillsboro Village, one of my Nashville neighborhoods. We debuted *XXX's and OOO's*, the CBS movie of the week slash backdoor pilot, at the Belcourt so I could introduce the film while standing on the stage where DeFord had performed. It was a way of hiding honoring him in plain sight, just like naming one of the Country stars in the show George Randall was a wink to my daddy only he would notice. Those days the Opry was peripatetic. It moved to East Nashville, then on to War Memorial Auditorium. That's the place I first saw Valerie June in a green room and immediately recognized her as a kindred spirit. We were there for a *The People Sing!* event (organized by Allison Moorer) that included Rhiannon, Valerie, me, and a lot of other folks who didn't look anything like Lil or DeFord. The Opry didn't move to the Ryman until 1943—after DeFord was booted out. The move to the Opry House, where DeFord would appear, notably to celebrate his seventy-fifth birthday, happens in 1974. To think about the history of Country Music through the lens of DeFord is to decenter the Ryman.

I'm starting to imagine Black Opry performances at the Belcourt. On the stage that DeFord frequently played around the corner from the shop where he often bought his harmonicas at Cotton Music, sometimes from owner Richard Cotton, sometimes from future Dixie Chicks producer and *Mother Dixie* champion Paul Worley.

And I am thinking of ways of making the Ryman a better place by getting DeFord back into the space. There are obvious and less obvious ways to go about this, including making available recordings from his extensive live interviews for visitors to listen to while they tour the building to inviting those who consider themselves to be heirs to his legacy and keepers of his flame to bring their twenty-first-century sounds to the nineteenth-century building.

A NEW NASHVILLE NOW, MICKEY GUYTON

There's already been a remarkable purification of sorts. I saw this on YouTube. Mickey Guyton and her father, Michael Eugene Guyton, are backstage, October 17, 2021, praying at the Ryman. They bow their heads and hold hands. Mickey's father speaks these words, "We ask, Lord, that you give us your strength, to God help us, Lord, to deal with all our might, Lord God, bless Mickey to sing her best, and the band to play their best, all for your glory, and for your honor, help her be receptive, and help the audience to be receptive to her, and to God we will give you the credit in Jesus name . . . Amen."

It's a vulnerable moment. It's a scary moment. It's a sober moment. So much needs to go right. She must sing—at her best level. The band must play at its best level. What is it the father is wanting Mickey to be receptive to? Is this a "If God is on my side who is against me moment"? That's the way I hear the prayer. The father is praying for Mickey to be receptive to God and praying that the audience be receptive to Mickey as an instrument of God. To know if they ain't on Mickey's side, they ain't on God's side. Before she goes onto the Ryman stage that has welcomed so many white girl singers and so very few Black girl singers, Mr. Guyton locates his daughter in the bosom of the Black church.

For a whole lot of reasons, Mickey Guyton would be a great addition to the Grand Ole Opry family. A student brought that home truth to me.

As I've told you, Mickey Guyton visited my class on Blacks and Country Music the first year I taught it. This was an advanced class, with a relatively small number of students, in a room just large enough for everyone to be on the first row. Guyton walked through the door flashing a mega-watt, bright, camera-ready smile.

Soon she was giving an insight-filled and candid recap of her career to that date. I was dismayed and perplexed to notice that one of my students was clearly on her phone while Guyton was talking.

I tried to indicate with eyes and eyebrows that the phone needed to be put away. Eventually I made my way around to the side of the seminar room where the seemingly distracted student was sitting and very subtly shook my head to convey "cease and desist." My student turned her phone so I could see a very young Black woman, beaming, listening, hanging on to every word. "My sister's a huge Mickey Guyton fan," the Howard Law School–bound senior whispered.

Long before she became a widely known celebrity who sang at the Super Bowl, Mickey Guyton was important to Black women in rural spaces and Black women who had to navigate white spaces.

Guyton grew up in Texas going to school with white people and church with Black people. Most of her early songs avoided the topic of race and her first videos situated her in groups of white girlfriends. Some Black girls watching Mickey in videos surrounded by white people read the image as Mickey retaining and flexing her power in spaces constructed to make her invisible and puny. They thought she was stealth. And they loved her singing. They thought she was smart. They thought she was a code-switching beauty. One of them said that in words I unpacked to notice that they thought she was beautiful at church and beautiful at school. So many of them were bruised by being beautiful at church but not beautiful at school. They loved Mickey and her voice.

Mickey Guyton. Super Bowl LVI. February 13, 2022. A beautiful cobalt blue, "Welcome four-time Grammy nominated Country sensation with the voice of an angel, Mickey Guyton." Oh say can you see, mermaid gown, tiny belt, slightly padded shoulders, long dark hair, long eyelashes, pale blue pageant girl pumps.

There are a few different ways to sing at the Super Bowl. You can sing "The National Anthem" before the game, you can sing "America the Beautiful," or you can sing your own songs at the half-time show. The first and the last are the preferred slots.

Some of the Country stars who have sung the anthem include Charley Pride in 1974, the first Country artist to sing at the Super Bowl; Garth Brooks 1993; Faith Hill in 2000; the Chicks 2003; Carrie Underwood in 2010; and Kelly Clarkson in 2012. Also that year, Miranda Lambert and Blake Shelton sang "America the Beautiful" shortly after they got married. Clint Black, Tanya Tucker, Travis Tritt, and the Judds all performed in 1994 in what is called a package show.

Mickey Guyton eclipsed all of that. She took us straight back to Pride. In my First Family of Black Country Music, Mickey is Charley's daughter. I dedicate her performance of "Black Like Me" to him. Actually, not the whole song. Just this line, "It's a hard life on easy street."

Pride is the only Black Country artist to get to any kind of Black Country easy street. His presence in America is contested—his presence in Country Music is not.

CIRCLING BACK, CHARLEY PRIDE

Charley Pride blasted twenty-nine songs to the top of the Country Music chart. He was an important Country Music publisher. He was an important real-estate owner on Music Row. In 1993, he had become the Grand Ole Opry's second Black member, quickly establishing himself as one of its biggest draws. There was no way to deny his superstar status, his influence, his excellence, his rural bona fides, his mainstream commercial Country identity.

Charley Pride was inducted into the Country Music Hall of Fame in 2000. DeFord Bailey was inducted into the Country Music Hall of Fame in 2005. Ray Charles was inducted in 2021. Pride paved the way into that Hall of Fame for the elders who had paved a way for him into a world of music. That was a hard row to hoe.

Sometime in 2019, I was sitting in an office on Music Row having false eyelashes applied to my eyelids and a whole lot of blush applied to my cheeks and thinking there are not a lot of people I would do this for, but Charley Pride is one of them. Being that I was born in 1959 I still don't associate writing books and teaching with being in front of a camera. But it has almost gotten to the point that you don't have the agency to teach and publish if you aren't willing to pundit a bit—if your face isn't seen on the screen. So, I had to say yes when invited to be part of the Charley Pride documentary, though I was feeling big as two houses. It was a very good thing. And not just because my students appreciated it.

Mr. Pride appreciated it. I discovered that a little later in 2019, at the debut of the PBS American Masters documentary of *I'm Just Me*, all about Charley. I had a few minutes of screen time in the finished doc and was invited to the preview on the Belmont campus and invited to sit in a VIP section but not the best VIP section. There were two. I chose a seat and my husband sat beside me. Guests streamed in. Eventually Charley arrived and took the seat next to mine, the seat in the lesser of two VIP sections, the seat not by Tanya Tucker or some of the big stars there, the seat by the one Black woman in the room.

He was dressed with a casual and immaculate swagger, body and face still looked gorgeous. He still looked athletic. His eyes flashed with the intensity of his demons and his intelligence; his smile flashed the irresistible charm of his simultaneously hunk of Black and Country-as-sweet-potato razzle-dazzle.

He still had it. I reminded him of the first time we met at that long ago ASCAP dinner. I told him that I taught him at Vanderbilt, and he appreciated that. When I came on screen he turned to smile and point at me like I was the star. Then the film was over, and he was ready to go to the bathroom. As he stood, he faltered just a little. He looked so vigorous, so timeless, but time told in his movement. His balance was off, his strength diminished, his coordination wonky, and yet grace, if fading, and grandeur, if creaky, were evident in every move he made.

I offered my husband David's assistance and Pride accepted it, and David and I both felt exalted by the opportunity to help the old man take care of basic human needs. We were proud to be his servants. We were charmed to be his audience: his edges were not sharp, his balance was off, some of the strength was gone, but his ability to thrill with his smile had not vanished. His dignity still awed.

In 2021, the RIAA (Recording Industry Association of America) wished to honor with a Lifetime Achievement Award the man who penned that succinct tribute to Aretha—Charley Pride. I was in the room, again with false eyelashes professionally applied this time above a Covid mask. The virus was going around taking names. There was a rumor the family denied that Pride had died of Covid that he had contracted at the CMA Awards. I did not want to believe that, but I feared that. Still, I who had barely left my apartment for months and months, who stayed in so much I lost quite a bit of weight, put on my mask, and went down to the National Museum of African American Music to share a stage with Garth Brooks and honor Charley Pride. Mr. Pride meant that much to me.

I got to meet Mr. Pride's son. Got to sit in the National Museum of African American Music and asked Garth this question: So, when Charley was pitching, he was known for his curveballs. I've got one for you in honor of Charley. I've been creating a Pride-Brooks playlist that puts your songs in conversation with his songs. Two of my favorite linkages so far: "Snakes Crawl at Night" and "The Thunder Rolls," or "Crystal Chandeliers" and "Friends in Low Places." If you were putting one of your songs into conversation with a Charley Pride song, which would it be and why? "All of them," Garth said.

Me and Garth we go way back. Him putting me on that stage is an acknowledgment of that. He asks me backstage, "Are you still with David?" I tell him, "No," and he doesn't look surprised. Trisha Yearwood is also backstage with her sister wearing a bejeweled mask. I thank Trisha for "XXX's and OOO's" and she demurs. She says the song has been as good to her as it has been to me.

CIRCLING BACK, LIL AND THE LINCHPINS IN A WILD WOMAN'S TOWN

When people tell the story of my life, when I tell this story of my life, Trisha doesn't get much space, but she is a linchpin. For me the linchpin is that tiny bit of aid that holds things together when they might otherwise fall apart that keeps you rolling down the road to where you were already going. It's not the engine, it's not the track. It's invisible but in the moment essential help. Midsummer was a linchpin in the career of Mark Sanders. I was a linchpin in the career of Rissi Palmer. Other hours, other rooms, I've been the linchpin for other careers in Country. Pat Halper and Karen Conrad were linchpins for me.

The linchpin is often invisible but always necessary.

This linchpin draws from legacy. I ask myself what would Lil, DeFord, Ray Charles, and Herb hear? What would they seek to see? Who would they care to help keep on keeping on?

As I am walking out of the door of the National Museum of African American Music and seeing how many people have come out to honor Charley Pride I am thinking this reception would have been hard for DeFord to imagine. And I am thinking the museum was very, very foolish not to include a Black Country gallery as I begged them to include. The First Family of Black Country deserves it. DeFord deserves it. And it will come.

I have seen a photograph of DeFord at the very end of his life. Sitting on his walking stick that converted into a stool. He is looking very old and very dapper. This is a family trait all the family shared. Old and dapper. Each of the First Family inhabited their body as original art, as proof against caricature and stereotype. I am hoping I inherited this trait. I am thinking this is another thing DeFord wouldn't believe, how many new Black artists and critics and songwriters have entered the Black Country space. I see Breland in the audience to honor Mr. Charley Pride and I am wishing the Covid wasn't raging and I could go out and introduce myself to him this young Black graduate of Georgetown University breaking into the Country spaces as a songwriter and singer. I'm thinking of a

Vince Gill song, "Young Man's Town" and the words "watch 'em burn it . . . to the ground . . . you built it" but "it's a young man's town."

These days I go to the Bluebird, and I can't get in. Sometimes even when they're playing my song. Usually, I don't even try to go. Even when my old friends are playing. Sometimes I call and they put me on the list. Matraca always does that for me and for all the family I want to bring.

Lil's unpublished autobiography has vanished. Let her recorded music, interviews, and photographs be a surrogate for that precious manuscript until it is found—but let it be found.

We know from letters she wrote, and comments published by her friends, that she completed the manuscript, sent it to publishers in New York, and had it rejected. If it is possible a draft of her rejected manuscript is in your relative's papers, check and see. And if you find it, shout it out. Her telling of her story is exquisitely valuable. Its loss is pure blues.

Lil understood the importance of archives. When she was living, she held on to her papers. And she took the time to write her life, refusing offers to collaborate on the telling. And yet the most important papers are missing. Have been lost now for almost half a century.

One of the things I want to read about? Her collaborations with other women. She formed and played in multiple all-female bands, the most successful being the Harlem Harlicans, which included Hazel Scott's mother, Alma Scott, on clarinet and sax, as well Leora Meaux on trombone. I want to read what she has to say about the music they made, the women they were, and the community they built.

That's why I am writing. A hundred years from now, or tomorrow, when the next person full of vim is curious to see Music Row from the perspective of a Black woman who worked for forty years on Music Row that story won't exist if I don't tell it.

The unbroken circle is a child's wish. The grown women know, the circle gets broken over and over again and on the best days it is remade, stronger, and more beautiful than before. We make sane like we make a bed, every day. We make art, like we make sane, every day. And this is how dreams become reality. Something too hard to bear becomes a song, and the song makes the hard bearable.

DeFord Bailey is the father of Black Country. Lil Hardin is the mother. Ray Charles is their genius child. Charley Pride is DeFord's side child. And Herb Jeffries is Lil's stepson. The way I figure it, all Black Country descends from these five people.

I don't know if I am a third cousin once removed or a cousin by marriage, but I chose this First Family of Black Country. I anoint this First Family of Black Country and I can feel this fictive family making a way for me as they had made away for so many.

When I claim these folk as kin, I am no longer creating or teaching Country in a predominantly white environment. I am working from the bosom of a badass Black artistic family.

I was born in one riverside music municipality, Motown, and will likely die in another, Music City. And I will die happy.

ENCORE

A SONGBOOK PERFORMED IN A WILD WOMAN'S TOWN

My end circles back to my beginning. It is a great disadvantage if you are a Country songwriter not to also be a singer. It is a greater disadvantage if you are a Country songwriter not to be a singer and to be Black and female. Entering my sixth decade as a non-singing songwriter, some amazing women in a wild symphony of red-butterfly effect, like those butterflies leaped off of Aretha's gown, swooped around the Ryman, and made their way to the Bomb Shelter, made their way to Moxxy studio, started inspiring some wild women to take a hard look at my catalog.

Nashville is no longer a young man's town. The era of my Country life that started with the publication of *The Wind Done Gone* has come to an end. The publication of *Black Bottom Saints* was the beginning of a next era, probably my final era, and women are defining it.

That novel is a deep dive into mid-twentieth-century Black Detroit in all its rooted in many arts splendor. Several of the Saints have a Black Country connection. Anna Gordy is a Black Bottom Saint who was closely involved with the development of the Supremes, who put out that

Country album I've told you about and Motown itself opened several Country labels. But LaVern Baker—one of my favorite Black Bottom Saints, the second woman to go into the Rock & Roll Hall of Fame—gets inducted just after Aretha.

Nwaka Onwusa, curator of the Rock & Roll Hall of Fame, hosted a conversation, Reckoning and Requiem, to honor Black Bottom Saint LaVern Baker. Nwaka invited me to co-moderate. On the bill: Siedah Garrett, Rosanne Cash, Margo Price, and Allison Russell, who had just released her first solo album *Outside Child*. One of the things we talked about either in preparation for the panel or on the panel itself was LaVern Baker recording an album of Bessie Smith songs.

Chelsea Crowell and Erin McAnally were catalysts for this extraordinary event. My connection to Chelsea goes back to meeting her grandfather Johnny Cash in the Ryman, back in the eighties. Over the years we've become dear friends and intimate colleagues. We were close enough to talk about what it meant to her that her mother, Rosanne Cash, discovered (on the Skip Gates PBS show) that she had African-American Heritage. Chelsea brought Allison Russell into my life.

It was like Aretha's red butterfly was getting busy and the butterfly effect was real. It may not be real in the physics of the twenty-first century. It's real in the magic of Black Country. Shortly after the Rock & Roll Hall of Fame cyber event I was coming out of Margot's, a woman-owned French and Tennessee restaurant in East Nashville located in an old gas station, and a usual for me at that time, Sunday hang just as Allison Russell was going in. Our paths crossed just about where the fuel pumps used to be. A flood of connecting words was exchanged, then she moved on into the restaurant, I believe to have dinner with Yola. That chance meeting sparked me to text to set up a phone conversation.

Allison is a superb catalyst of pop-up communities. She is also gracefully outspoken. She emphatically told me that Ebonie Smith was the person who should produce *The Alice Randall Songbook* and that it shouldn't be a single artist singing my songs like the LaVern Baker sings Bessie Smith project—it should be a collection of artists.

My daughter had an evolving project with Rhiannon and had done a takeover of Fiona Prine's Instagram in which she sang "Sam Stone" in honor of Swamp Dogg and talked about his cover of the John Prine standard. She knew that if this project was going to happen it had to be on Oh Boy Records because it was a songwriter's label. John Prine was a songwriter's songwriter. And I knew one of his Country songs had companioned me through the hardest weeks of my life. Caroline said I had to get on the phone with Fiona. I told her I was a Black woman who had never once heard my songs sung by someone who looked like me or who looked like who I had imagined my characters to look. She made the pitch to her boss, Jody Whelan, her son. Oh Boy was our label!

Then Ebonie was in. From the moment she signed on, she created a fortress of thought, theory, technical knowledge of recording, expansive knowledge of recorded American music, insight into the preservation of cultural heritage in nonacademic and noninstitutional settings (she was at the time helming the Atlantic Records studio in New York where Aretha recorded); she took deep dives into the individual lyrics and melodies; and she immersed herself in my private and public story, including reading rough drafts of my memoir but seeking out independent sources. Then she distilled all of that into a pitch deck for our artists. It was bright yellow and black with clear, clean contemporary graphics that evoked a sense of vegan family barbecue . . . it was a barbecue, this project was Southern and homecoming and Country but was pure Sankofa, looking back to move forward, we were deep in the move forward. I loved the deck she was sending out to the artists so much I asked if I could add a note to be included.

It was an "Ain't too proud to beg moment." It was a standing on my feet head turned to the sky tears streaming down my face moment. And you know I will cry again in the studio, and I am not a crier. I did not cry when I was told I needed a mastectomy and was advised to have a double. But I saw the names of the women Ebonie was inviting to be part of the project and I knew I wanted to be a songwriter again for the first time in two decades because I wanted desperately to hear something I thought I would never hear, my songs sung by people who had walked some of my walk, who could have been my daughters, my nieces. So Ebonie completed the pitch deck. I wrote my begging letter to the artists. Caroline started working her text threads.

I felt like Moses looking out on the promised land suspecting he would never get to set foot in it. My head started swirling with desire to have this project come to fruition. I didn't want any rabbits eating these strawberries. I didn't want to just be able to do one or two like I had hoped when folks started to talk about this thing as even a long shot half-possibility. Now I wanted the album. And it would be a minute before it got figured out. It was a lot of busy people to coordinate, a lot of possibilities to run down, a lot of competing projects in the air, in Nashville, nationally, globally. I told myself the truth that it wasn't likely this was going to work out. And the first set of studio days we attempted to make happen no one was available.

The whole thing got put off for minute . . . But I noticed Ebonie was uniquely determined to do for me what I have been wanting to do for Lil. That shook me. Lil inspired me with her words and music. Ebonie took care of me and my project; she did that thing Quincy promised to do for Miles, laid down a velvet carpet for her pearl. I didn't know I was a music pearl till I rolled in Ebonie's sound velvet. I thought that was something only the boys got to do, or only white girls got to do. I had to live long to see a Black woman get studio time to do something as crazy as this project and discover a whole lot of brilliant generous women, and a few brilliant men, signing on to a Country album project like no other.

An artist spots an artist at a far distance then closes the distance. That's my rewrite of a Russian proverb that I put in *Pushkin and the Queen of Spades.* The Russian translated is a fisherman spots a fisherman at a distance and moves away because there won't be enough fish if another fisherman is present. It's a scarcity mindset proverb. My rewrite is Country and it's inspired by my return to enjoying being a songwriter. These women have game, have each independent startlingly amazing music game, and they came together. Seeking to create, to amplify, to harmonize, to fund, to encourage, to do whatever needs doing for art to shine and joy to rise—for artist and for audience. This is not a myth. This is not a wish. This is reality with receipts. I got the album, rough but I got it.

My Black Country: The Songs of Alice Randall presents eleven of my songs reimagined by a collaborating community of artists, mostly Black and female. These women did not show up because they were offered a big payday; or because they had nothing better to do. They were not offered a big payday; and they did have a lot of important things to do. They showed up because there was a need that they understood. The need of a writer who had worked in Nashville for four decades and been erased from the history of the city, been erased from the sound of my own recorded songs.

Because these women had walked a mile in my shoes, they had some ideas about why that might be. They know what it is to be the "unexpected songwriter" in Nashville; the "unexpected body" on Music Row crowned by "unexpected (never seen on CMT) hair." They know, so they show up.

On May 1, 2023, I received an email from Ebonie with a link to the rough completed tracks. The original song sequence: "Went for a Ride" performed by Adia Victoria, who is in the Blair House poetry collective with my daughter, Caroline. "Get the Hell Out of Dodge" performed by Saaneah Jamison, who has worked in my favorite gritty museum, the Jefferson Street Sound Museum, and grew up living at her beginning in housing provided by the same landlord that housed DeFord at his end. "Girls Ride Horses, Too" performed by Monique and Chauntee Ross, who I know from watching them in performance with Brandi Carlisle and Allison Russell. "Small Towns" performed by Leyla McCalla, who I have watched on YouTube, fascinated as I have been by her homage to Langston Hughes. "I'll Cry for Yours," a song I co-wrote with Robert Jetton while walking through a Confederate graveyard, a Union graveyard, and a graveyard of the enslaved is performed by Miko Marks with a raw urgency that makes it the theme song of many global conflicts and this project. "Who's Minding the Garden" performed by Rissi Palmer in crystalline voice just in time to be the climate change anthem we need right now, one that will change the hearts and minds of Evangelicals not concerned about climate change as the planet experiences record breaking heat. "The Ballad of Sally Anne" performed by Rhiannon Giddens as reckoning of lynching so exquisite it does not retraumatize though it explicitly holds murderers accountable and paints lynching as terrorism. "Solitary Hero" performed by Sunny War is a song the co-writer took to Kerrville Folk Festival and won a songwriting contest with it and never even told me. I didn't know till I heard *The Women of Kerrville* album years later. Sunny War's searing performance of bigger troubles and bigger triumphs made me want to happy holler about getting past hard things. "Big Dream" performed by Valerie June is just as I had imagined it before Valerie June was born—ethereal, ineffably trippy Black hippy Country. Closing down the album and bringing us home on a high, "Many Mansions" is not only performed by Allison Russell, but she also evolved and improved the lyric.

Each performance is fecund, life bringing, life sustaining. The voices are wildly and widely varied, in pitch and tone, as well as in accent and inflection. I know these songs. Each cut carved new layers of meaning into the lyric. Each cut was sung theater, embedded lit-crit and music-crit. Each was a substantial feast of sound, voice, and instruments. Ear candy if your idea of candy is a perfectly roasted to caramelized perfection sweet potato.

An album is a heavy lift. Ebonie Smith did much of the heaviest of the lifting, from selecting songs, to matching the artists with songs, to casting and inviting additional musicians, but most ambitiously charting an inclusive course through the audioscape of Country that implicitly honors Lil, DeFord, Ray, Charley, and Herb as it explicitly honors the capacity of this community to form at this time.

The whole accents and amplifies the value of the independent parts. The community sends us back to savor the performances of the individual. We, the women of Black Country, are not a monolith. Our beauty and power is most visible in our varieties and variations.

After reckoning can come reconciliation. Covering the sign was reckoning, removing the sign was reckoning, Black prayer warriors in the green room reckoning, the emergence of the Black Opry a reckoning, realizing that the Opry was not born in the Ryman a reckoning, making audible what was muted a reckoning. More reckoning to come, but between reckoning and reconciliation is renaissance.

Ebonie, Adia, Allison, Caroline, Fiona, Leyla, Miko, Rhiannon, Rissi, Saaneah, SistaStrings, Sunny War, and Valerie showed up, collaborated, created, and did the work that allowed me to hear, for the first time ever, songs I had co-created as they had sounded in my head—but not on record. It was the end of imagining.

The Alice Randall songbook gets recorded backed by an independent record label, Oh Boy Records. Solo, duo, and community collaboration make my public and personal history audible. The bonus track will be "XXX's and OOO's (An American Girl)" performed by the original American Girl, Caroline.

I have returned to imagining. I dream a concert. Where would it be? The Ryman? War Memorial Auditorium? The Opry House? I think War Memorial Auditorium. It is the most intimate space and DeFord sang there most often. Fisk Chapel. Lil attended Fisk, home of the Jubilee Singers. Must be Fisk. There will be a Hatch Show Print. They made posters for Aretha, and DeFord, Ray, and Charley Pride. In honor of Lil, we will pay special attention to the costumes and collaborate with dressmakers of color.

We will remember to invite Linda Martell and her granddaughter Marquia Thompson, who has directed and filmed a documentary telling of the living woman who did the most to pave the way for those who will take the stage. They will be seated in the front row center and when I take my seat between Linda and Ebonie I lean toward Martell and whisper that I am as proud to be in her documentary as I was to be in Pride's. As the houselights dim I ask Ebonie if I can squeeze her hand. She says, "Yes."

In the dark we hear DeFord blowing his "Swing Low, Sweet Chariot," a few bars of Lil, then silence.

Adia steps to the stage in a costume by Sami Miro, or Fe Noel, or maybe it has to be a creation by mother and daughter Rebecca Henry and Akua Shabaka of House of Aama. Yes, the "Southern Girl Cotton Mini Dress." And then she will sing "Went for a Ride." We will invite Radney Foster and Justin McBride. They can sit in the back and listen. They can contribute by respecting being decentered. They are not sharing the mike. They are witnessing that the mike has been taken from them. Women who are heirs of Lil, DeFord, Ray, Charley, and Herb are sharing the mike. And it starts with Adia embodying the beauty of being Black as the sky on a moonless night.

It's Saaneah's turn. No one in the audience knows who she is. She does not throw away her shot. She sings better than Sarah Vaughan and better than Dinah Washington because she got to sing championed by Ebonie. Every flip of Saaneah's mermaid hair reminds me of a myth that rose in Detroit. Pregnant Black mothers who jumped off the slave ships, gave birth to babies who could breathe water after their birth, as they had inside their mama's bodies. And infants thrown off the slave ships, immediately after birth had this power. According to the Motown myth, mermaids are born from their mother's radical refusal to be owned; born from their mother's radical belief in the power of their daughter's breath; born from a mother's faith in their offspring's ability: to riff, to evolve, to agilely escape, what would confine. Mermaids know how to get the hell out of Dodge. They call the hardest projects in Nashville Dodge City. Saaneah grew up near, and DeFord grew old in Dodge City. Mermaids know the first step of getting out of Dodge is to imagine getting out of Dodge. And when Saaneah comes to the close of her performance we know it, too.

Chairs are placed. Atop one is a violin, atop the other a cello. SistaStrings walk into the spotlight holding hands, languid. Usually, they don't sing. They play strings behind the singers. Tonight, they will sing. And they can sing. "Nothing in the desert is what it seems. I ran the numbers in my dreams." Literal real-world calculations are involved in the song, calculations born from my days being a little girl whose favorite and most intellectually stimulating uncle was an illegal numbers-racket banker. As SistaStrings sings "Girls Ride Horses, Too," the song is in a sweet conversation with "Pancho and Lefty" as sung by Willie and Merle and SistaStrings is holding up the more interesting side of the conversation.

Leyla's next. She holds the center of the stage, powerful as a honeybee. The banjo-playing brainiac who shined a spotlight on Harlem Renaissance poetry in her best solo album sings "Small Towns" wearing a sheer linen dress by Haitian designer Azede Jean-Pierre that features stenciled quotations from Leyla's own lyrics. Images of female tweens of color living in small towns around the globe flash behind her.

Now Miko, who grew up in California down the road from the Pointer Sisters, our better than Brenda Lee, our little Miss Dynamite, is claiming the universality of the Black and female and Country. Raw and ready, she sings the necessity of mourning; the truth we damage each other, and we can redeem each other; the water of tears, is water we can breathe.

In the center of the show Rissi Palmer steps to the mike. She's a bona fide Country star who played the Ryman with a song on the Country charts. She carries the banner that links Lil Hardin, to Linda Martell, to Rissi, and she's hoping there's someone singing along in the audience she can soon hand it off too. Glen Campbell, the man who handed Charley Pride his entertainer of the year award, originally recorded "Who's Minding the Garden" and invited me and my daughter to the studio. He declared the song, "'Galveston' big." The way Rissi sings it that might be true. She asks a hard question in sweet, sweet tones. Are we doing enough to protect God's green earth? Note for note, Rissi beats out Glen. Rissi's version of the song is more beautiful thanks to how her voice; the complex Country track Ebonie constructed; and the edit co-writer Bruce Bouton and I implemented where we ripped out our own stupidity about drug lords, improving the lyric.

Nobody can follow Rissi, except Rhiannon Giddens, Rhiannon who got her Pulitzer Prize. Rhiannon who plays fiddle and voice and started off singing opera. Rhiannon takes down the best recording ever made of one of my songs: John Cowan singing and Mark O'Connor fiddling on "The Ballad of Sally Anne." The song reaches a new level when a brown woman, a real Sally Anne, is singing witness of the lynching of her husband between their wedding and their reception. Rhiannon's got all kind of skin in the game. John Cowan sang the bejesus out of the song; and Mark sawed the bejesus back into it. Dear Rhiannon, pigtailed, unpretentious, knit while the others drink; talk deep into the night; write ballets with my all grown up baby daughter, Rhiannon was something more. She eclipsed the Cowan and O'Connor brilliance like the sun eclipses other stars. So bright you don't even know the sun is a star.

Sunny War follows up with a moon, "Solitary Hero." This song contains the theme of the album, theme of the process of the project, and theme of my life: woman as simultaneously solitary and working in community. We witness Sunny War as a solitary hero, and as a woman working in community with the other women in the album. We witness her knowing all about hard transactions. Selling art for money is a hard transaction. Selling your body for money is a hard transaction. The women on this album, like the women in the world, learn to see the difference between hard transactions and impossible transactions. Bodies and songs you can sell. Dignity, no. Integrity, no. Freedom, no.

The night starts to move to a close. The lights come down. It's time for a hippy, trippy, lullaby. It's time for the song Rissi Palmer first heard on a teenage trip to Mexico, "Big Dream," the song I once stole from my child. The song that reminds me often it's not too late to fix things, to mend up your broken heart so torn, the song that make me think, God's a woman, just like the women on the stage, like Valerie June delivers it singing like it got whispered to her by ghost church voices.

But we won't always be on the stage. We end not on sleep but on death with another song about God being a woman. The song Allison Russell rewrote and improved is the song one of my co-writers consistently wrote me out of the story of, "Many Mansions." Moe Bandy sang, "in my father's house are many mansions." Allison sings, "In my mother's house are many mansions." And on this stage, we have inhabited so many of them and built more spaces to inhabit where we are seen and heard, in our power and beauty, in warmth and movement. Allison Russell enters into conversation with Emily Dickinson by singing "hope is the thing with feathers." And we all benefit. Allison uplifts us. Allison overturns our understanding of what is and isn't a classic text. She creates new classics and inhabits old classic like mansions. "Wild Woman's Town," a new song written by all of us, is the encore. *It's a wild woman's town full of wild women's dreams . . .* Followed by "XXX's and OOO's" spoken by Caroline on a track that samples DeFord. We held the fort. We are the linchpins.

NOTA BENE

Memory is mutable, perspective is subjective. Read this as a packet of love letters to the First Family of Black Country, to Our Native Daughters, to the Wooten Brothers, to train rides, to the Black West and Black and brown cowboys, to the Black Opry, to Color Me Country Radio, to the young woman I used to be, and the old woman I am thrilled to be. Read it as an invitation to explore histories and concerts and albums and academic articles and acres to bring you other pictures of the time. But remember, people lie to the census taker, census takers can have poor hearing or poor spelling, proven with evidence is not always true. Trauma, therapy, and aging all impact memory and observation. This is a portrait of how I remember what happened to me, now, which may be different from how I remember it tomorrow, or how I remembered it yesterday. Palimpsest. Kaleidoscope. Memyth. Having Our Say. Confabulation. Memoir. Cocktail Chatter. I have written this taking something from all these genres of life-telling. I write aware that telling my story in therapy, at dinner parties, over coffee, on paper, through the years, alters memories. As time passes events fold upon each other, details from one day imprinting on another, telescoping on occasion, umbrella-ing on occasion, kaleidoscoping often.

ACKNOWLEDGMENTS

My grandmother, Georgia Minnie Litsey Randall, taught me the most significant things I know about narrative craft.

When I was a very young girl in Detroit, she would watch *General Hospital* or *Days of Our Lives* while I took a nap on a pallet made of patchwork quilts she had hand sewn. The patches were squares cut from her old party dresses. Some afternoons to woo me toward sleep, she would tell me the story of the dress the patch came from, which swirled into the story of a long ago in Alabama party, that swirled into the story of her life before she migrated north.

The story each patch told was individual and distinct, yet mutable. The patches that surrounded a patch sometimes gave whole new meanings to the patch they framed. The quilts cocooned me in moments of Black social and economic triumph and anchored me to her understanding that context matters.

And, eventually, as I grew into a woman who knew more about life than what the quilts told, to the power of the edit.

Shame, pain, and difficulty were all a part of shopping while Black in Selma in the 1930s when my grandmother was first wearing those party dresses. She admired a dress displayed in the window of a store that would not allow her to enter. It became inspiration—to make a better dress—with fabric bought from a store she could enter. That store where she could shop carried fabric and dresses, but there were so few dresses she wanted to buy. The shopkeeper's concept of what Black women wanted to wear and what my grandmother wanted to wear had very little overlap. And when she found something that reflected her taste there was no simple triumph in the purchase. If a white person entered the store, to shop or just talk to the store owner, while my grandmother was paying, she had to abruptly step back, be silent, and wait, for her disrupted transaction to complete. Hanging whole in her closet, pretty dresses told a hard story that had everything to do with bruising encounters with Jim Crow racism. Reformed into a pallet quilt, the dresses became the radical act that is unmitigated Black triumph and beauty.

This book is more than a little like that quilt. Patches of memory, more this than anything else, but also patches from my songs, academic chapters, lectures, articles, and even a patch from a museum guide for an exhibit that was never created, are juxtaposed to create a quilt that might cocoon present and future Black Country listeners and artists in catalytic instances of Black triumph and joy.

I repeat myself. That is part of a Black aesthetic. Martin Luther King, Jr., gave more than one version of the "I Have a Dream" speech. Some of the words in this book I have used before, but never quite like this. Never as part of a Black world of my creation. Never to the purpose of cocooning.

I am grateful to the academic presses, journals, institutions, and editors that have published some of my evolving thoughts about Black Country over the years. There are a few editors who put me in particularly fertile conversation. Holly Gleason edited *Woman Walk the Line* for the University of Texas Press. It was within those pages that I first published thoughts on Lil Hardin. Jada Watson and Paula J. Bishop edited *Whose Country Music? Genre, Identity, and Belonging in Twenty-First-Century Country Music Culture* for Cambridge University Press. It was on their pages that I previewed some of my Black Country money story that had been written for this memoir. The *Oxford American* has a history of publishing important articles on Southern music. I was pleased to celebrate and honor Linda Martell on the pages of the *Oxford American* way back in 2010. More recently, the *Oxford American* has entered into a new era ushered in by powerful female editors. Working with Danielle A. Jackson, after she expressed interest in publishing my reflections on watching *The Johnny Cash Show,* was an education and an honor. Dina Bennett edited my contribution to the National Museum of African American Music catalog. Though many of the editors who made space for me on their pages were women—they were not all women. Caine O'Rear gave me space to make the argument that "Daddy Lessons" was a Country song in the pages of *American Songwriter* magazine, Lisa Konicki, the current editor-in-chief, signed off on my using that material in this book.

Most of the earlier uses have a kind of howl in the wilderness tone. In all of those publications, the Black voice I celebrated, and the Black voice I have, was in a distinct minority. Within the pages of *Woman Walk the Line* and *Whose Country?* white female voices dominated. In the pages of *American Songwriter* magazine, which has a majority male audience, I understood myself to be shouting against the prevailing wisdom and opinion when I argued "Daddy's Lessons" was indeed Country. When I share my "Is it Country checklist" in this book, I understand myself to be whispering truth accepted in *my* Black and feminine Country world.

My grandmother made a memory quilt that centered her frivolous and foundational Black triumph—as a political act—that would overturn existing hierarchies. My grandmother's quilt has been a model for this memoir.

Jan Miller and Ali Kominisky are able allies and extraordinary agents—starting with they live in Texas not New York—that supported me through transforming sixty-four years into less than three hundred pages. They introduced me to Atria. There, Nick Ciani, senior editor, engaged my text and my life with rigor and respect; Shida Carr proved to be an insightful and tireless publicist; and Hannah Frankel kept us all coordinated.

Charlamagne tha God links words on paper to words in air with genius, generosity, and profound power. He is that rare star burning bright in their prime who makes a way for old heads at the table of essential cultural conversations. I am grateful to be his invited guest.

Everett Bexley first read this manuscript when it was over six hundred pages long. My human and literary debt to this young fiction writer who asked so many very good questions and has a keen proofreading eye is large.

My daughter Caroline introduced me to Jan, Ali, and Everett; lived with me through many of the events in the memoir; and inspired my biggest country song. My debt to her is vast.

Edith Gelfand, Bob Doyle, Matraca Berg, Ray Kennedy, and Bobby Braddock have traveled forty years with me on my Nashville music journey. Together we didn't just make music and money, we made hours of joyful life that defied the powers that would divide us if they could. They couldn't.

The journey wouldn't have started without Gloria Messinger. You know all about that if you've read this book.

Mark Sanders, Steve Earle, Robert Jetton, and Ralph Murphy are the four songwriters who taught me the most about writing songs by writing with me. Bobby Braddock, Bob McDill, and Guy Clark are the three songwriters who taught me the most by example and by giving me mini-lectures on the art. All my co-writers: thank you.

Paul Worley was the first person in Nashville who understood what I was trying to do with *The Mother Dixie Project* and Quincy Jones was the first person in Los Angeles. The Wooten Brothers are the people who gave life in sound to the project creating beauty that is at once disruptive and foundational.

Working on Music Row in the twentieth century I made some true friends (not already mentioned) who were witness and helpmates in the business of life. Allison Moorer, Bruce Bouton, Callie Khouri, Diana Haig, Harry Stinson, J.C. Crowley, Karen Conrad, Kevin Welch, Manuel Cuevas, Marshall Chapman, Mark O'Connor, Michael Woody, Pam Tillis, Pat Alger, Pat Halper, Rachel Whitney, Radney Foster, Rodney Crowell, and T. Bone Burnett, I thank you for the hours you companioned me on the adventure. Walter Hyatt, I thank you, too, and I miss you.

Kimberly and Brad Paisley became friends and powerful allies in the 21st century.

Trisha Yearwood and Garth Brooks changed my life forever and for the better. Trisha by singing "XXX's and OOO's" and Garth by being a truly fair and equitable businessman who cut a square deal with Midsummer Music. After some twentieth-century bad deals it was good to arrive in the twenty-first century with a square deal.

And in the twenty-first century I rode with the posse of my dreams, Adia Victoria, Allison Russell, Caroline Randall Williams, Ebonie Smith, Fiona Prine, Leyla McCalla, Miko Marks, Rhiannon Giddens, Rissi Palmer, Saaneah Garrett, SistaStrings, Sunny War, Valerie June, and made the *My Black Country: The Songs of Alice Randall* album.

Vanderbilt University has been a strong partner for me in my work with, and on, Black Country and Country. From supporting the development of two different academic courses: Country Lyric in American Culture and Black Country; to committing dollars and curatorial resources to the development of a Black Country archive, to hosting Black Country stars in our classrooms; to developing programs with the National Museum of African American Music, Vanderbilt has made a positive difference in how Black Country is understood, created, remembered, and honored around the world. Chancellor Daniel Diermeier, Provost Cybele Raver; Tracy Sharpley-Whiting, vice provost for Arts and Libraries; Holling Smith-Bourne and Jason Schultz of Vanderbilt Library staff, and former students Kenyon Glenn and Mac Hunt have been particularly supportive of my work in and on Black Country.

Barbara Ching was the first scholar to publish extensively on my work in Country music. Her chapter, "If Only They Could Read between the Lines: Alice Randall and the Integration of Country Music," published in *Hidden in the Mix*, the iconic and still authoritative academic text on Blacks in Country Music, emboldened me to keep on keeping on. At the turn of the millennium, journalist Pamela Foster published *My Country,*

Too: The Other Black Music that deserves to be read and remembered. I was honored to be included in her pages.

Elizabeth Alexander, Thadious Davis, Michael Eric Dyson, Kiese Laymon, and Nell Painter have inspired me and sustained me as scholars and humans.

Steven W. Lewis, Kelly Elaine Navies (both of the Smithsonian), and Julieanna Richardson, of the HistoryMakers digital archive, have provided a particular flavor of encouragement and provoked new insights—by working to document my life in Country music. Their process, their passion, and their discipline inspires me. The Country Music Hall of Fame and Museum has long sustained, sheltered, and catalyzed me.

Jeff Colvin, attorney, Jennifer Alexander at the Sports and Entertainment Division of Truist, and Trina Smith-Dort at Me Gusta Music bring joy to my experience of business. Matthew Clark is my secret editorial and business strategy weapon.

There is an emerging community of Black business voices reshaping the ecosystem of Music Row. Shannon Sanders at BMI, Ruby Amanfu and Armand Hutton at the Recording Academy, Chuck Harmony and Claude Kelly with Weirdo Workshop, Rissi Palmer with Color Me Country Radio, Marcus Dowling, writing for *The Tennessean*, and Holly G. of the Black Opry are all a part of a Black Country Renaissance. And The National Museum of African American Music is an anchoring and educating presence that propels the Renaissance.

If Black Country has an OG, ongoing, highly visible, and all-about-Nashville pioneer of Black Country activism it is Candi Stanton. She's done it all from sing on the Opry to give Black Country music tours. She is an asset and a resource that will help support the Renaissance.

The week after this book is published an album, *My Black Country: The Songs of Alice Randall*, produced by Ebonie Smith, executive produced by Fiona Prine will be released on Oh Boy Records. I thank Jody Prine, president of the label, Ebonie, Fiona, and the entire Oh Boy Records team, including Eileen Tilson, for making the dream of hearing my songs recorded as I imagined them a reality. And a special thanks to Dan Knobler for producing the XXX's and OOO's homage track.

I have adopted some siblings and cousins and some mamas have adopted me over my sixty-five years. My family circle includes Alex, Ali, Amanda, Anita, Ann, Anton, Bill H., Bill C., Bob, Carter, Chelsea, Courtney, David F., Deborah, Debra, Diana, Edith, Edwin, Elena, Everett, Florence, Gail D., Gail W., Helen, Jay, Jim, Julia, Jun, Justin, Kaeli, Kate, Kazuma, Keisha, Leslie, Marc, Marq, Mathew, Mary Jane, Mimi, Nadine, Neil, Perian, Ray, Reggie, Rex, Rick, Robert, Sam, Siobhan, Takuma, Tanya, Taylor, Thad, and Vandana. I love you. Truly.

My family is my rock and a rainbow. My daughter Caroline Randall Williams recently married Tim Darrah. The people invited to fill the six tables—yes, only six tables—to celebrate afterward are the people we consider family. They know who they are. And I love them. Mimi Oka and Jun Makihara co-hosted that party with me and named a scholarship in my father's honor at Harvard so I can say they all up in the founding of this family of choice feast. And a thing about this family? It is actually Black, and white, and Asian; it is rooted to wealth and to poverty; it is straight, queer, questioning, and evolving—but it shares a commonality: We lead with love and fight, when possible, with art.

AUTHOR'S NOTE

Some ideas, language, and events included in this book first appeared in earlier publications. The *Oxford American* published "Linda Martell's 'Color Him Father'" in 2010; it contains a portion of the Linda Martell material and snapshots from my early Nashville days. "Beyonce's 'Daddy Lessons Is Classic Country," published in 2016 in *American Songwriter*, contains a version of my "Is it Country?" checklist and thoughts about Country. *Woman Walk the Line*, published by University of Texas Press in 2017, contains the chapter "That's How I Got to Memphis"; some of the Lil Hardin material further developed in this book as well as some of the reflections on Motown first appeared in that publication. *Rivers of Rhythm*, published by the National Museum of African American Music, contained my essay "From Lil Hardin to Lil Nas X." Concepts and language from my class lectures and talks were published for the first time in that essay, notably but not only ideas about Lil Nas X, the dandy, and Rhiannon Giddens, as well as some snapshots of teaching Black Country. "Music from the Magic Box" was published in 2021 by the *Oxford American* and contains my first published reflections on listening to Johnny Cash in rural Maryland. *Whose Country Music?* published by Cambridge University Press in 2023, includes my chapter "Mailbox Money," which contained some of the business history that appears in this book. I am grateful to the museums, magazines, and presses that allowed me to preview bits and pieces of my life work in progress along the way to completing this work.

INDEX

C

F

G

H

ABOUT THE AUTHOR

ALICE RANDALL was born in Detroit, Michigan, on May 4, 1959. She wrote her first country song sitting high in the branches of a cherry tree overlooking a Motown highway. In 1983 she drove to Nashville and founded Midsummer Music, a company that still exists, and played a role in launching the career of Country superstar Garth Brooks. Randall, the first Black woman to cowrite a number-one Country hit, Trisha Yearwood's "XXX's and OOO's," had songs recorded in the eighties, nineties, aughts, teens, and twenties. Some of the stars that have recorded Randall's songs include: Glen Campbell, Marie Osmond, Holly Dunn, Moe Bandy, and Radney Foster. She is the Andrew W. Mellon Chair in the Humanities at Vanderbilt, where she teaches the course Black Country.